Advance praise

Good Small Business Planning Guide

'I find this book a delightful change from the technique-heavy fare that often comes across my desk in the name of business strategy and planning. This book is distinctive for the remarkable way in which it speaks directly to the business planner, addressing in a highly accessible – and always in an engaging and entertaining fashion – the issues that he or she will face as they construct their future. There are few business books that you might describe as a page turner, but this could well be one. The author's deep empathy for his reader jumps off the page. I would unhesitatingly recommend it to the new business starter, or to those who were looking to expand or diversify their existing enterprise. Quite brilliant, so lucid and different.'

Daniel Doherty, Programme Director, MSc in Strategic Management,
School of Economics Finance and Management, University of Bristol

'This is one of those books than can change your life ... it has practical insight and wisdom for all small business owners. Taking the time to plan and do it with an open mind and honest challenge of yourself (the owner) has been the key to success for many of our growing and profitable business customers.'

John McGoldrick, Finance Director, Lloyds Banking Group,
Commercial Banking

'This truly comprehensive analysis of all the key factors behind successful business planning is to be thoroughly recommended.

Importantly, it deals with the underlying behavioural and "people" issues that impact on what makes efficient planning and effective execution possible and is to be commended to businesses of all shapes and sizes.'

Richard Boot, Chairman, Institute of Directors, West Midlands Region

'I wish I had the ability of John Kirwan to enthral with words. His stories draw you in, his explanations spark your imagination and his takeaways inspire you to action. If you are an entrepreneur, or thought you had it in you to be one, then read this book and make it happen! I doubt there is another text which will add so much to the entrepreneurial cause unless, of course, John decides to write another bestseller.'

Cary Adams, Business Leader

'At last! A book on business planning that makes sense. A book that's full of insight, and wisdom. That uses anecdotes and stories. That really helps. And hardly a spreadsheet, 2 x 2 matrix or trite acronym in sight. Thank you, John. Thank you for writing a book that speaks to human realities. That is a delight to read. And that goes far, far beyond business-planning-as-taught-at-business-school.'

Dennis Sherwood, Managing Director,
The Silver Bullet Machine Manufacturing Company Limited

'As a soldier well used to planning to achieve success, I find in this book the essence of how company executives should plan for their success in the challenging world of competitive business. It is pragmatic, comprehensive and easy to read. For existing companies who are perhaps losing focus or facing unexpected challenges, this is essential reading. And just as there are no prizes for coming second on the battlefield, companies are not destined to fail ... most often, it is humans who cause the failure. By learning the lessons so eloquently outlined in this book, business success is much more assured.'

Major General JHT Short, CB OBE

'At last, a book on business planning that not only covers the process involved but also explains the personal journey involved. An essential read for those starting a business for the first time and equally for those established leaders who are looking to rejuvenate their businesses.'

Mike Teasdale, Partner, Strategic Planning Solutions

GOOD SMALL BUSINESS PLANNING GUIDE

How to make a successful business journey

John Kirwan

First published in Great Britain 2009

A & C Black Publishers Ltd
36 Soho Square, London W1D 3QY
www.acblack.com

A CIP record for this book is available from the British Library.

ISBN: 9-781-4081-0948-9

This book is produced using paper that is made from wood grown in
managed, sustainable forests. It is natural, renewable and recyclable.
The logging and manufacturing processes conform to the environmental regulations of the country of origin.

Design by Fiona Pike, Pike Design, Winchester
Typeset by Saxon Graphics Ltd, Derby
Printed in the United Kingdom by
Martins the Printers, Berwick-upon-Tweed

Contents

Acknowledgements

It is only when you write a book that you realise how much of yourself goes into it.

Memories of distant childhood events, recollections of facts learned at school, re-lived debates from university studies, insights prompted by the articles and books of thoughtful writers, the stimulation of clients and colleagues, the wisdom of good friends, the love of parents and wife, the illumination shone by my children's wonder.

All of these make me who I am, and this book what it is.

I acknowledge the special place of them all. I have also made every attempt to acknowledge throughout the book all the quotations that I have borrowed to share with you.

In my view, my role is to pull together for you the best opinions and practices on business planning that I have seen validated in the course of my business experience as the most likely to lead you to success, to create the best business you can.

It feels to me to be like an act of sharing which I count as a privilege to have the opportunity to do.

In this regard, I readily thank Lisa Carden, my editor at A & C Black, who has been unfailingly encouraging and patient.

I also thank my colleagues in SPS South West: Mike Teasdale, Peter Heath, James Short, Mark Garnier, Claire Marshall and Andy Booth. They kindly read the manuscript throughout its composition and offered numerous improvements as well as much encouragement. They also practise what they preach: a total commitment to supporting their business clients.

Much of my business education I owe to the opportunities given to me by my former employer, Lloyds Bank. It is there that I was blessed with the happy fortune of working with my good friend, Cary Adams. He is the most accomplished leader and inspirational person I have ever worked with. Whenever I spend time with him, I always leave his company with ideas I have never had before.

It is also only when you write a book that you realise how much hard work it is.

In every way, it would have been beyond me without the unconditional love and support which amazes me every day and which I am more than blessed to receive from my wife, Julia, and our children: Sean, Dominic, James and Hannah.

Introduction: About This Book

'Whatever you do, or dream you can, begin it. Boldness has genius and power and magic in it.' – Goethe

You are on a wonderful, delicious, awesome, bittersweet journey.

You are making an ending and embarking on a new beginning. You are wriggling to emerge from your history in order to create an exciting future. As the philosopher Demosthenes said, 'Small opportunities are often the beginning of great enterprises.'

Being in business is all of these things. It will take you to the highest highs and the lowest lows. There will be times when you will not be able to imagine doing anything else; and there will be times when you are on your knees pleading to exchange places with just about anyone.

You will be buzzing with energy and you will be sagging with exhaustion. You will be lit up and also let down. You will be beaming and seething. Your business will succeed; and at times it will just suck.

I congratulate you in your endeavour. I really want you to achieve success in whatever terms you define it. You are important. Your spirit of enterprise is an example to us all. Of course, there exist poor examples in the world, examples that diminish us. But my assumption is that you are not like that. My assumption is that you want to build something that matters – that matters to you, to those closest to you, to those who depend on you, and to those whom you will serve as your customers.

And, sure, if you increase your wealth, then that is wonderful, right and proper.

You are driven to accomplish something significant in business and, since it is *your* journey, the significance is personal to you.

I've worked with hundreds of businesses for more than a quarter of a century, and I am convinced that a proper engagement with the process of business planning is essential to success. This book describes how best to engage in successful business planning and is here to help you.

I have been trying to form a picture of who you are, but my determination not to pigeon-hole you is denying me any specificity of image.

You are someone who is *anyone* (any age, any sex, any ethnicity, any education, any socio-political class). Whatever, you are unique. You might be someone who is thinking about the possibility, the 'maybe', the 'perhaps' of starting a business. You might be someone who has already started and it is early days. You might be someone in an established business who is considering the future. You might be part of very sizeable business wondering how best to work out its future or the future of one of its divisions. You might be someone who works with people in business as an adviser, consultant, coach or mentor. You might be a student of business. You might be *anyone* who wants to know more about business planning.

Unique though you all are, if you do have something in common, it might be that you are at least half-asking some questions along the lines of:

- How do I make my business grow?
- What's the best strategic direction for my business?
- How do I achieve more sales?
- How do we best launch our exciting new product?
- What's the key to successful expansion into a new market?
- How do I sell my business for the best price?
- How can I get my business to run faster?
- How am I going to get this merger and joint venture work?
- How do I tell the wood from the trees?
- How do I give my people the leadership they need?
- How do develop some new thinking?
- How does my business get a new sense of purpose and new energy?
- My business is at a crossroads: which way do I go?
- How do I best communicate the strategy?
- My nose is always at the grindstone and all I'm getting is a bloody

nose. How do I step back?

- I spend time *in* the business but not *on* the business. How can I change that?
- I need to raise my team's performance – how?
- How do we achieve a meeting of minds?
- How would I franchise my business?
- Supply and distribution flows are erratic: How does my business improve?
- How do I improve my processes? Would outsourcing help?
- How do I reduce my costs?
- How do I make a success of trading overseas?
- How do I get the financial backing my business needs?
- How do I improve the customer experience?
- What projects should my business invest in? How do we implement them effectively?
- How do I survive?

You might be asking questions like these because you are in business, or because you advise businesses, or because you study businesses, or because you are simply interested. Whatever your reasons, these questions are important.

In fact, they are so important that they must be – can only be – answered within the context of business planning.

You need this book and it's here to help you. By the final chapter, you'll know how to engage in successful business planning. This will help you find a way to answer all these questions and the thousands of others that are posed to business people all the time.

You'll also understand:

- why the process of business planning is absolutely vital;
- that the *process* of business planning is different from the output of a business plan;
- that the process of business planning is continuous, evolutionary and craft-like;
- how a business plan is best structured and presented to a variety of audiences;
- that producing a business plan dramatically enhances the quality of the process of business planning;

- how best to identify, analyse, evaluate and communicate a business opportunity so as to engage commitment from others: potential investors, shareholders, bankers, collaborators, purchasers, your own people, customers, suppliers;
- how best to implement your business plan and make your business journey happen;
- how to make your business a successful locus in a network of relationships;
- how to deal positively with the inevitable setbacks along the way and keep your business journey vibrant;
- how to be the best servant of your business vision that you can be.

In your hands, these nuggets of understanding will combine to build a golden future.

I wish you every business and personal success.

John Kirwan

Chapter 1

The Principles Behind Successful Business Planning

'If you think you can do a thing or think you can't do a thing, you're right.' – Henry Ford

WHAT'S THE *POINT* OF BUSINESS PLANNING?

Is there a part of you that wonders what's the point in all this business planning? Is there a voice that says: 'Look, I'm too busy running my business to take time out on academic stuff – I've got customers to serve, suppliers to be nice to, and my bank is moaning at me – plus the fact that my best worker has phoned in sick and we've got this order to deliver – so I can't stop when all this is going on; and anyway another thing ...'?

Is there also a voice which says: 'Besides, what's the point? It's not like it'll make a difference anyway. *Che sarà sarà.*'

Such comments are understandable – I have heard them (and similar) many times in my career. They seem to resemble each other in that they are both 'anti-planning', but in fact they come from quite different directions.

The 'I'm-too-busy'-objection

The first type of comment, which I shall call the 'I'm-too-busy'-objection, is a plea about the pressures of being a small business elbowing aside what are viewed as luxuries more appropriate for big business. 'It's alright for your big PLCs, they've got lots of people who can do this'; or 'my business isn't a complicated PLC, it's a simple small business – I've got it all in my head'.

And yet the people who think such thoughts rarely go on to wonder how such businesses became big with lots of people, in the first place. There is also the presupposition that real work necessarily involves physical activity or a sense of fevered 'rushedness', whereas thinking is not real work, but some sort of indulgence that masquerades as work. According to this view, it is like a free-revving engine: thinking and planning can, to some, make the sound and noise of considerable motion, whereas actually they believe it's a con without any real traction on physical reality.

To be honest, I don't have a lot of patience for the 'I'm-too-busy'-objection. To such people whining that there is too much on their plate for them to be able to think and plan, I say make the time (and get a bigger plate!). In my experience, the trouble with people who keep their noses to the grindstone is that they always – and only – end up with bloody noses.

'But *how* do I plan for my business?' Now *that's* a very fair question and I am going to help you answer that question very effectively with this book. So all you readers who are former I'm-too-busy-people, and those of you who are, all along, yes-I-do-believe-planning-is crucial-for-my-business-people. So let's go.

The 'che-sarà-sarà'-objection

There is an important group still to engage. These are the proponents of the *che-sarà-sarà* objection. This has a different basis from the 'I'm-too-busy' argument. Whereas that one presupposed a superior value in physical work over thinking and planning, the *che-sarà-sarà* objection assumes a fundamentally chaotic world that is indifferent to the rationalised hopes and plans of puny humans. When the fluttering of a butterfly's wings in the Amazonian jungle, so the argument runs, can cause a hurricane in south-east Asia, what's the point of a business in Cleethorpes hoping to plan to double its profits?

This is a dangerous anti-planning argument. Part of its danger is that it seems to inject some up-to-the-minute thinking about the deepest nature of the universe into shoring up what is essentially destructive pessimism. 'I may not like it', so the argument runs, 'but that's just me failing to be a mature adult in this precarious modern world. I am simply clinging on to a childish and ultimately forlorn assumption that my hopes and aspirations actually matter. It is a delusion to think that the chaos of the universe can be bent or moulded to my tiny purposes.'

'Just do the best you can', the *che-sarà-sarà* people would recommend, 'and if you are fortunate you won't go against the grain of the benign indifference of the universe and you'll get by. In fact, that might fool you into thinking your own plans make a difference, but actually you've just got lucky.'

So, the *che-sarà-sarà* objection has its attractions: it seems to be the mark of modern adulthood and it looks like it copes with contrary evidence. This is why it is so dangerous.

And that is also why it is so flawed. It is not the mark of modern adulthood; it is in denial of our basic human nature.

The ancient Greeks understood that people are essentially 'teleological': in other words, purposeful, goal-setting creatures. We have to have goals. So strong is this need, if we don't give ourselves new goals, then we shall simply continue with the ones we already have, and nothing much changes. Or we take on someone else's goal and then find ourselves joining our colleagues down the pub because we might as well; we have nothing better to do. Or, tragically, if our goal-orientation is taken away, we just curl up and die. We see this among some of those who retire – irrespective of the age at which they retired[1] – or among prisoners of war who are otherwise given enough sustenance to survive; or among surviving spouses who, being so dependent upon their partner in life, often live only a short while after their death.

When it comes to the inference that should be drawn about business planning; the essential nature of humans as teleological trumps any insights into the universe as chaotic. What does this mean for you as a business person? If you don't have goals for your business and make plans on how to achieve them, then either you will take any old goal that comes your way, or your business will eventually curl up and die. So, better to set your own goals, consciously and deliberately and with intent, and plan on how to achieve them. In a complex, ambiguous world *that* is the truly adult thing to do!

We shall say more about the power of goal-setting and planning in Chapter 2, which is where former *che-sarà-sarà*-objectors can join their former I'm-too-busy-counterparts. Meanwhile, there is one last group with whom we must engage otherwise they, too, would remain as a ball in a pinball machine: plan-less and so knocked hither-and-thither by whatever levers and springs they happen to bounce into. Points amassed are scored by others; the ball itself is just struck and scratched.

The 'my-business-is-already-good-enough'-objection

Your business is successful. Turnover is growing: has done for years, still is, and looks like it will for years. Customers are happy – at least they always tell you they are when you ask them and besides, they are rewarding you with increasing sales. With costs growing more slowly than turnover, you feel very happy with your rising profits. Indeed, your business is lauded as a model example pored over as a case study by students at what many would call the world's foremost business school. *Fortune* magazine says you are top for innovation. With such success, what need have you of new goals and new plans?

Your business, called Enron, looks poised for stellar success[2]. And yet it became the largest corporate bankruptcy in American history with repercussions still being keenly felt today. Corporate history is littered with the broken dreams of businesses that once flew high – and not just airlines like PanAm or DanAir. I remember as a child looking in wonder at the myriad of Airfix models at the toy shop I cycled to on my Tri-ang tricycle before racing home to meet my dad who had just driven home in his Hillman Imp. More recently, instead of typing this on my Samsung laptop, I might have been using a Tiny computer before checking my shareholdings in Marconi and Northern Rock.

Of course, it is not necessarily the absence of plans that did for these companies, but the quality of the plans – and most especially the quality of their implementation. A plan stands or falls not by the quality with which it is written or by the quality of its research and insight but by the quality of its implementation.

Sure, all businesses – from the smallest to the mightiest – can be seriously knocked about by external forces: a new competitor, a change of fad that pulls away customers, a technological breakthrough that banishes your product to obsolescence, a stroke of the regulatory pen that re-writes the rules of the game and takes away your ball. And it is because that these risks exist that business planning is all the more imperative.

No business is 'already good enough' to withstand such shocks. A business that thinks it is 'already good enough' will find no reason to change. Its goals will become more and more short-term until the business focuses just on maintaining the status quo. What started as successful experiments will be routinised unhindered by any fresh thinking but propelled by complacency all the way to orthodoxies, doctrines and dogma.

Such a business will be smugly gazing in the opposite direction from the juggernaut of change that brutally runs it over. Or, if it does catch sight of the headlights, it will not have the abilities, resources or time to leap to safety; and the spasm of the last-minute attempt will simply add to the anguish.

Yet forces – including forces of change – form trends and trends can be tracked and extrapolated. The outside-in attitude that proper business planning encourages will help you to anticipate future changes and allow you to prepare your actions in good time. The forces of change are not stopped, but you are better able to steer them towards your chosen goals. Noah did not wait for it to rain before building the ark – just as it is easier for a healthy person to exercise in order to stay well.

One of the ironies of our age is that, as the life expectancy of individuals in developed economies is rising, that of businesses is falling. One accomplished business practitioner, thinker and writer, Arie de Geus, has studied this area. He found that a third of the Fortune 500 companies listed in 1970, had gone by 1983 (acquired, merged or broken up)[3]. De Geus goes on to quote a Dutch study showing that the average corporate life expectancy in Japan and Europe was only 12½ years. Another study found declining business life expectancy in the major European economies between 1987-89 and 1999-2001: it had dropped from 9.7 to 4.1 years in Britain; from 13.3 to 9.2 years in France; and from 45 years to 18 years in Germany[4].

Achieving sustained success in business is extremely difficult. The *Fortune* list of top companies began in 1955. Just five years later, only 82 of the original list were still in the top 100. After a further 25 years, fewer than half, that is 44 companies, were still among the top 100. By now, at the time of writing – 2009 – can you guess how many of the top 100 companies in the world in 1955 are still among the top 100 in 2009? Astonishingly, it is just 9!

Note that these are established, substantial businesses, so it is easy to understand that success is also extremely elusive for small businesses. In the UK, only about half of small businesses are still trading after their first three years from initial set-up[5]. To survive in business, let alone flourish, is hard enough without making it impossible by failing to plan[6].

Of course, unexpected changes have their part but my experience of observing thousands of businesses over the years and the accumulated wisdom of other students of business is that there is a high correlation between successful businesses and those with coherent, well-implemented business plans, and also between failed businesses and those with no or poor business plans. And more: the degree of success reflects the degree of quality of the plan and its implementation.

So you have a stark choice: do you want to increase significantly your chances of failure? If yes, don't bother with a business plan. Do you want to increase significantly your chances of success? Then let me help you form an effective business plan.

As far as I have found in more than a quarter of a century of working with businesses and in the accumulated experience of hundreds of my colleagues and friends, only the late Sir John Harvey Jones, the former Chairman of ICI and wise TV business guru, has found, with heavy irony, an advantage in not bothering with business planning:

'The nicest thing about not planning is that failure comes as a complete surprise, rather than being preceded by a period of worry and depression.'

Oh one more point: whether you are a start-up business seeking investment or an established business seeking funding, you will not get the monies unless you have a business plan. So forget the debate and let's get going!

Key takeaways from Chapter 1:

1 Say NO to 'I'm-too-busy-to-plan'.
2 Say NO to 'che-sarà-sarà'.
3 Say NO to 'my-business-is-already-good-enough'.
4 Say YES, YES, YES to success through business planning.

Notes and References

1 Tsai S.P., Wendt J.K., Donnelly R.P., de Jong G., and Ahmed F.S. 'Age at retirement and long term survival of an industrial population: prospective cohort study'. *British Medical Journal*, 2005, **331**, p. 995.

2 For example: 'Enron is one of the world's leading electricity, natural gas and communications companies. The company, with revenues of $40 billion in 1999 and $30 billion for the first six months of 2000, produces electricity and natural gas, develops, constructs and operates energy facilities worldwide, delivers physical commodities and financial and risk management services to customers around the world, and is developing an intelligent network platform to facilitate online business. *Fortune* magazine has named Enron 'America's Most Innovative Company' for five consecutive years, the top company for 'Quality of Management' and the second best company for 'Employee Talent'. In addition, Enron ranks in the top quarter of *Fortune*'s 'Best 100 Companies to Work For in America''. From an Enron press release, 4th October 2000. In fairness to *Fortune*, many people in the business world were fooled by Enron, from hard-nosed Wall Street analysts to sober-minded academics. And it was *Fortune* that ran an article entitled 'Is Enron Overpriced?' by Bethany McLean on 5th March 2001, which unpacked the comment that 'Enron's financial statements are nearly impenetrable'.

3 De Geus, A. *The Living Company*. Boston: Harvard Business School, 1997.

4 Seifert, W. G. 'Neuer Markt: that damned economic miracle or the return of Dr. Mabuse'. *The Finance Foundation News*, 2002, **3**, pp. 46-57. www.fondation-finance.com/ff/ff.nsf/EN/p46p57

5 For example: 'It is a fact that only about 50% of small businesses are still trading after their first three years from initial set up' (www.bizhelp24.com). And 'Start up businesses have a very high failure rate in this country with as many as 1 in 2 failing in their first two years' (www.thetimes100.co.uk). And 'On average only slightly over a third of start-ups survive five years, and less than one in five survive ten years', *Small Firms in Britain, 2007: A Review by Barclays Local Business Banking*, October 2007, p. 5.

6 The necessity of having a business plan and the contribution that the absence of business planning makes to business failure are well understood. See Chapter 2, Survival (p. 9).

Chapter 2
The Benefits of Business Planning

'Plans are useless, but planning is essential.' –
Dwight D. Eisenhower

SURVIVAL

Allow your imagination a free rein for a moment.

Transport yourself to a parallel world that in every respect exactly resembles this one – except for one thing. In this parallel world the benefits of business planning are being considered by a bizarre fusion of the erudition of Benjamin Franklin with the musical rhythms of *Saturday Night Fever.*

We can bring back the resultant insight to our own world. For when the unassailable wisdom of Franklin's axiom 'By failing to prepare, you are preparing to fail', fuses fantastically with the strains of the Bee Gees' 'Stayin' Alive', we instantly understand that one of the benefits of business planning is ... survival.[1]

We learned about the crucial role played by planning in increasing the chances of survival in Chapter 1, and this is widely recognised. For example:

- 'It is essential to have a realistic, working business plan when you're starting up a business.' www.businesslink.gov.uk
- 'Lack of planning and preparation before starting up is number one of the "Seven Deadly Business Sins"', according to www.learndirect-business.co.uk
- www.thetimes100.co.uk cites 'poor business planning' as one of the key reasons for business failure.

- 'To maximise your chances of success, it's key to do your research and have a solid business plan first.' *Barclays Bank Start-Up Business Guide.*
- 'To be a successful business owner you must focus on your strategy and your business plan – you need to know where you are going.' www.talktosps.com

You might be wondering why I am stressing this point so much. The reason is that only a minority of businesses survive beyond their first five years and, of these, far too many are under-achieving – that is, performing way below their potential.

I passionately want your business not just to survive, but to flourish because I know how important it is to you and to those who depend on you.

You want the same. And, therefore, you want business planning.

BUSINESS PLAN AND BUSINESS PLANNING: DOCUMENT AND PROCESS

Notice that my previous sentence was not 'You want a business plan', but 'You want business planning'.

Far too often, businesses see the object of the exercise as the production of a particular document called 'XYZ's Business Plan'. The consequence is that they become overly fixated on issues such as layout, chapter headings and presentation, and when such issues are resolved, the job is regarded as done. The business plan is therefore regarded as finished and is then kept in a drawer – rarely, if ever, to see the light of day.

Of course, there is a genuine point in producing an end-product, a document that is known as the business plan. The discipline of committing one's thinking into tangible form 'out there' is irreplaceably useful in making sense of the context in which the business is operating, the vision for the business, and the means by which the objectives of the business are to be achieved.

Furthermore, there are important audiences – such as investors, bankers, the business's leaders – who need to see 'the business plan' so that a specific outcome can be achieved: obtaining equity finance, getting an overdraft for working capital, directing and motivating the team. These outcomes are indeed important and so, therefore, is the document that helps to achieve them.

But the real importance is in the *process* by which the business plan is created in the first place and then kept fresh in the light of real world events: progress and setbacks. This is why Eisenhower valued planning over plans. Properly done, business planning is an unending iterative process that is gestured towards by a business plan, but is realised fully only when it becomes part and parcel of how the business is run.

When you undertake business planning, you are, like the potter working with clay, undertaking a craft process. You start with an idea of what you will make, but at the same time you respond to the exigencies of the situation, just as the potter's hands respond to the moving form of the clay on the wheel. And the business reacts to the changes you make and the actions you take, just as the clay yields to the potter's hands. There is a continuous, reciprocal interaction. Even the most meticulous description of the finished pot would not do justice to what the potter is really doing. Likewise, an exclusive focus on the business plan would miss out where the true power lies: in the benefit of business planning on helping the business to succeed by continuously affecting behaviours and outlooks.

Always remember that it is the people who make the numbers – not the other way round.

AVOIDING CRISES

Have you: got married, started a family, got divorced, changed jobs, sold your house, bought a new house, emigrated, repatriated yourself, suffered a bereavement, changed your car, started a new hobby, joined a club, become a vegetarian, had cosmetic surgery and started a degree course, *all in one year*?

Would you ever plan, deliberately, to do all this in one year?

Such upheaval is barely imaginable. We humans are superb at initiating and coping with change – but within reason. We need some continuity, some routines on which we can graft change in order to maintain our orientation, our energy – even our sense of who we are.

Fundamental, root-and-branch revolutionary change is hard for us. It is disorientating, wearing and can give us an unsettling sense of uncertainty as to who we are or who we are becoming. We begin to long for things to settle down, to go back to 'normal'.

Yet while the string of major changes compressed into one year may indeed be unimaginable, we do recognise that a crisis is often the trigger for revolutionary change. A business in crisis, for example, will often act drastically. Factories are closed, jobs are cut suddenly, stress levels are high. 'Desperate times call for desperate measures' and such actions may indeed save something of the business for the longer term, but there will have been huge dislocation and tragedy.

Crises do happen, but they are best avoided. Humans are not naturally made to cope with the 'desperate measures' that 'desperate times' may call for. Yet the pace of change is so great that what starts as a modest disconnect between a business and its market can very quickly escalate into a major breakdown, a crisis.

There is no guarantee, but the way to reduce the likelihood of crisis and the resultant problems of revolutionary change is to engage in business planning.

This is not particularly because a business plan is a good predictor of the future (it is not necessarily), but because the process of business planning creates resilience in the business. It equips its leaders with the understanding of the levers of the business to take serial actions that maintain congruence with the market.

With business planning, fewer of the dramas that are the inevitable lot of modern business life will become full-blown crises.

SPOTTING DANGER SIGNS

Have you ever tried to boil a frog?

Even if you have not, you may well know that it is said that if you were to drop a frog into boiling water, it would leap out with some alacrity – and probably cross you off its Christmas card list.

However, if you were to put the frog in cool water, and then gradually increase the temperature, it is said that the frog will take no notice until it becomes groggier and groggier as the temperature continues to be increased. Finally the frog will die. So you will stay on the list, although still not receive a Christmas card.

I have not actually tested this with a real frog, but the point is clear. Although there was no one moment of decisive change that obliged the frog to take action, nonetheless we can see, with hindsight, that the frog was caught up in a dangerous trend. But it did not seem like that to the frog.

And so, for example, at what point should it have occurred to the leaders of the British motorcycle industry – the foremost such industry in the world – that they were caught up in a trend that would ultimately lead to their business's demise and the domination by the Japanese motorcycle of the UK and world markets?

The threat seems obvious to us as outsiders, but the industry leaders, caught up on the inside of the story, were like groggy frogs. Or in banking, at what point should Northern Rock have changed its business model instead of traipsing all the way to disaster?

Failure or a material decline in business fortunes is such an ever-present danger, that another of the key benefits of business planning is the ability it gives to leaders and managers to spot warning signs more quickly. This is not about predicting the future. It is about so understanding the capabilities and resources of the business and the path that it is on that a potentially harmful departure from that path can be identified early and corrective action taken.

Every seaman knows that a small early correction to one's course is much easier to make than a later radical one. It is partly about avoiding crises, which we discussed earlier, but it is also about avoiding the grogginess that makes the business unable to save itself. Alertness to what is going on and to what that means for the business is an essential business planning skill.

GENERATING ENERGY AND CREATIVITY

Business planning is about how and why goals will be accomplished. Goal-setting, as we learned in Chapter 1, is intrinsic to human nature. Our well-being and, indeed, survival, are bound up with having an ability to have goals.

So there is something fundamental to the human condition about business planning. And goal-setting – integral to business planning – gives other benefits as well.

You notice a picture hanging crookedly on a wall. You feel compelled to straighten it. Why? Because it is not as it is supposed to be. This mismatch between how something actually is, and how it ought to be, generates energy in you to fix it. Goal-setting mimics exactly this phenomenon. The goal is an expression of how you want things to be. Things are not yet like that. Energy is generated in you to 'fix it'. And, moreover, it is generated in your team.

The goal-setting that is integral to business planning not only generates energy, it also generates creativity. You will be surprised at how, when you have a clearly visualised business goal that you care passionately about, your mind will be awakened to find all sorts of help, resources and ideas to help you achieve it.

Have you ever noticed that, after buying a car, the road seems suddenly full of cars just like yours? Did scores of people coincidentally decide to buy the same car as you at the same time? No, of course not. The truth is that these cars were there all along, but the act of purchasing one yourself has awakened your mind to their presence. You are now alert to them.

Goals produced by business planning (that is, goals that are clearly defined and arouse passion) awaken the energy and creativity of those within the business to accomplish them. It is as though people are self-guiding missiles: once a target is set, they have a self-correcting guidance system that keeps them on course even if the target moves about. This process can be quite unconscious. We become open to anything and everything that will help us reach our goal, help keep us on course.

In business, we see hundreds of ifs and maybes every day. For example, should I prospect for this business? What price shall I charge? Should I develop this new product, or that one? Is it better to train or hire?

We fail to see thousands of others.

The way to cut through this confusion, to separate the cul-de-sacs from the genuine half-chances, is to view them with the perspective of the business goals. You will recognise them for what they are when you look at them from the perspective of the last page – the end in view.

CELEBRATING SUCCESS

Why is it that it is the children's grandparents, and not the parents, who always remark on how much they have grown? Because the parents are with the children all the time, they do not notice the incremental progress that their offspring are making. This is why some parents make a mark on a wall to show a child's height as soon as he or she can stand, and then at every birthday thereafter.

The point is that progress cannot be celebrated unless there is a reference point and subsequent monitoring – all of which are integral components of business planning. In the case of business planning, however, there is a crucial difference between the reference point for a business and that for a child's growth.

It goes back to goal-setting. In business, as in life, it does not matter where you have come from. What matters is how you stand in relation to where you want to get to. Turnover growth of 10 per cent halfway through the year is to be celebrated if it keeps the business on course for achieving 20 per cent year-on-year growth. And this is to be celebrated if it keeps the business on course towards the goal of doubling turnover in three years which itself matters only if it is part of the goal of achieving market leadership and being the number one choice for customers. The key relationship is between where the business is now and where it is headed, as articulated by the business goals and vision that are part of business planning.

Spotting success, and harnessing its motivational power, are only possible with business planning.

ACHIEVING A SPECIFIC OUTCOME

We have discussed already that one of the benefits of business planning is that the process does produce a (living) document that is essential to achieve certain specific outcomes, such as funding from investors, overdrafts or loans from bankers, or a sale when exiting and selling on the business.

These canny audiences know full well that a neatly presented business plan is just what it appears to be: a nice piece of paperwork. The real significance is in the business that the plan seeks to represent. 'What are the real live processes that underpin the business plan?'; this is the question that actually concerns them. Quality business planning will stand a much better chance of achieving the specific outcome.

Key takeaways from Chapter 2

1 Remember that the benefits of business planning are:

    a. helping a business to survive;

2 The strength of the business plan comes from the quality of the process of business planning;

    a. avoiding crises;

    b. spotting danger signs;

    c. generating energy and creativity;

    d. celebrating success;

    e. achieving a specific outcome.

3 In business, people make the numbers, not the other way round.

4 Start with the end in view.

Notes and References

1 The link between the Bee Gees' song 'Stayin' Alive' and survival is actually not so bizarre. On the 19th October 2008, BBC's online news carried a story headlined 'Bee Gees hit could save your life: US medics have found the Bee Gees' 1977 hit 'Stayin' Alive' is an ideal beat to follow to perform chest compressions on a victim of a cardiac arrest.' Apparently, the catchy song contains 103 beats to the minute, which is close to the recommended rate of 100 chest compressions per minute. A spokesman for the American Heart Association was reported as confirming that 'Stayin' Alive' has been used as a training tip for cardiopulmonary resuscitation instructors for the last two years or so.

Chapter 3

The Process of Successful Business Planning: Its Form

'Planning is bringing the future into the present so that you can do something about it now.' – Alan Lakein

THE FRUITS OF YOUR MIND – AND A LEMON

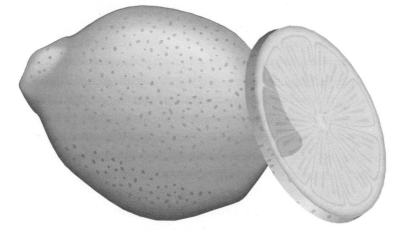

Imagine that you are in your kitchen. You decide to get a lemon. So you go to where you would find a lemon and pick one up.

You pause for a moment as you feel the lemon in your hand. You can feel its firm shape, its dimpled skin, its fat, slightly yielding middle, and its tapered pimples at each end.

You decide to cut it. So you reach for a cutting board and a knife. You grip the lemon firmly with one hand and the knife in the other. Bringing down the lemon to the surface of the chopping board, you begin to cut.

A sudden spurt of juice almost catches your eye. The fresh, fragrant smell of lemon zestiness is now strong in your nostrils. As you complete the cut, more juice starts to weep onto the chopping board.

You bring the cut half of lemon closer to your face and the transected yellow segments stand brightly in their white surrounding duvet of pith. The scent is really strong now.

You bring the lemon close to your mouth, which opens, and your tongue reaches out and licks the full face of the cut lemon. Immediately your tongue is stung by the tartness and you recoil.

'LEMON-ENTRY, MY DEAR READER'

Did you actually register the smell of the lemon? Did you physically react to the taste? I've talked through this scenario with roomfuls of people and by the end, I can see some tongues, certainly a few throats bob up and down as the imagined lemon juice is swallowed, and also some grimaces!

The point is that powerfully visualising a possible reality can have a real, physical impact on actual reality. Of course there isn't really a lemon, and no lemon scent, and no bitter lemon juice – and yet our bodies respond as though it were actually happening.

If the visualisation is detailed and vivid enough, then we can actually affect the present. But for the visualisation to have an impact on the here and now, it must be as comprehensive and as emotive as possible. Do not build half a dam.

HARNESSING ENERGY FROM THE POWER OF PURPOSES

Try pulling on one end of an elastic band.

Easy, isn't it?

There is little energy in this simple system because there is no anchor at the end opposite to the one you are holding. To get some real energy, there has to be a real interplay between two strong points: opposite pulls at each end of the elastic band.

It is the same for people and for businesses. Neither will choose to move from where they are unless they are discontent with the here and now. They have to be dissatisfied with the status quo before they act to create a new status quo.

We shall come back to say more about the here and now, but at this stage let us note that one way to generate discontent with the current situation is to compare it unfavourably with how good things could be. But this discontent will be proportional to how attractive to you the possible future state is. As ever in an iterative system we have to start somewhere, so – as one of our takeaways from Chapter 2 exhorted us – let us start with the end in view.

In Chapter 2 we talked about how a picture, hanging crookedly on a wall, can move you to action to straighten it. Why? – because it is not as it is supposed to be. It is the same feeling as when you observe someone wearing a jacket where the back of the collar is half-folded up, or when you see text that is out of $a^{li}_{g}n^{me}n_{t}$. When the world looks out of kilter with how you think it ought to look, energy is created in you to put the world right.

Now, we are very familiar with how a picture should hang on a wall, or how a jacket should be worn or how text should line up, but how should your business be? There is no ready-to-hand pattern of 'how my business is supposed to be', no pull on this end of the rubber band – until, that is, you create it or *visualise* it.

We have seen that the power of a vivid visualisation of an imagined reality can have a tangible affect on the here and now. If we make ourselves create a vivid mismatch between how we think the world ought to be and how we see the world actually is, we shall generate energy to set about changing the world and putting it right.

This is the purpose of creating a vision for your business: to imagine vividly and in detail how you want – how you really, really want – your business to be in the future so as to generate energy and creativity in the present to get you there.

Peter Senge, a noted writer on how businesses can achieve their full potential, has developed our rubber band analogy[1].

Imagine stretching a rubber band between two points: an upper point called 'Vision' and a lower point called 'Current Reality'.

Vision

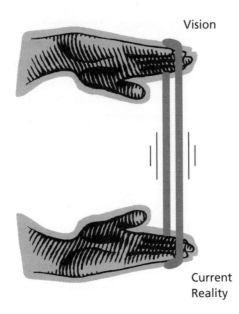

Current
Reality

'Vision' represents a vivid visualisation of a possible reality, of the world as it ought to be. 'Current Reality' is the world as it actually is.

There is tension in the rubber band. The tension needs to resolve itself.

If the pull of Current Reality is stronger than that of the Vision, then the rubber band will be pulled back downwards in the direction of Current Reality. If, on the other hand, the pull of the Vision is stronger than that of Current Reality, then the rubber band is drawn towards the Vision and Current Reality starts to change and move towards the Vision, becoming more and more like it.

Now, if the Vision is too outlandish, too far out, then the rubber band will not stretch that far and it will be pulled back – perhaps sharply, snapping at your fingers. That hurts! It is the disappointment and disillusion that comes from falling short of a dream.

But notice, too, what happens to the rubber band as it pulls Current Reality to the Vision. The tension goes, the energy is dissipated. This is why, as a vision is being approached, so it is imperative to set a new vision with new goals. The successful business works not *to* goals, but *through* goals.

This is how the successful business planning process gets started: you manufacture and then direct energy to move from current reality, to initiate and drive change, towards the vision, the goal – and new goals are continually set as each one is approached.[3]

But remember how there is little energy if nothing anchors the other end of the rubber band? To get some real energy, there has to be a real interplay between two strong points: opposite pulls at each end of the elastic band. The Vision provides pull, but only if we have a detailed understanding of the Current Reality we are pulling against. This understanding is like the anchor at the other end of the rubber band – but not an immovable anchor.

SOME REALLY SIMPLE MATHS – HONEST!

I find the following formula very helpful here:

D x V x I > R

That is: **Discontent x Vision x Implementation > Resistance (or inertia)**[4]

I work to this formula whenever I am writing a business case, or when seeking to persuade someone, or when explaining the need to change to a group.

It is about so describing the current situation with all what Jim Collins calls its 'brutal facts'[2] so as to arouse discontent with the present reality. It is about showing that we cannot continue as we are.

Then it is about showing how good a changed situation could be: that there is a possible reality that would be so much better than where we are today – the 'V' of 'Vision'. This starts to generate energy and creativity.

Once it is understood that the vision is not fantasy or too far-fetched – by showing that there are early implementation steps that can get us on our way – then inertia or resistance is overcome. This is the part of the formula with the beckoning finger, the 'come hither' look. ('Inertia' is not necessarily no movement at all. Rather, it is really the same as 'resistance' once the actual pace of change becomes slower than the required pace of change.)

MATURITY: CENTRAL TO THE PROCESS OF SUCCESSFUL BUSINESS PLANNING

This is why what is central to the process of successful business planning is not your intelligence as a person, nor your skills as a business owner/leader, nor the number of hours you spend working, but your maturity.

This essential maturity is the ability to hold simultaneously a vivid visualisation of a future reality for your business at the same time as a strong grasp on its current situation – and then act effectively to close the gap[5].

Why? Because as we have already noted: To get some real energy, there has to be a real interplay between two strong points: opposite pulls at each end of the elastic band.

Key takeaways from Chapter 3:

1   The heart of the process of successful business planning is maturity: the ability to hold simultaneously a vivid visualisation of a future reality for your business at the same time as a deep and detailed understanding of its current situation.
2   Your business needs energy: a vision you feel absolutely passionate about, and a constant discontent with the status quo.
3   Don't just work *to* your business goals, but *through* them.
4   Your business outlook must exhibit maturity at all times.

Notes and References

1   Senge, P.M. *The Fifth Discipline: The Art and Practice of the Learning Organization.* pp. 150 ff. London: Random House Business Books, 1993.
2   Collins, J. *Good to Great.* Chapter 4. London: Random House Business Books, 2001.
3   For the moment I am not defining any distinction between vision and goals. Such a distinction will be needed (plus others besides), however, and will come in Chapter 4.
4   This is based on what is called 'Gleicher's formula' (D x V x F > R) where:
     D = dissatisfaction with the status quo
     V = vision of what is possible
     F = first (or next) concrete steps that can be taken towards achieving that vision, and
     R = resistance to change

5   Martin Luther King, for example, did not have a critical path schedule. He had a *dream*. He held out a vivid visualisation of a different and better reality while at the same time vividly describing the appalling here and now so as to generate the energy and creativity that started to change the world: 'Just as Socrates felt that it was necessary to create a tension in the mind so that individuals could rise from the bondage of myths and half-truths to the unfettered realm of creative analysis and objective appraisal, we must we see the need for non-violent gadflies to create the kind of tension in society that will help men rise from the dark depths of prejudice and racism to the majestic heights of understanding and brotherhood' (*Letter from Birmingham Jail*).

Chapter 4

The Process of Successful Business Planning: Starting at the End

'No wind favours him who has no destined port.' – Montaigne

THE VISION THING

I cannot tell you what the vision for your business should be. In fact, no one can, other than you: your business's vision has to be *your* vision.

Your vision is very specific not only to your business and its marketplace but also to you as a person. It represents a vivid encapsulation of where you want to take your business in the future. It is your idealised interim end-state (an 'interim end-state' because it is in the long-term future and, as we noted in Chapter 3, as we later approach our vision, so we set ourselves a new one.)

Making it happen will make huge demands on you and you will have to work very, very hard. Your vision has to be so alluring to you, so powerful for you, that it will get you out of bed every morning, even when you are longing simply to pull the duvet back over your head.

Write your vision down. You will need many attempts before you get it how you want it – how you need it – to be. But it will not only clarify your thinking and your true dreams, it will also get you out of bed with a bound.

So, your vision is essential to captivate you and so generate the creativity and energy you need to bring it about. It will also help to clarify key business issues for you. You will not know what your marketing strategy, for example, ought to be, or what skills and talents you will need, or how to organise your business operationally, unless you know the vision that all these are designed to achieve. In this way, your vision is like a beacon towards which to navigate your whole business.

And so you now have a vision: a written statement of where you want your business to be in the long-term future, a vision that clarifies your thinking and captivates your heart. It is so vividly articulated that you are absolutely confident you will get there and that, every time you read it, you are full of excitement. The ideal future state for your business has to matter to you very, very much. Don't commit yourself to anything less.

If you are running your business with others, then the vision will do the same for the whole team. It is a very personal thing.

This is why I cannot write your vision for you – but I can give you some examples of what other businesses have set as their vision, and I can also give you some tips as to how to write your own.

SOME EXAMPLES OF OTHER BUSINESSES' VISIONS

There is a story that US President John F Kennedy visited the NASA space station in the 1960s to look at progress. He spotted a guy sweeping the floor with a broom. Going towards him, he said: 'And what do you do around here?'

'I'm helping to put a man on the moon, sir.'

Putting a man on the moon (by the end of the 1960s) was a vision that aimed, quite literally, very high, and no one had any idea at the time how it could possibly be achieved. It also inspired people and, for the man who was sweeping the floor, it contextualised his activity in a way that connected to his sense of what was deeply meaningful for him. It got him out of bed in the morning.

Imagine if the vision had been something like 'let's build the best rocket we can and see how high we can transport a crew. It lacks something, doesn't it? Something crucial.

Or what if Karl Marx, instead of finishing his *Communist Manifesto* with 'Workers of the world unite! You have nothing to lose but your chains', had penned something like: 'All you workers out there, it would be greatly beneficial for you to get together'?

Such an insipid vision would not have had anything like the power to inspire and rally people.

Vision statements are brief and usually capture something fundamental. One of the shortest ones I have come across that also gets to nub of things is IKEA's: 'to create a better everyday life for the many people'[1].

Like its products, IKEA's vision statement has no ornament, yet it is wide-ranging in its scope, part of the fabric of day-to-day existence and irrepressibly upbeat. It guides everyone inside and outside the company about what IKEA wants to achieve. Products are functional – they are part of everyday life. They are available to as many people as possible – they are low priced. They are low priced because they are low cost to produce. And so, from marketing through pricing to supply chain and manufacture, the vision is informing IKEA's entire business model.

Pithiness seems to be a retailer's hallmark. Morrisons, the supermarket chain, goes for something even briefer and is the shortest vision statement I have come across: 'Food specialist for everyone'[2]; which is eminently punchy, no-nonsense and straightforward – and highly ambitious! Similarly, it also signals to staff, customers and suppliers what it wants to achieve and informs how it aims for distinctiveness in its marketplace. Morrisons sources most of its meat and produce direct from farms and prepares and processes it itself, which is how it aims to combine freshness with affordability and meeting individual customer needs[3].

In other companies, their vision incorporates the judgement of key stakeholders. For example, the vision of the Lloyds Banking Group (the resultant entity from the combination of Lloyds TSB and HBOS) is 'to be recognised as the best financial services company by customers, colleagues and shareholders'[4]. There is an assertion of self-identity here, effectively: 'We are a financial services company'. Not only is this vision about how the company is seen by others, but it is unendingly open-textured given the indefinability of 'best' and the different agendas of the three stakeholder populations[5].

Merck, the global pharmaceuticals company, also acknowledges the multi-agendas of its stakeholders, but provides some more substance. It calls its vision a 'mission': 'The mission of Merck is to provide society with superior products and services by developing innovations and solutions that improve the quality of life and satisfy customer needs, and to provide employees with meaningful work and advancement opportunities, and investors with a superior rate of return'[6].

Striving to triangulate the company's vision seems to me to be a growing trend. For example, 3M, who developed the iconic innovative product the Post-it™ note, writes under the heading 'Our Vision': '3M's commitment is to actively contribute to sustainable development through environmental protection, social responsibility and economic progress. To us, that means meeting the needs of society today, while respecting the ability of future generations to meet their needs'[7]. This vision statement is about achieving difficult balances: 'development' but it has to be 'sustainable'; 'economic progress' but with 'social responsibility' and mindful of 'environmental protection'; 'meeting the needs of society today' but 'while respecting the ability of future generations to meet their needs'. It reflects a very 21st century preoccupation: boldness – if that's alright with everyone else!

TOP TIPS FOR CREATING YOUR VISION

1 Give yourself time and peace and quiet – and lots of paper!
2 Aim high and do not worry about the 'hows' – they will come later.
3 Think about what and who really matters to you – and make lists:
   a. What do you want to be?
   b. What do you want to do?
   c. What do you want to own?
   d. Who do you want to be with?
   e. If you were looking back, what would you be really proud of?
4 Score each item you have listed out of 10, with '0' being a nice-to-have and '10' being very important.
5 Select the top-scoring items (say 3 or so) that relate to your business (as distinct, say, from your personal health or relationships, etc.).
6 Craft a statement that vividly expresses these top-scoring items. This might take several attempts. Keep it **brief** and **simple** – a sentence or two. Google's vision for example, is big, arresting and challenging – and just 12 words: 'To organise the world's information and make

it universally accessible and useful'[8]. Marx's rallying cry is just one word longer.

7   Review your vision:
   a. Does it truly inspire you? (It must get you bounding out of bed every morning. For as long as it takes.)
   b. Is it very, very important to you? (It must be **your** vision, not someone else's or something you think others will approve of, or put together because this book says so!)
   c. Does it really stretch the rubber band – without snapping? (It must be ambitious and challenging, but not fantastical – and yet, do not let the fear of failure constrain your vision.)
   d. Is it infectious? (It must get a positive, passionate response from others. Customers. Colleagues. Suppliers. Investors. Spouse.)

8   If you answer 'no' to any of the review questions, then start again. Remember: a vision is a very personal thing. Would BAT's vision do it for you: 'Our vision is to lead the tobacco industry through growth, productivity and responsibility'[9]?

Key takeaways from Chapter 4

1   Your vision will be bold, ambitious, emotive; something you care deeply about to get you out of bed on the darkest, coldest mornings.
2   Use the eight top tips to create your vision.

Notes and References

1   See www.ikea.com/ms/en_GB/about_ikea_new/about/index.html. Unilever has a vision (they call it a 'mission statement') which also talks about the quality of life for people rooted in the everyday: 'Unilever's mission is to add vitality to life. We meet everyday needs for nutrition, hygiene and personal care with brands that help people feel good, look good and get more out of life'; (e-mail from the company to the author dated 16th January 2009).
2   E-mail from the company to the author, dated 12th January 2009.
3   Another major supermarket retailer, J. Sainsbury, also encompasses within its vision statement (which they call 'Our goal') references to customers, products and everyday lives: 'At Sainsbury's we will deliver an ever-improving quality shopping experi-

ence for our customers with great products at fair prices. We aim to exceed customer expectations for healthy, safe, fresh and tasty food, making their lives easier every day' (see www.j-sainsburys.co.uk/index.asp?pageid = 14). More richly, perhaps, J. Sainsbury does not refer to customers as a group, but to their 'shopping experience' and to their 'expectations'. You may feel that this resonates more with what your own business is striving for.

4 Internal Lloyds Banking Group document *Our New Bank*, p. 4.

5 The main elements in this vision statement are interesting: first, there is reference to how Lloyds Banking Group is seen by others, in this case customers, colleagues and shareholders. Their perceptions will not necessarily be the same, however, as to what counts as being 'the best financial services company'. Indeed it is a moot point whether they ever could be the same, and so you might consider the extent to which the Lloyds Banking Group has articulated here anything that could ever be a *common* vision. The second element is the expression of self-identity as a 'financial services company'. It is important for every business to know what they stand for, to know what business they are truly in. Do you think this does it? Compare it with Tesco's statement of what they call their 'core purpose', which they encapsulate in just 10 words: 'To create value for customers to earn their lifetime loyalty' (see www.tescoplc.com/plc/about_us/values/). The third element in this articulation of Lloyds Banking Group's vision is in the list of those who are party to the vision as recognising the Lloyds Banking Group as the best. It is a fairly conventional list of stakeholders – customers, colleagues and shareholders – and not only might you ponder whether it is possible to have these three groups all recognising the same financial services company as being the best, but also whether this is the right list of stakeholders. The government is not mentioned, although it might be counted as among the shareholders. The regulator is not mentioned – a huge figure in the future lives of banks – unless it is included among a very broad interpretation of the word 'colleagues'. Nor is 'society' mentioned. I say all this because it might stimulate your own thinking as to what would be the right articulation of your own business's vision. Note that, in the case of the Lloyds Banking

Group, their articulation of their vision as quoted contrasts with what was stated in the Annual Report & Accounts for the Lloyds TSB Group for the year ending 31st December 2007: 'To be the best financial services organisation in the UK'. It is proclaimed on the opening page of text of the document under a large-font heading 'Our Vision'. It pre-dates the combination of Lloyds TSB with HBOS and so pre-dates the creation of the Lloyds Banking Group. There is the same expression of self-identity, but notice that 'to be the best' is not at all related to the recognition of any stake-holder. Furthermore, there is a geographical dimension to this vision statement: 'in the UK'. A year later, the Annual Report and Accounts are – rightly – full of discussion about the acquisition of HBOS (although the date of the accounts, the 31st December 2008, technically precedes the formal acquisition date of HBOS, 16th January 2009). After the list of contents, there is a sub-heading on page 1 'Our Vision', although it is less prominent than in the 2007 Annual Report and Accounts. The 2008 document has the same vision statement that we have been discussing – but with the addition of the geographic element: 'to be recognised as the best financial services organisation in the UK by customers, colleagues and shareholders'. Later in the 2008 Annual Report and Accounts, there are two further references to the vision which read like the 2007 version: 'being the best financial services provider in the United Kingdom' (p. 10), and 'being the best financial services organisation in the UK' (p. 40). I have spent quite some time on this because I believe a business's vision is very important. More than that, I believe that *your* business's vision is very important. So spend time, thought and effort to craft it to mean something that is truly important, meaningful and engaging to *you*; and be consistent about how you articulate it!

6   See www.merck.com/about/mission.html

7   See solutions.3m.com/wps/portal/3M/en_US/global/sustainability/ceo-statement/our-vision/

8   See www.google.com/corporate/

9   E-mail from the company to the author dated 8th January 2009 and also see www.bat.com/group/sites/uk__3mnfen.nsf/vwPagesWebLive/DO52AD6H?opendocument&SKN=1 (Also see 'Our vision is to achieve leadership of the global tobacco industry in order to create long term shareholder value' at www. bat.com/group/sites/UK__3MNFEN.nsf/vwPagesWebLive/ DO659LCX?opendocument&SKN = 1)

Chapter 5

The Process of Successful Business Planning: My Marketplace

'There are no facts, only interpretations.' – Friedrich Nietzsche

HEALTHY DOSES OF REALITY

'All the analysis in the world will never generate a vision ... the natural energy for changing reality comes from holding a picture of what might be that is more important to people than what is. [But] vision without an understanding of current reality will more likely foster cynicism than creativity' (Peter Senge[1] in Segal-Horn, 1998 p. 297).

This reminds us that a vision must not only have emotive power, it must also and at the same time emerge from an understanding of current reality.

Understanding current reality? There could hardly be a bigger topic! So what does the busy business planner do? Fortunately, there are well-established processes that you can usefully go through in order to get an understanding of reality that will help your business.

PEST IS BEST OR WRESTLE WITH PESTLE

PEST is a useful tool to structure how you get a grasp of the forces at work in the world that can help and hinder your business. It stands for:

P = political
E = economic
S = social
T = technological

So working through the PEST tool obliges you to consider, in turn, the key political, economic, social and technological forces at work in the world – or, at least, that portion of the world relevant to your business, i.e. your marketplace.

You may come across STEP which is simply PEST in a different order. Some writers extend PEST to become PESTLE which adds 'legal' and 'environmental' (or 'ecological'); for others, 'E' is 'ethical'. One business school lecturer I have heard likes to add 'M' for 'media' on the basis that newspapers, radio, television and the Internet can influence the perceptions of customers, businesses, regulators and many others besides. These perceptions, in turn, affect your business.

You should choose the tool that works for you. To my mind, PEST is helpfully straightforward and can be understood broadly enough to include all of the additional forces if necessary. Besides, you may find it more fruitful to consider the additional forces in the context of the four core PEST ones. For example, suppose you judge that customers will focus more and more on ethical issues. Ask yourself what that might mean for PEST forces. Could this focus translate into a politically-inspired legislative programme that will affect your marketplace? Or could there be an economic opportunity to position your business as an overtly ethical enterprise – like the Co-op Bank, for example?

And similarly, you might reckon that concerns with carbon emissions will be a growing force. Yet these might be reflected in technological developments that promote low-carbon alternatives, or in political developments that constrain the transportation of goods across vast distances, or in planning decisions that go against the development of airports. Such forces could affect your business if your UK operations source materials from, say the Far East, or if you depend on large-scale construction projects.

The point is that these additional forces need to be understood in terms of their generative effects on the PEST forces, which is why the PEST tool, broadly understood, is helpful enough.

I said earlier that this tool is about helping you to understand the forces at work relevant to your marketplace. Using the tool will be most illuminating when you have an idea of the marketplace that is the subject of these forces. A marketplace could be:

- the market in which your business operates;
- the market in which a particular unit of your business operates;
- the market in which a particular product or service of your business is offered;
- the market in which your business, or an offshoot of your business, or a new product/service could potentially operate;
- the market in which a business you could acquire or invest in or collaborate with operates or could operate.

So, how do you use the PEST tool? The easiest way is to come up with four lists of factors at work under four headings – one heading for each of the four PEST forces. You may need to do some research and data-gathering. Of course, you can do all this as a team with colleagues and trusted advisers – as you wish.

Next, review your lists and as you look at what you have written, ask yourself the following:

- Do I judge this force to be major or minor?
- Is this force strengthening or weakening?
- What are the trends?
- Is this force unpredictable?
- Do any of these forces interact? How?
- Which forces could most impact my business?
  - Positively?
  - Negatively?

Once this is done, write all the most impactful forces on a simple grid, like the one opposite:

POLITICAL	ECONOMIC
The local, national and international government actions that can affect your business, including legislation and regulation	*The fiscal and monetary policies and developments that can affect your business (e.g. economic conditions – local/national/international; tax; interest rates, exchange rates, etc.)*
SOCIAL	TECHNOLOGICAL
Social and demographic trends that can affect your business (e.g. attitudes to, or demand for, your product, 'green' issues, availability and skills of workers, etc.)	*Technological developments that can affect demand for your product or the activities of your business*

Note that these forces can act in concert or in conflict. For example, Internet technologies can drive demand for online purchasing of your product while also providing your business with the very means to meet that demand and capture useful intelligence about the buying behaviours of your customers: more books are bought online than ever before and Amazon, as one provider, captures information on its customers' purchases in order to recommend other books in related fields.

Alternatively, the availability of local grants might make setting up your business in a particular locality attractive, but this might need to be weighed against unfavourable demographics and the scarcity of appropriately skilled workers. After all, it might be because of negative factors such as these that grants are available in the first place.

So what might your PEST analysis look like? An example is shown overleaf (and it is by no means definitive), but do please be sure to make your PEST analysis your own, as only you can consider PEST forces that are pertinent from your chosen marketplace perspective. And it is your judgements about strength, relevance and trend that you, ultimately, have to back. Besides, judgements about key trends are liable to change over time.

POLITICAL	ECONOMIC
• General election due – change of government • Government action makes credit more available • Increasing regulation • Local pressure groups growing • Transportation increasingly difficult • Current overseas markets becoming more volatile • Increasing political uncertainty • Growth of Chinese economy	• Recession until, say, first quarter 2010 • Low interest rates, low inflation, weak £ (more expensive imports but export opportunities) • Rising taxes driven by 'green' and health issues • Changing weather affecting demand patterns • Grants available • Banks more selective in providing credit • Have the agendas of our customers or investors changed?
SOCIAL	TECHNOLOGICAL
• Ageing population – but local demographics? • Growing consumer protection legislation • 'Me-now' generation v. social consciousness • Rise of ethical, health and environmental issues • Flight to trusted brands and value-for-money • Desire for bespoke solutions • Changing working patterns • Growth of diversity and multi-racial society • Growing media attention to our activities	• Rise in internet and mobile technologies and e-commerce, and developing AT (advanced technology) • Pace of technological innovation quickening • Proliferation of media channels, including growth of internet-enabled social networking and viral marketing • New materials being patented • Technological advances reducing the optimal size of firm

Be pragmatic in your use of the PEST tool. Remember, its role is to help you get a handle on the current 'reality' end of the continuum to complement the 'visionary' end. The contents of each of the quadrants is very marketplace-specific: for example, if you are a munitions business, you may well have more to consider in the political quadrant than if you manufacture ethically-responsible cosmetics, where you might concentrate rather more on the social quadrant; or your PEST analysis might look different if you are currently providing a care home service in the UK for the elderly and you are weighing up new market possibilities in, for instance, the US or Germany or Russia or China.

'OH MR PORTER, WHAT SHALL I DO...?'

So far, you are painting 'current reality' on a broad canvas – albeit a highly informative one. You now need to bring your thinking closer to home by looking at the forces at work specifically in your industry. Fortunately, we have an excellent guide to help us since we can pick the brains of a very eminent business guru, Michael Porter. A Google search will give you a gaggle of information about him; what we are concerned with are those ideas of his that will help you undertake effective business planning.

Porter's Five Forces tool[2] is useful in helping to understand the industry forces that your business has to contend with. Indeed, it is Porter's contention that the level of profitability of a business is, in the long run, determined by how these forces operate. It is therefore very important both to understand them and, where possible, to influence them. In effect, Porter says that there is a finite amount of value in an industry – your industry, for example – and it is the nature of these five forces that determine how that value is divided up among players, suppliers and buyers. It is like a cake which is cut up and shared out. What size of slice can your business look forward to? It depends on the five forces at work in your industry, says Porter.

The five forces are:

1 bargaining power of suppliers
2 bargaining power of buyers
3 threat of substitute products or services
4 threat of new entrants
5 rivalry between existing players

They can be portrayed pictorially:

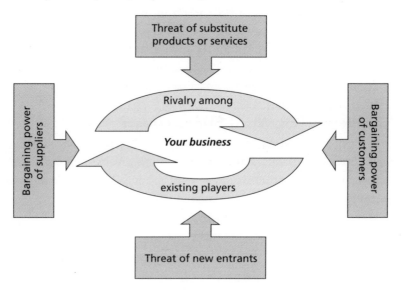

Figure 5.1

That these forces can affect your business's prospects become intuitively quite straightforward once we unpack them:

- **Bargaining power of suppliers**: ask yourself how easily could your suppliers drive prices up. If your suppliers are strong, relative to your business, then this will be a constraining force on your business's performance. This might be because your business depends on them more than they depend on you (you have few alternatives, but your suppliers have many), or because their supplies are much more crucial to you than your purchases are to them. Perhaps they are a vital component in your own product or service, or perhaps one of your suppliers accounts for a huge proportion of your total purchases, or they are financially stronger and can dictate terms of trade, or they have access to key information denied to your business, or they could readily take over your business if it suited them to do so. Naturally, there is an argument for you to reduce these asymmetries of power as best you can: for example by seeking alternative suppliers, keeping them in balance so that you do not become beholden to any one of them. If you feel vulnerable, then you may well wish to include a programme of actions in your business plan to address this vulnerability. Essentially it will come down to the quality of your relationships, but more on that in Chapter 14.

- **Bargaining power of buyers:** Unsurprisingly, this is the obverse of the bargaining power of your business's suppliers. Ask yourself how easily could your customers drive prices down. If your sales depend in very large measure on one buyer who has many alternatives, then this will be a constraining force on your business's performance. Of course, if the reverse holds then you will be able to achieve superior profits – but probably for a limited period only. Attractive profits earned over a prolonged period, will inevitably attract new entrants to the market. How your customers respond to this new opportunity for them will in large measure reflect how they feel your business has treated them. So once again, understanding this force in your marketplace can inform the contents of your business plan, but not in a simplistic way. The wilful leveraging of undue power over a buyer is likely to sow the seeds of your business's downfall in the longer run. After all, how would you feel if you were on the receiving end? A captive customer is not the same as a loyal one and the fundamental issue remains the quality of the relationship.

- **Threat of substitute products or services:** if your business is, say, a cinema chain, you might be vulnerable to the home DVD market if consumers judge the experience to be sufficiently similar and start to prefer the lower cost and easiness of a night in. Note that the threat of substitutes is in the eye of the beholder. This is why, as the business provider, you need to be broadminded to spot threats from possible substitutes. As a cinema owner, you may well be right that the audiovisual experience in a modern cinema is very different from what a home TV can produce, but it is the consumer's assessment of the relative benefits that counts. After all, many people switched their leisure activity from reading books to watching television, and they are now switching again to computer games and the Internet. These are quite different experiences, but with only finite leisure time, consumers can treat them as substitutes for each other. Or consider another example: makers of stage coaches, when they first saw the spluttering attempts at making horseless carriages in the 19th century, did not know they were looking not only at their own demise but arguably also at the single most significant piece of technology of the 20th century. Substitutes for your products or services can be hard to perceive, but trying to do so is highly illuminating for your business because it requires that you understand the real reasons why your customers buy from you. The growth in sophistication of telecommunications might be a substitute for car use: drivers buy fuel because they need to drive to work. If this need diminishes because of greater home-working, then those businesses dependent on car use could see their business contract. This sequence of causes and effects makes sense, but is not necessarily immediately obvious. What are the substitutes for your products and services? What would tip your customers over to preferring them? In short, why do your customers buy from you?

■ **Threat of new entrants:** if you are successful, then other entrepreneurs or businesses may wish to get in on the act. Let us suppose you set up a store specialising in ties and scarves. If you become very successful, there is nothing to stop the established clothing chains extending their offering to include an enhanced range of ties and scarves. You now have a new, tough competitor, and your customers have greater choice of provider. Or perhaps your business has come up with a new invention. You can protect this intellectual capital through patents and thus create high barriers of entry to your marketplace. Or you can feed the profile of your brand so that new entrants are kept at bay. There are many brands of baked beans, for example, but for some consumers only Heinz baked beans will do. Potential providers may give up before they even start. Or you can seek protection from regulation: only a fizzy drink from a certain region in France can call itself 'Champagne'. Or perhaps you have such a strong local relationship with your consumers – the local farmshop for instance – that even when a new Lidl store opens in the vicinity, your own business's trade remains undiminished. However, the barriers to becoming a new Lidl are formidable: it requires huge economies of scale, planning regulations inhibit the construction of new supermarket stores, and existing players would react fiercely. Consider another example: before Internet banking came along, the need for an extensive network of expensive branches was a considerable barrier to entry into the retail banking industry. Now there are more providers of financial services than ever before. Yet the impacts of technology do not stop there. The Internet means that the millions of buyers of financial services, individually relatively powerless compared with the large providers, are very well informed about alternatives and, through the numerous cost-comparison sites, can easily compare prices of insurance products, loans and mortgages. Technology is a two-edged sword: it can create a temporary barrier to entry (you have the technology and others do not), but technological advances can change the rules of the game and allow others to leapfrog you. The Sony Walkman, for instance, was an innovation that allowed people to enjoy music on the move and was fantastically successful. But then came along the iPod … As the science fiction author William Gibson is quoted as saying: 'The future is already here – it is just unevenly distributed'[3]!

■ **Rivalry among existing players:** How do your competitors behave? Are you in an industry where no quarter is given? You can expect intense rivalry if there are several equally-sized players, or in a relatively new industry with too many suppliers vying for market share. If exit barriers are high (that is, it costs a lot to remove oneself from an industry), or if running costs are high with only cyclical sales to cover them, or if your market has low growth or is even declining, then competition will be fierce to win what precious sales there are. Or it may be that your business has a competitor who does not read the market as you do or has insufficient grasp of either the forces at work or of its own organisation's structure and so behaves irrationally. Such a player will buy market share at cost or less either because it does not realise it is losing money or because it believes that this is the approach to win out in the longer term. Some say that the whims of a few rich individuals are distorting sensible economics in the soccer business, pushing the prices of its workers – soccer players – to unsustainable levels that meanwhile are impoverishing the majority of rivals (other football clubs). Understanding the mind-sets of your competitors and how they read the marketplace – indeed, knowing what their vision is – is crucial information to inform your own business planning. You can anticipate move and counter-move, and lay your own action plans accordingly.

So what might your Porter Five Forces analysis look like? Before giving an example below (and it is by no means definitive), just as with your PEST analysis, do please be sure to make your Five Forces analysis your own. Only you can judge how power is distributed between buyers, customers and competitors in your industry. Once done, only you can then prioritise what actions your business needs to take.

I am reminded by a farming business I visited. It comprised a couple of dozen acres and was devoted to growing organic produce (fruits and vegetables). The owner wanted to sell the business after building it up from nothing over the last 10 years. A prospective buyer might well have undertaken a Porter Five Forces analysis as part of the decision-making process whether to buy the farm or not. How might that analysis have looked?

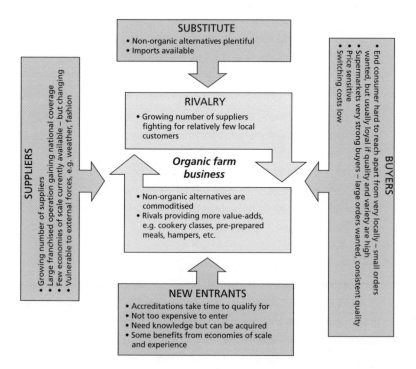

Figure 5.2

So prospective buyers of this organic farm business, unless they are buying into a lifestyle, are going to have some worries. The need for proper accreditations gives the business some protection from new entrants, but only some. If profits become high, other players can enter the market relatively straightforwardly, such as large non-organic producers and overseas suppliers. In times when spending is tight, as in an economic downturn, buyers can easily switch to much cheaper – and plentiful – non-organic alternatives. Economies of scale are difficult to achieve as farms are often constrained by physical features which caps their size or by processing techniques that are hard to industrialise. In these circumstances, rivalry is growing in intensity, with a constant need to provide innovative added value for ever more discerning consumers. So serving the consumer directly is difficult for organic farms as distribution beyond the locality is problematic. The alternative buyers – supermarkets – are comparatively very powerful.

The upshot is that this looks like a tough industry to prosper in and, unless the would-be buyers of this farm can exploit some peculiar local niche, then any entrepreneur is more likely to be motivated by seeking a particular lifestyle than by making a fortune. And it is this lifestyle that it is difficult to find a substitute for, and so is the farm's unique or special proposition.

Key takeaways

1   Your vision must not only have emotive power, it must also emerge from an understanding of current reality.
2   Use PEST as an analytical tool to help you understand the forces at work, shaping the macro-environment in which your business operates:
    a.   political
    b.   economic
    c.   social
    d.   technological
3   Use Porter's Five Forces as an analytical tool to help you understand the dynamics of your business's industry:
    a.   bargaining power of suppliers
    b.   bargaining power of buyers

   c.   threat of substitute products or services

   d.   threat of new entrants

   e.   rivalry between existing players

4   The fundamental issue is the quality of the relationships that your business forms and sustains.

5   Keep going until you get a true insight into exactly why your customers buy from you.

Notes and References

1   Senge, P.M. 'The Leader's New Work: Building Learning Organizations' (1998), printed in Segal-Horn, S., *The Strategy Reader*, p. 297, Oxford/Milton Keynes: Blackwell/Open University, 1998.

2   Porter's Five Forces are discussed in several of his works, beginning with 'How Competitive Forces Shape Strategy', *Harvard Business Review*, **57**, March-April 1979, pp. 86-93; or more accessibly in, for example: Porter, M.E., *Competitive Strategy: Techniques for Analysing Industries and Competitors*, New York: Free Press, 1980.

3   William Gibson, quoted in *The Economist*, 4th December, 2003.

Chapter 6

The Process of Successful Business Planning: My Business

'Look well into thyself; there is a source of strength which will always spring up if thou wilt always look there.' – Marcus Aurelius

FLY WITH SWOT

From Chapter 5, you now have an understanding of the macro-forces at work affecting your business, plus a sense of the dynamics of your industry. Already, you will be thinking of some actions that you need to take to harness the forces that are beneficial to your business and other actions to counteract or mitigate some of the more negative forces.

We shall need to pull together this growing action agenda but there is another piece of analysis of 'current reality' to undertake first. This is a called a SWOT analysis and SWOT stands for:

S = strengths
W = weaknesses
O = opportunities
T = threats

A SWOT analysis is more effective when undertaken after you have used the PEST and Five Forces tools. For example, if you are in the business of manufacturing next-generation batteries, the prospect of increasing legislation against, and taxation of, hydro-carbon based cars and lorries will represent an opportunity for your business. Moreover, any patents on your technological breakthroughs that create barriers to entry will constitute a strength.

Arguably, however, a SWOT analysis is the most challenging of these tools to use. This is because it calls for complete objectivity and absolutely no hubris or wishful thinking. Trying to discern 'current reality' through rose-tinted spectacles will give you a view with an unnatural colour.

I have referred to strengths and weaknesses about 'the situation'. This is too vague: for you to get the best value from using a SWOT analysis in your business planning, you need to be clear as to what the slice of 'current reality' you are SWOT-ing actually is.

If your business is fairly uniform and uncomplicated, then you can SWOT your whole business. You can also SWOT a division of your business or subsidiary or team or discrete activity, or a particular product or a service, or a location or geographic market. The subject of the SWOT analysis can be about the existing situation, or a situation you are considering becoming a part of. So you can SWOT what you sell (product, service, the customers who buy or use it, the customer experience), how you sell it (processes, distribution, profiling, organisational set-up, your people, sourcing, the finances around it), where you sell it (location, channel), your relationships (with customers, suppliers, shareholders, stakeholders, regulators, legislators, politicians, media, etc.), and how well you fare by comparison with your competitors. It is important to be clear what you are SWOT-ing and you can always do more than one SWOT to get a complete picture.

Thus the SWOT tool is highly flexible, potentially very illuminating, and a strong source of important actions (naturally you will want to capitalise on strengths, minimise key weaknesses, mitigate threats, and seize opportunities). Of course, it is your strengths that will enable you to take advantage of opportunities and it is your weaknesses that leave you vulnerable to threats. This is why you might like to picture the SWOT tool thus:

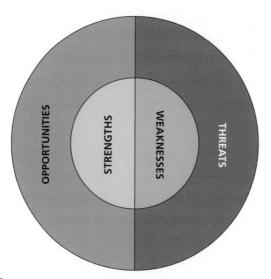

Figure 6.1

So how do you pull your SWOT together? First of all, decide upon your unit of analysis. As discussed earlier, is it your business as a whole, or a particular team, or a particular marketplace, etc? Then brainstorm four lists under a heading for each of the four SWOT components. You may well wish to do this as a team, especially involving those who have some knowledge of the product, market or competitor that you might be SWOT-ing. Use the insights from your PEST and Five Forces analyses to inform the contents of your SWOT analysis. Is your business or service or product (whatever) one for which an ageing population, for example, represents a threat or an opportunity? Is the cachet of your brand such that the threat of substitutes is low, and therefore a strength? And perhaps you have opportunities to extend the brand into complementary products or services?

It is important that this is a genuine brainstorm. You should not spend time assessing or critiquing what you or the others come up with. Keep the flow moving and keep honest!

Once your brainstorm is complete, review each item and consider each one for impact on, and pertinence to, your business aims. You will then have a distilled list of the key strengths, weaknesses, opportunities and threats relating to the aspect of your business that you have been considering. You will then be in an excellent position to begin action-planning.

DIGGING DEEP WITH SWOT

But you feel you want more help to construct your SWOT? This is fair enough, and shows that you really do want to optimise this tool for understanding that reality which is closest to you: your business itself. With this thorough grounding, you can truly set the 'as-is' against your vision, know fully the size and nature of the gap between one and the other, and then set about the most telling actions that will close the gap for you. You are doing the process of business planning!

Knowing your business is an absolute must. This is more than just knowing the 'what' of your business – what it does, what it earns, what customers and suppliers it has, and so on – it is also about the 'why', the 'how' and the 'who'. You have started to answer the question why your business exists with your work on the vision. You need also to understand how it works and what the levers are that makes cause 'C' result in effect 'E'.

For example: among the inventory of what you consider as items for your SWOT analysis must be the competencies – and incompetencies! – of your business. What are you good at? What are you not good at? Perhaps you have poorly trained frontline staff. The consequence of this could be that the quality of service that you provide is inferior. The results could be a high level of complaints, little repeat business, a poor reputation and falling sales.

So, in completing your SWOT analysis, you might count as a threat the fact that your turnover is declining. However, your SWOT analysis would be incomplete if you left it there, since the real value of this analysis comes when you seek out the root causes. This is what is meant by truly understanding the levers at work in your business. Why is turnover declining? Let's say it's because existing customers are not giving you repeat business, and potential customers are increasingly choosing to go to one of your competitors. And why is this? In the case of foregone potential customers it is because – to continue the illustration used above – they have picked up on your business's reputation for poor customer service. Why does your business have this reputation? It is because existing customers are spreading the word about their unsatisfactory experiences – and they are also not coming back to you. Why are their experiences unsatisfactory? It is because of the nature of their interactions with your business's frontline staff. And why are these interactions so unsatisfactory? It is because your staff are poorly trained. These poorly trained staff constitute a weakness in your business which sets in motion a cause-and-effect sequence that ultimately results in a threat to your business.

This example of a root-cause analysis illuminates some key dynamics in your business:

■ Your customers make buying decisions on the basis of their experiences with your frontline staff (whether directly or vicariously by reputation).
■ Your customers will recount their poor experiences to others.
■ There is a clear causal relationship between training of frontline staff ➜ the customer's experience ➜ the customer's buying decision ➜ the level of sales (turnover).

It might require you to get comments from customers in order for you to have all the data you need – after all, any system needs a feedback loop – and the existence or absence of a process to gather customer views could be another strength or weakness of your business, as the case may be.

However, it could be the case in your business that the opposite holds: that is, the competence of your frontline staff in dealing with customers is very high and is therefore a strength. Yet still sales are falling. How could this be? Well, it might be that too many of the products that you sell are faulty. In this case, you would then seek out root causes in, say, your manufacturing process and quality assurance and inspection procedures.

In sum, crucial to undertaking an effective SWOT analysis are:

■ seeking out root causes by asking 'and why is that?' over and over until the digging spade of your relentless enquiry hits the bedrock of a root cause;
■ pressing through to significant consequences by asking 'with the result that ...?' over and over until you reach an outcome that bears materially (for good or ill) on your business goals.

QUESTIONS, QUESTIONS, QUESTIONS ...

Let me give you yet more help with your SWOT analysis.

Here is a list of questions that you can use to interrogate the current reality of your business. Pick and choose which questions are pertinent – it will depend on the unit of analysis of your SWOT and on your business's particular situation. Feel free to amend the questions or add your own – the list here is not definitive – and do not forget to include any relevant points from your earlier PEST and Five Forces analyses. As you work your way through the questions you have selected, note down which truth about your business that your answer reveals is a strength, a weakness, an opportunity or a threat. Then review each of the four lists and pick out what you regard as being the most important examples of their kind. You will end up with a powerful SWOT analysis that is genuinely illuminating of your business and readily generative of important actions that you will need to take.

I have grouped the questions into eight areas:

- Customers
- Offering (Products/Services)
- Suppliers
- Operations
- People
- Financials
- Risk
- Competition

The reason I picked these eight areas is because they reflect the key issues that businesses, in my experience, fail to give due account to. Even among those businesses that do embark on business planning, there are some who struggle mightily, and they struggle mostly because of one or more of the following reasons:

- They persist almost pathologically in continuing to seek to provide a product or service that no one wants or too few want.
- They risk all their eggs in one basket by becoming overly reliant on one customer or one supplier.
- They allow their working capital cycle to become awry by paying suppliers far more quickly than they are, in turn, paid by customers, leading to unsustainable cashflow pressures.
- Their people – most often the leadership team – are not up to the job.

- They organise their business, taking on costs and postponing painful, yet essential, decisions because of hugely over-optimistic sales forecasts or because of persistent, but groundless and unfocused, hope.
- They ignore warning signs or new risks in the ostrich-like belief that the same activities will produce a different – and better – result tomorrow from the one they produced today and yesterday, and the day before ...
- They ignore competitors and fail to respond to competitor action.

These questions are not academic. Knowing the answers to the questions that relate to your business, and taking appropriate actions as a result, could well mean the difference between success and failure.

Questions about my business's customers

- How many customers does my business have?
- Is this number growing or falling? At what rate?
- Who are my main customers (or customer groups)?
- Of all customers for my product/service, what is my share?
- Is my market share growing or falling? At what rate?
- What sorts of customer does/could my product/service have? Are these changing? How?
- Are there different types of customers?
- Do any customers account for a particularly large proportion of my total sales? (say, 15 per cent or more)
- ... and profits?
- Are any key customers struggling?
- Who are my unprofitable customers? (Or how many?)
- Where are my business's customers based?
- Where are my business's customer numbers growing fastest and falling fastest?
- How do my business's customers buy? What channels do/could they use?
- How does my business acquire new customers?
- What new customers could my business acquire?
- How many new customers does my business acquire? Is the rate growing or falling?

- How many customers does my business lose? Is the rate growing or falling?
- Why do my customers buy from me? What is important to them?
- How many of my customers come back? Why? Why not?
- How do I measure customer satisfaction?
- Does my business act on customer feedback?
- If my customers could change one thing about my business offering, what would it be?
- What do my customers complain about?
- Are complaints falling or rising?
- Why do I find any of these questions very difficult/very easy to answer?

Questions about my business offering

- What are my business's main products and services?
- What share of sales is accounted for by each or each type?
- Which shares are growing and falling? At what rates?[1]
- Do any products/services count for a particularly large proportion of my total sales? (Say, 15 per cent or more.)
- ... and profits?
- How important to my business's customers is my product or service?
- Is my business's product or service protected? (e.g. patents, exclusive contracts, trademarks, etc.)
- Which are my unprofitable products or services?
- How does my business develop new products or services? How long does this take?
- What after-sales service does my business provide?
- What is my pricing policy?
- How do I profile my offering?
- What is the reputation of my business?
- How well known is my business's brand? How is it regarded?
- How do most customers hear about my offering?
- What channels are used, and in what proportions? Are these proportions changing? In what ways and at what rates?
- What new products or services could my business develop? New territories?[2]

- Why do I find any of these questions very difficult/very easy to answer?

Questions about my business's suppliers

- Who are my main suppliers (or supplier groups)?
- What sorts of supplier does/could my business have? Are these changing? How?
- Are there different types of suppliers?
- Do any suppliers account for a particularly large proportion of my total purchases? (Say, 15 per cent or more)
- Are any key suppliers struggling?
- Is my business missing any opportunities for deals? (e.g. volume discounts, free trials, promotional support, etc.)
- Who are my most difficult suppliers? In what ways are they difficult?
- Are there many alternatives?
- Where are my suppliers based?
- How do my business's suppliers supply to us? What channels do/ could they use?
- How does my business acquire new suppliers?
- How many new suppliers does my business acquire? Is the rate growing or falling?
- How many suppliers does my business lose? Is the rate growing or falling?
- Why do my business's suppliers supply to me?
- How does my business regulate and monitor supplier performance?
- Does my business act on supplier feedback?
- Does my business address supplier issues, e.g. tackling under-performance, recognising extra added value?
- If my suppliers could change one thing about the relationship with my business, what would it be?
- If my business could change one thing about the relationships with my suppliers, what would it be?
- Why do I find any of these questions very difficult/very easy to answer?

Questions about my business's operations

- How well do my business's operations work?
- In what ways are my business operations working well? And not well? What is the state of the buildings/machinery/vehicles?
- What would have to be different to improve productivity by 30 per cent?
- What is my business's right-first-time ratio? How much re-work is there?
- Is there idle time?
- What are the main systems that run my business? (This is not just a question about IT but also includes financial, HR, sales, and logistical processes.) What problems are there?
- What are my business's control mechanisms? How are they monitored and evaluated?
- What are the key processes in my business? Are they mapped and monitored?
- How good is my business at initiating and implementing operational improvements?
- Could others do aspects of my operational activities better/cheaper than my business does them?[3]
- Does my business truly understand the key processes on an end-to-end basis?[4]
- How do I spend my own time within the business? (Do a detailed breakdown.) Are my priorities right?
- Why do I find any of these questions very difficult/very easy to answer?

Questions about my business's people

- Does my business have enough people for what is needed? Or too many? What is the right number?
- Does my business have enough of the right skills for what is needed?
- What skill-shortfalls are there?
- What do my business's people do best? Worst?
- Do people understand my business's vision? Have they appropriated it?
- What are the values in my business?
- What is the culture of my business?

- How good is the leadership team?
- How does my business find and recruit new talent?
- What is the level of staff turnover? Is it rising or falling? At what rate?
- Why do people join my business?
- Why do people leave my business?
- How are my business's people motivated?
- How are my business's people rewarded?
- How is the performance of my people managed, reviewed, assessed, and incentivised?
- Does everyone know what is expected and how they are performing against what is expected?
- How do people learn and grow within my business?
- What is the level of morale? How engaged and confident are the people in my business?
- How collaboratively do people work together?
- How effective is communication?
- Is my business highly dependent on any key individuals?
- What succession planning takes place?
- What is the capacity of my business's people to initiate, effect and embed change?
- Why do I find any of these questions very difficult/very easy to answer?

Questions about my business's financials

- How does my business's working capital cycle work? What is the average time for customers to pay? Any customers paying especially slowly/quickly? What is the average time for my business to pay suppliers? Any suppliers paid especially slowly/quickly?
- Does my business have enough funds to finance:
  - its existing operations?
  - its ambitions?
- Is my business carrying too much stock or any obsolete stock?
- Is the level of investment sufficient for the business's future?
- Is the business investing in the right projects?
- Is pertinent and actionable management information (e.g. budgets) available within the business and is it used? (KPIs = key performance indicators)

- How is my business performing? What are the main trends?
- How are my business's key financial ratios? (e.g. gross and net profit margins, gearing, etc.)[5]
- How much debt does my business carry?
- How supportive are my business's investors?
- Does my business generate and use forecast information? Any financial pinch-points forecast?
- What are my business's 'good costs' and 'bad costs'?[6]
- Are proper financial controls in place?
- Are robust financial appraisals made at appropriate times?
- Does purchasing/requisitioning follow due process?
- Why do I find any of these questions very difficult/very easy to answer?

Questions about my business's management of risk

- Does my business understand the different types of risk?
  - project risk
  - operational, business-as-usual risk
  - systemic, enterprise-wide risk
- Are the specific risks identified?
- Is there clear accountability for each one?
- Are there counter-measures in place for each identified risk?
- Are these risks and counter-measures monitored and reviewed?
- Why do I find any of these questions very difficult/very easy to answer?

Questions about my business's competition

- Who are my business's main competitors?
- What are their relative market shares? Are these growing or falling? At what rates?
- How do my business's competitors behave? (e.g. complacently, lazily, aggressively, irrationally, etc.)
- How great is the threat of new entrants?[7]
- How easily could my business's product or service be copied? Or substituted?
- What are my business's competitors good at? Strengths? Better than my business?

- What are my business's competitors poor at? Weaknesses? Worse than my business?
- In what ways are my business's competitors getting better? And worse?
- To which competitor(s) do the customers that my business loses go?
- What is different about my business?
- Why do I find any of these questions very difficult/very easy to answer?

Examples of SWOT analyses

Your SWOT analysis is, and necessarily must be, your own. To give you further help in producing a SWOT analysis that truly illuminates your business, here are some examples of SWOTs that actual businesses have produced. In fairness to the businesses themselves, their identities are not revealed.

This is the SWOT that a private company running a council service came up with:

STRENGTHS	WEAKNESSES
• Customer care – go the extra mile for customers	• Finance/pricing – ensure all costs are allocated correctly
• Technical knowledge and expertise – national awards	• Annual challenge on business plan and numbers but limited challenge during the year
• Reporting – are better at MI (management information)	• Lots of ideas – which ones are the priority? What are the cash-flow implications? Need to look at opportunities as a whole business not individually
• Governance – improvements in company board	
• People – multi-skilled	• Customer care – commercial considerations
	• Improvements still required in MI
	• Communicating success
	• Cash-flow – needs further focus
	• Financial monitoring
	• KPI (key performance indicators) usage needs improving

OPPORTUNITIES	THREATS
• 94 per cent of income is from parent company – potential to grow other income sources • Basket of services and competiveness	• Capacity to grow and deliver • Core basket – potential to lose this at a time of moving to ALMO (arms length management organisation) status • Speed to market • Customers – increase from one customer to many customers and ability to respond • Capacity to deliver • Clear strategy required

This is a SWOT analysis that was completed by a specialist dessert manufacturer:

STRENGTHS	WEAKNESSES

• Committed flexible team
• Out-sourced model
  o manufacturing/distribution not core
  o no need for in-house expertise
  o provides flexibility
  o releases management time for core activities
  o spreads risk
  o low capital requirement
• Good order-handling processes
• Good customer relationships/ reputation
• Service generally good
  o (but problems are big ones)
• Flexible operations
  o easy to react
  o not controlled by system
  o very close to data
	• Relatively inexperienced team
	  o within industry
	  o with (X Ltd) (18 months max.)
	• Poor forecasting processes
	  o no long-term forecast
	  o unclear accountability/ measurement
	  o what's important
	  o poor sales data availability (France)
	• Systems
	  o manual
	  o not integrated/double keying
	  o time consuming
	  o information immediately out of date
	• Raw materials/packaging management
	  o unclear responsibilities
	  o time-consuming

	o doing work of suppliers
	o major cause of service failure
	• (Specific newly taken over supplier) relationship
	o difficult relationship
	o who is customer?
	o run parallel systems for acquired supplier and others
	o planning/project management poor
	• Short-termism
	o vision/plan (1 year)
	o operating plans (weekly only)
	• Manufacturing partners
	o unstructured/unclear responsibilities
	o communications poor with some
	o scattered locations = complexity
	• Cost of service not fully understood
	o write-offs
	o packaging
	• Shelf life not maximised
	• Insufficient involvement in new product development/new suppliers

OPPORTUNITIES	THREATS

• Leverage outsourcing skills
  o flexibility
  o speed to market
  o entry into new sectors
• Cost reduction from closer align-ment to
  o partners
  o suppliers
  o currently no incentive to improve
  o project 'headmaster'
  o efficiency drives on current SKUs (stock-keeping units)
	• Suppliers/partners are also competitors
	• Limited exposure to suppliers
	  o out of touch with marketplace
	  o miss NPD (new product devel-opment) opportunities
	• Exchange rate risk from European partners
	• Fuel surcharges unrecovered
	• Acrimonious 'divorce' from partner
	  o no contractual structure in place
	• Small player to (supplier of logis-tics service)
	• (Supplier of dairy products) v. (procurement company) clashes

This is an example of an issue-specific SWOT: it relates to the exit-planning exercise of a business in the pharmaceutical industry which, for the purposes of this illustrative exercise, is called 'Ph Ltd':

STRENGTHS	WEAKNESSES

• Recession-resistant segment of pharmaceutical industry
  o ensure that investment compa-nies are included in potential purchasers, as those already in Ph Ltd will take this element for granted
• Consistent predictable sales and profit
  o low-risk and immediate oppor-tunity to focus on growth
	• Project-based rather than recur-ring revenue
	  o database revenues will comple-ment the existing project revenues
	• No formal sales/prospect follow-up
	  o potential growth opportunity for purchaser to focus on exist-ing clients and identified new market opportunities

- Professional customers
  - o low risk, high level of integrity and respect
  - o longstanding relationships should enable smooth transition
- No bad debt
  - o sums are comparatively small for clients, and services are significant to clients' future revenue streams
- 12-month order book
  - o secure cash flow and ease of managing resources and related costs
- Limited competition in external service providers
  - o price and service has some elasticity, sales revenues are reliably forecastable 12 months ahead
- Pan-European
  - o access to the European market, no national restrictions – 80 per cent of sales are non-UK
- Breadth of services offered
  - o can offer full-service project management for clients, and a more fully developed service offering
- Good spread of customers – no over-dependency
  - o can resist price and delivery pressures, and can spread resource and cash risks
- Generates around £400k free cash annually
  - o high return on sales, consistency provides security to investor/purchaser

- Limited US activity
  - o potential to expand sales activity into the US markets
- Limited experienced senior staff members create dependencies
  - o in-house system provides operational support for all client activity, ensures that key staff are well remunerated, and appropriately trained
- No sales growth in last three years
  - o poised for growth in both established and new identified markets – limited proactive sales activity in the past, sales generated by client loyalty
- CEO dependent – the figurehead, the marketing image
  - o potential for further delegation on operational matters to key managers, increasingly focus CEO on non-core activities, including development of database, speaking/training opportunities, and other business development opportunities
- Limited competition reduces potential purchasers
  - o ensure that sales broker spreads search sufficiently wide to incorporate agricultural, human service providers and investors
- Location in South West reduces access to experienced people
  - o retain and develop existing staff

• Location in South West reduces people turnover
  o client relationships are maintained with key members of staff, training costs reduced, service continuity is maintained
• In-house system provides operational backbone
  o systematic approach to operations allows accurate and regular reporting on sales, resources and client projects; allows management to only focus on key operational and business issues
• Well-organised resource allocation
  o accurate resource forecasting from in-house system, client expectations are met, costs are controlled
• No investment capital required
  o working capital requirements are low, no depreciation costs
• Loyal and committed staff
  o competitive remuneration and benefits package, eight training days plus professional subscriptions
	• Space for expansion limited in current location
	  o space has been optimised for existing business size, and alternative space is available within 2-mile radius of existing site

OPPORTUNITIES	THREATS

• High-value outcome from services = high value-add
  o for existing suppliers to industry enhance their offer and increase their sales of existing services; for new suppliers, position them to sell high-value services to company's clients
• Direct client contact not via purchasing
  o cost of sales is lower due to more direct communication and relationships, limited competitive bidding, limited formal purchasing bid processes.
• Strong market presence
  o strong brand and quality reputation can be used to expand sales
• Database
  o establish wider and deeper market presence, become the authority in industry for all regulatory matters.
  o generate new recurring revenue stream
• US expansion
  o generate new sales.
• Agro-chemicals
  o generate new sales
• Synergy with human healthcare
  o generate new sales
• The animal health market is available for sales growth
  o generate new sales
	• High staff turnover – after 2-3 year training investment
	  o offer pleasant, informal flexible working environment, competitive salaries for new graduates.
	• staff dissatisfaction at sale
	  o ensure good clear timely communications regarding intent and future security for staff
	  o CEO to ensure that he has one-to-one sessions with all staff, advise them of plans and the potential opportunities that will result
	• Customer dissatisfaction at sale
	  o ensure good, clear, timely communications regarding intent and future continuity and quality
	  o arrange one-to-one meetings with top 10 clients
	• Limited opportunity to find purchaser in UK
	  o will need to ensure that sale agent/broker has international reach and experience

Key takeaways from Chapter 6:

1 *Do:*

- involve the wider team (even outsiders) in brainstorming the contents of your SWOT analysis and prioritising the key items;
- create the conditions for free-flowing thinking: give the process due time and keep factual;
- use a skilled facilitator (it might not be you!);
- be clear on the unit of analysis and ensure the team is well-briefed;
- be honest: be objective, combine an insider's perspective with an outsider's view;
- draw on the key findings of your PEST and Five Forces analyses to inform your SWOT;
- take information from a wide variety of reliable sources;
- be specific;
- keep action-orientated: build action plans based on your finalised SWOT;
- refresh your SWOT analysis regularly – at least annually.

2 *Don't:*

- do the SWOT on your own;
- overstate positives or gloss over negatives – *you* might be a source of some of your business's weaknesses!;
- evaluate prematurely by critiquing or ignoring ideas while brainstorming;
- get bogged down in petty detail or over-analysis, or side-tracked by picky arguments;
- make inferences beyond what the data will support;
- just count the items, *weigh* them!;
- make simple lists and ignore root-causes.

Notes and References

1 You might find it helpful here to consider your products/services in the light of what is often called the 'Boston Matrix' or 'BCG Matrix' (see Henderson, B.D., *The Logic of Business Strategy*, New York: Ballinger Publishing Co., 1984). What it is called is not terribly important, and that it is taken from the world of management consultancy should not put you off. It is simply a way of thinking about and classifying what your business is offering to your customers. It can be used with different units of analysis – for example, by a parent company to view its main subsidiaries – but that does not matter here. In fact, once you catch on to the fact that consultants and MBA students simply love analysing situations with 2-by-2 grids, then you, too, are well on your way to becoming a business guru!

In using the Boston Matrix to assess your products or services, you are thinking about them in terms of their existing market share and the prospects for market growth. If your offering holds a high market share in a market with high growth, then clearly that is a very desirable situation and you would count such products or services as your stars. You would naturally be encouraged to support such products or services with a large measure of your resources – time, personal energy, people, finances and future investment.

Of course, the reverse would hold in the opposite circumstances. If you have little presence in a market that is contracting or has only low growth, then you would want to divert your finite resources away from these products or services and probably withdraw them.

The Boston Matrix considers the main combinations of market share and market growth:

You can see that the products or services that you would likely withdraw are 'dogs'. Where your products or services enjoy a high

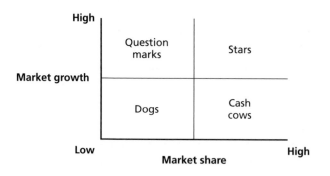

market share but the market itself has little growth, then it is not worth putting a huge amount of resources – just basic 'care and maintenance' – into these, and your business might as well enjoy the revenues they generate for as long as you can. This is milking your 'cash cows'.

If your products or services have little presence in a market that is high growth, the right course of action is less straightforward. It boils down to your assessment of the prospects to generate suffi-cient revenues on the rising tide of the market, despite the fact that you have only a small boat. In this context, you would have to weigh up alternative opportunities that might be more deserving of your finite resources. And you should consider whether there are actions you can take to grow your market share: that is, what could you do to shift your 'question marks' rightwards into the 'stars' quadrant?

So, in considering the products or services that you offer, ask yourself which ones are rising stars, and which ones are dogs. It is a useful perspective to take, although bear in mind that, in a reces-sion, more than the usual number of products or services have a canine yelp about them. Just one note of caution: one of the limitations of this perspective is that it does not on its own take into account innovations or market developments that can change the dynamics. For example: to some analysts, years ago the ice-cream market looked well developed with established distribution channels dominated by a couple of major players who brought out new products only to the extent that they needed to reflect the latest fad prevailing in the world of the children who were the consumers. It looked like a care-and-maintenance approach would suit what was reckoned to be a fairly static market. This resting-on-one's-laurels meant that the established players had to engage in a catch-up when Häagen-Dazs showed that ice-cream could be very much for adults and extended the nature of the market. This was not the only novelty, and confectioners started to bring out ice-cream versions of their most popular chocolate bars. Existing paradigms are always vulnerable to new thinking. This is one reason why some writers (e.g. Johnson, G., Scholes, K., *Exploring Corporate Strategy*, 6th ed., Harlow: Prentice Hall, 2002) say that the Boston Matrix 'should be applied to *strategic business units*, not to products' (see p. 286, their emphasis). I think that is too prescriptive, and if you find that the perspective of the BCG Matrix prompts useful thoughts about your business's products or services, then that is all that matters.

2   Another 2-by-2 to help you! This one is called the Ansoff Grid and is a way of considering the options for your business's products or services and markets (see Ansoff, I., *Corporate Strategy*, revised ed., New York: McGraw-Hill, 1987).

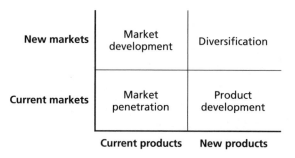

	Current products	New products
New markets	Market development	Diversification
Current markets	Market penetration	Product development

The Ansoff Grid invites you to consider whether your existing products or services (e.g. new customer groups, new territories, etc.) could be taken into new markets – 'Market development'. Or perhaps your business is already serving markets to which you could introduce new products or services – 'Product development'. Or, perhaps after your work with the Boston Matrix, you are resolved to concentrate on milking your cash cows and backing your stars, in which case you will focus on 'Market penetration'. Bringing new products or services to new markets would be 'Diversification' – often the riskiest approach.

The purpose of using the Boston Matrix and the Ansoff Grid is, in SWOT terms, to help you consider aspects of the current reality of your business so as to identify strengths and weaknesses which, respectively, constitute opportunities and threats. Once identified, pertinent action plans can be formed. In sum, this is all part of business planning.

3   This is posing the question whether there are opportunities for outsourcing certain of your business's existing activities (this can entail offshoring, but not necessarily so). An example could be HR processes such as payroll or even recruitment. How to identify and then assess potential candidate activities for outsourcing is beyond the scope of this book.

4   An example of understanding a process end to end would be the sales process, which would start from the act of enquiry through order capture through order processing through invoicing through payment collection through goods/service delivery and up to after-sales follow-up. An understanding entails detailed metrics at each key step-point; for example, how many enquires turn into sales negotiations, how many sales negotiations turn into actual orders, and so on.

5   There will be more on understanding the financial aspects of your business and the role of financial analysis in business planning in Chapter 9. So do not worry!

6   As in physiology, it is not just the weight of the human body that is important but the proportions between fat and muscle. Healthy weight loss is about losing fat, not muscle.

It is the same for a business. It is not just the totality of the cost base that is important but the proportions of 'good costs' and 'bad costs'. Good costs are those that will bring in greater savings elsewhere or extra business and thus income, or are simply what it takes to have a seat at the table in the business's chosen market (i.e. keeping what you've got).

Good costs are muscle. After all, if your costs were zero, what do you think your income would be? Yes, zero!

Bad costs are fat. These are the inefficiencies in the business. Inefficiencies most notably accumulated during benign trading conditions when the business was driven for indiscriminate growth: the legacy customs, the tortuous processes, the re-work, the ex gratia payments to complaining customers.

7   Remember 'new entrants' does not solely mean a new start-up business encroaching on your marketplace. A new entrant could be a large, long-established business that sets up a new activity which competes with your business.

Chapter 7

The Process of Successful Business Planning: An Illustration

'We learn by example and by direct experience because there are real limits to the adequacy of verbal instruction.' – Malcolm Gladwell *(Blink)*

LIGHT FROM A BORROWED TORCH

After working through Chapters 5 and 6, and then taking the processes to your own business, you will have a telling understanding of the current reality of your business and its marketplace to set beside your vision. There will be a gap. The next stage in business planning is to set out what is required to close the gap.

However, before we move on to that stage, you may find it helpful to see an example where the PEST, Porter's Five Forces and SWOT analyses have been done. This is not, of course, for you to copy the contents slavishly, as your business is your own and its reality will be very different. It is just that, sometimes, it is helpful to navigate with reference to a landmark or feature even though you have absolutely no intention of making that your destination.

It is in that spirit that I offer to you a set of analyses I did some years ago on the car-maker Peugeot-Citroën. Naturally, it reflects its time and was looking at Peugeot-Citroën and the car industry as they were in the 1980s and 1990s.

This means that you can add the perspective of hindsight. In what follows, think about whether the analysis is a proper reflection of the facts. Also, look out for implications of the situation being appropriately addressed by: the options going forward, the actions actually adopted, and the suggested future course. Key to your own business success will be your skill at making good interconnections between analysis, insight, and action.

On the other hand, if the car industry of 20 + years ago feels too remote from your own business, then do please feel free to skip this chapter and move on to Chapter 8.

Peugeot-Citroën: a summary

The car industry is marked at this time (as today) by chronic over-supply. Volume-players invest heavily in plant and machinery to achieve economies of scale. They also spend considerable sums on advertising and profile in order to stimulate demand for their products.

Price competition is intense. This is because supply is concentrated in little more than half a dozen volume-providers and the industry cost structure is heavy on fixed costs and low on variable costs. (See Chapter 9 for more on fixed costs and variable costs.)

Peugeot-Citroën has been able to create image-differences among buyers but, in common with its rivals in its strategic group, these differences do not amount to sustainable differentiation.

Peugeot-Citroën has moderate, but not class-leading competencies in the required areas of cost-efficient volume production, speed to market, and entrance to new markets whether developed (the US and Japan), or emerging (e.g. China and India).

Peugeot-Citroën has relative strengths, however, in diesel and new-fuel technologies, and in the French and Western European markets.

The long-term future of the car industry (20 years plus) will need Peugeot-Citroën's existing strengths, but the company will have to acquire additional core competencies if it is to succeed in the recommended hybrid strategy of a low cost base supported by expanded demand in new markets, with reinvestment in maintained price competitiveness and differentiated products.

These additional core competencies are set out later but chief among them are:

- developing collaborations and alliances, most likely entailing a merger as well, both to open up markets more effectively and to generate cost-efficient economies of scale;
- managing a complex set of relationships with suppliers, distributors and customers;
- actively using the political dimension to support commercial activities.

While the industry will become even more fiercely competitive driving further consolidation, and environmental pressures are likely to grow yet stronger, the underlying fundamentals in the market for powered personal transport solutions are for growth.

Being successful will require low-cost production, technology-led innovation, and global reach.

The macro-environment as illuminated by PEST

We can consider the large-scale forces that were affecting Peugeot-Citroën in the 1980s/1990s by using a PEST analysis. Much of the analysis holds good today.

Political (including legal and environmental) forces

It is difficult to separate these. For example, the increasing concerns about the environmental impacts of the production, running and disposal of cars is leading to tighter legislation on fuel emissions (e.g. in Europe and California), which, in turn, is reflected on taxation rules (e.g. ratcheted petrol taxes in the UK and benefit-in-kind taxation rules that have changed from favouring high usage to placing the emphasis on low CO_2 emissions).

There are also the increasingly stringent standards of safety that cars have to meet.

The relevance of these issues of environment and safety is that previous bases of differentiating between products might diminish, but others could increase.

For example, if all cars have to meet ever more exacting standards of safety and crash protection, then Volvo, for instance, could be affected. It may find the way it has been differentiating its products – on the very basis of safety and so on – could lose much of its power. Indeed, Volvo has been stressing the style and performance aspects of its vehicles.

On the other hand, preoccupations with the environment can open new potential bases for differentiation along the lines of fuel economy, or alternative fuels, or less resource-hungry smaller cars. This, in part at least, has stimulated the continued development of diesel technology (diesel fuel is less heavily taxed in the UK, for example) in which Peugeot-Citroën is a market leader. We also see cars being marketed that use other fuels (e.g. the Japanese Prius, which is a combination-fuel car), and also smaller, lighter city cars – why use the family car for a short trip? – such as the Smart car.

Concerns with safety can not only drive car design; they can also penalise certain product features. For example, 4x4 vehicles with prominent bull-bars at the front were heavily criticised for harming pedestrians. Thus we see that politico-legal and environmental forces are affecting the bases on which competition is waged, and the nature of the product in the showrooms.

However, some politico-legal forces apply pressure on all cars. For example, London's congestion charge is taxing cars that enter the centre of the city in the hope of moving travellers into alternative means of transport. Other cities are watching London closely and have their own plans ready. The legal framework is in place to allow this.

Economic forces

Key here is the relationship between demand for cars and national levels of income. We see that there is a very dynamic relationship in that changes in GDP give rise to proportionately far higher changes in demand for cars – perhaps twice as great or more.

Thus, in a recession with a 5 per cent reduction in GDP, we would previously have expected to see around a 10 per cent decline in car sales. In fact, a decline of 30 per cent and more has been experienced during the most recent (2009) recession – even amongst mainstream manufacturers. Expectations are that during an economic upturn, rises in GDP will be accompanied by even greater rises in car sales. However, it is likely that these averages hide important differences between car segments. For example, in a recession, we would expect the sale of expensive luxury and performance cars to decline relatively more than sales of budget vehicles.

The opposite might hold in more prosperous times, except that we might see an increased market for second, or even third, vehicles which, in combination with the politico-legal forces we have noted above, could point favourably towards smaller, budget cars.

Economic forces are very important to the car industry. We shall observe when we discuss the nature of the industry in the context of Porter's Five Forces, that the economics of car production are very heavily geared towards global production, based on high-volume output yielding economies of scale. This entails heavy capital investment and a high fixed-cost structure – but with comparatively low variable costs as a proportion of the end-price. Thus when demand falls, as in times of economic downturn, this can lead to serious overproduction. Given the cost structures of car makers, the temptation to embark upon potentially ruinous price wars is often impossible to resist.

Indeed, throughout the period 1994-2000, we see that world production of cars exceeded demand (measured by new registrations). This put a downward pressure on prices and thus on margins as well, and so focused car-makers' attention even more on reducing costs of production on an ever-greater scale (especially in searching for new markets) and improvements in production efficiencies (e.g. global models and shared components and car platforms).

If some economic forces are pulling the car industry towards lower costs, then others are pushing it towards yet lower prices. Free market movements are making it harder for car makers to charge more for their products in one country than in another – especially in Europe where government-backed enquiries have led to car firms (e.g. Fiat) being punished by fines.

There have also been enquiries into the dealership system, and commentators are widely predicting that dealers will no longer be beholden to one or two car makers. Instead they will be able freely to choose whose cars they sell. Peugeot-Citroën might want to consider forward integration: i.e. acquiring its own dealership distribution network.

Social forces

With the rise in households seeing two incomes, each earner has needed a car to support their lifestyles (commuting to work, taking children to school, doing the weekly shop at the supermarket, etc.). The demand for second cars has thus grown over time. Moreover, as the price of cars has, in the long term, fallen as a proportion of disposable incomes, so parents are increasingly buying cars for their children as soon as they are old enough to drive.

In developing economies cars are seen as a ready means to generate wealth: labour costs of production are relatively and attractively low, and factories (which have to be large scale) are a major source of much-needed local employment. Indeed, this is true of developed economies such as the UK, where subsidies were made available to Nissan to build their car factories in areas requiring economic and social regeneration such as the North East.

But cars are also seen as the breakthrough symbol of personal wealth and success, and as such are highly aspirational for people in developing economies.

Hence, there are social forces supporting car demand which run counter to the environmental forces that are seeking to depress it. The question for Peugeot-Citroën is not so much which force will win out, as what type(s) of personal transportation will be needed as a result of all these forces.

Technological forces

Heavy investment in technology has enabled the car industry to reduce the costs of production[3] (e.g. continuous production flows, robot-workers etc.). IT has thus had a critical role in supporting important changes at both the supplier end and the customer end of the car industry. For example, there has been the move towards high-volume production at low cost, shared components, and common design platforms. At the customer end, there has been an ever-growing specification of the product. Cars are more highly equipped than ever before and yet more reliable. Engines are no longer maintained by an overall-clad mechanic with an oily rag, but by wafers of silicon in an engine-management chip.

Technology has also made possible an ever-growing specification of product at the customer end of the value chain. Cars are more highly equipped than ever before and yet more reliable. Engines are no longer maintained by an overalled mechanic with an oily rag, but by wafers of silicon in an engine-management chip.

As Peugeot-Citroën addresses the question posed when considering social forces, it is likely that technology will continue to make these sorts of changes happen. Given the economic forces, ever-lower costs of production are likely to be crucial to survive going forward and IT will feature there. And, yes, cars will become ever more cleverly equipped, not less so – and technology will figure there as well.

But to address the macro-economic forces at a fundamental level, it is likely that car makers will again look to technology for the answers. How can a car be powered so that it performs like a petrol car, but uses environmentally benign fuel with emissions (if any) that are eco-friendly? Car makers are investing huge sums in new sources of power (e.g. hydrogen fuel cells), new hybrid engines that can run on different types of fuel, and new materials (which are themselves eco-friendly to make and which, being lighter, require less power and are more recyclable).

In some markets, e.g. California, only car makers who succeed in developing these technologies in a commercially viable way will be able to sell their products at all. If a car maker shows it can be done, they are bound to encourage legislators to earn votes from the environmental lobby and restrict vehicles to the new technologies. Thus, car makers who do not have products reflecting the new technologies could well find themselves without any markets.

Of course this is just one scenario, and an extreme one, but it does serve to illustrate that Peugeot-Citroën needs to consider a range of possible scenarios to stimulate its strategic thinking.

Summary of macro PEST forces
Given the nature of the relationship between the demand for cars and levels of income, the car industry (or at least the strategic grouping of which Peugeot-Citroën is a part) has locked itself into a highly fixed-

cost structure which drives to seek volume and engage in severe price competition. This is a rational response when you want to maximise revenues in times of economic growth and protect yourself in times of economic downturn.

However, while there are clear social trends that appear to support an expectation of overall demand growth, there are also powerful political and environmental forces, that are starting to attempt to curb this demand and certainly to affect its shape, i.e. towards certain *types* of car-solution and away from others.

We may also see a diversity of geographical markets based on their stage of economic development.

Technology will figure prominently thus requiring continued high levels of investment from car makers. Such is the scale of investment required in non-familiar technologies that we may see car makers not only consolidating or teaming up with each other, but also with non-car makers, e.g. battery technology businesses, lightweight materials businesses, and small-scale design specialists (e.g. as Mercedes teamed up with Swatch).

PEUGEOT-CITROËN AND PORTER'S FIVE FORCES

Porter claims that it is an industry's structure that determines the profitability of the average player, and his Five Forces determine how economic value is divided up between competitors, customers, suppliers, etc.

Let us consider these forces in turn:

Threat of substitute products

Obvious substitutes are public transport, other modes of transport, alternative 'car solutions', etc.

However, other substitutes, not necessarily in the transport business, could nonetheless have profound impacts on Peugeot-Citroën and others within its strategic group. The rise in homeworking and Internet shopping with home deliveries might mean people will feel they no longer need a car.

Stricter laws on drinking and driving, and the growth in health-consciousness, might see fewer people using cars for recreation and leisure. Indeed, perhaps the growth in sophisticated home entertainment systems will mean more 'nights in', with advanced telecommunications allowing people to share the experience with friends as if they were there, without them actually having to be physically in the same place.

In other words, a proper examination of the threat of substitutes rests on an analysis of the reasons why individuals use cars at all. If these reasons were to change – and some of them appear to be changing – then cars, or whatever future variants on cars there might be, will need to fulfil new roles for consumers and their changing lifestyles.

Peugeot-Citroën has been investing heavily in electric car technology and in exploring ways in which consumers' needs might be met differently, for example by its old Tulip project in which small two-seater Tulip cars could be rented by subscribers in several places in a town.

Bargaining power of customers

On the face of it, with millions of individual buyers who are not co-ordinated as a group there seems little power here.

However, such is the degree of over-supply as a consequence of over-production that individual buyers are habitually able to negotiate discounts and additional product features. This is because, buyers have choice, switching is straightforward and suppliers are desperate to sell. Internet technologies also mean that buyers are very well informed about prices.

Discounts are even higher for fleet buyers, who have the buying power (and, in the case of driving schools, for example, the profile) to exert even more pressure on sellers.

As for Peugeot-Citroën, it has the added complexity of competing with itself: separately incentivised dealerships selling Peugeot will fight for a customer's business against those selling Citroën, and vice versa.

It is also highly concentrated, with its single most important market being France, and most of its other sales being made elsewhere in Western Europe.

Threat of new entrants

Here we make a distinction between the threat of substitutes, which could see non-car makers enter, and the threat of new entrants into volume car production.

There are classic barriers to entry:

- scale economics and experience
- high capital requirements
- access to distribution (tied dealerships)
- branding (takes years to develop)
- high level of retaliation could be expected

However, even these are not insuperable; we would have said the same in the 1960s/1970s, since when Japanese car makers were able first to enter, and then become a dominating force in, the world automobile industry. Many commentators believe other Asian producers – in Malaysia, Korea or India, for example – might be able to repeat the same feat within the next couple of decades.

As for Peugeot-Citroën, it has some additional scale opportunities: components are increasingly shared, allowing also joint purchasing, and research and development (R&D) expenses are shared. However, maintaining two brands means that sales, marketing, promotion and dealership costs are higher.

One result is that it is proportionately a far greater effort for Peugeot-Citroën to renew its model range. To renew eight basic models (four Peugeot and four Citroën) every six years, means the company has to launch one or two models every year.

Bargaining power of suppliers

The power of suppliers is relatively weak. Historically, car makers have been able to impose reducing prices on their suppliers. Long-term contracts and joint research programmes (which raise their costs for switching suppliers) tie suppliers in further.

Peugeot-Citroën implemented productivity plans with its suppliers and reduced their costs accordingly. Most of the company's suppliers are located in France; if Peugeot-Citroën is truly aspiring to be a global player, it needs to consider whether this means it needs a global source of supplies.

Competitor rivalry

We see rivalry coming out in brand and price. This is typical of a market controlled by a few strong, global players.

Spec-for-spec, a car from Vauxhall (Opel in mainland Europe), Renault, Fiat, Ford and Peugeot-Citroën will be similarly priced. The nature of competition and the price-sensitivity of consumers mean that marked price divergences will be punished in favour of the lower price.

Car makers nonetheless do seek to cultivate separate images for their cars. Renault, for example, is known for its design chic, Fiat for its Italian bravado, Peugeot for its quality driving experience, and Citroën for its individuality.

However, that price competition is so fierce suggests that car makers have not been able to turn these image differences into a tangible point of differentiation. They are more about keeping up.

Peugeot-Citroën has an added difficulty by comparison with say, Volkswagen. The top-range Peugeot is still called a Peugeot, and the top-range Citroën is still called a Citroën. However, a top-range Volkswagen is called an Audi, which has much greater cachet among the customer segment to which it is targeted.

Volkswagen has a suite of marques against which Peugeot-Citroën must contend. If it goes for lower prices, it is up against Volkswagen's Skoda and Seat brands, which already have a reputation for value for money. If, on the other hand, it goes for higher prices backed up by higher perceived quality, it finds itself against the Volkswagen name itself or Audi, which are both well established in that market space. So Peugeot-Citroën remains among the desperate mass of brands, fighting out amongst themselves on price, with image eking out a difference without being a differentiation, so that each can keep up with the other. And Peugeot also fights with Citroën and vice versa!

Such rivalry is one reason why car makers are supportive of trade barriers that protect their home markets, although of course they seek removal of barriers to trade with markets they are trying to enter.

Jacques Calvet (Peugeot-Citroën's leader at the time), for example, strongly advocated protection of the EU market from the Japanese, both against their imports into Europe and against their setting up manufacturing plants within Europe.

Thus Calvet was using recourse to trade barriers as a means by which to limit access to Peugeot-Citroën's strategic group. The argument for reciprocal trading freedom is specious bearing in mind how few were the sales into Japan after concessions were achieved; it is entirely about one player seeking to use whatever tools it could to jockey for position against a rival.

Summary of the Porter Five Forces analysis

From our consideration of the nature of Peugeot-Citroën's market, we have noted that:

■ On the supply side, economies of scale and scope are important, not so much as a source of enduring competitive advantage, but as a pre-requisite to 'get a seat at the table' – the key players are global in scope (in terms of the reach throughout their value chain).
■ On the demand side, demand is highly sensitive to income levels, general economic prosperity and prices.
■ As for competitor rivalry, Peugeot-Citroën's group of volume providers is operating as an oligopoly (i.e. the top six suppliers account for 75 per cent of the market in Western Europe), and only short-lived advantages are being gained by exploiting scale economies, product and image differentiation, and trade barriers.

The nature – or deep structure – of the market is profoundly and enduringly affecting Peugeot-Citroën's performance, yet is largely outside its control and cannot be fundamentally altered by any strategic actions it might take.

But – and this is an important but – the same deep structure also holds for the other members of the oligopoly, so the question for Peugeot-Citroën is: how does it avoid ejection from the oligopoly? How is Peugeot-Citroën to survive?

To achieve this, Peugeot-Citroën must manage, even if it cannot fundamentally alter, this deep structure better – or less badly – than its rivals. Competitive advantage is about delivering superior value to customers and, in doing so, earning an above-average return for the company and its stakeholders.

This cannot be bought simply by cutting prices, nor by simply growing costs by adding quality without a higher price.

It is about delivering differences from competitors of a kind that consumers value. These differences can be sustained if Peugeot-Citroën:

- has crucially relevant resources that rivals do not have, or cannot identify, and which are hard to acquire;
- cannot be caught up easily;
- keeps finding other differences of value to consumers.

Of course, rivals will be considering the same issues, and so Peugeot-Citroën faces intensifying competition against a background of challenging environmental forces in its traditional markets, potentially large new markets opening up, and endemic over-supply.

HOW COULD PEUGEOT-CITROËN HAVE RESPONDED?

This is how the industry looked in the 1980s. (It is not very different from today.) So what options did Peugeot-Citroën have in response?

- Reduce costs by:
  - improved productivity by rationalising manufacturing, and better production processes (increased speed to market);
  - sharing components-purchasing and R&D expenses between Peugeot and Citroën;
  - cutting procurement costs with suppliers;
  - tighter management of inventories;
  - reduction in staff.
- Investment in products and skills by:
  - continued investment in development of diesel engines (to maintain its No. 1 position);
  - investment in electric car technology;
  - training programmes for staff (spending to be doubled as a proportion of wages).
- Develop new markets by:
  - expanding its network of dealers in Germany;
  - acquiring Chrysler's operations in the UK;

- – making HQ-subsidiary relationships more sophisticated so that some adaptations to important foreign markets could be accommodated. However, this would require a fair degree of local-market autonomy;
- – entering markets overseas, especially Asia, India and South America, with smaller markets around the Mediterranean and in Africa. In 1995 Calvet said: 'Our ambitious goal in this area is for Peugeot and Citroën to progressively make 25 per cent of their sales outside Western Europe.' In 1986, Calvet set the goal of becoming the leading car manufacturer in the European market in terms of number of vehicles sold. By 1995, Calvet had not achieved that strategic goal, yet the focus of his strategic attention appeared to have broadened to include select overseas markets;
- – considering a return to previous markets, especially North America.
- ■ Maintain parallel branding of Peugeot separately from Citroën.
- ■ Resist incursion from overseas – especially Japanese – manufacturers by enlisting governmental action to impose trade barriers.

In Peugeot-Citroën's case, we can say that its scope at this time was relatively narrow: although broadening to include overseas markets, it was primarily focused on Western Europe and especially France. We might regard Ford's scope as broader.

Although not operating in a 'commodity' market, Peugeot-Citroën clearly has maintained a fervent cost focus. We might regard Mercedes as having a differentiation focus based on perceived quality and prestige; its development of smaller models is encroaching on Peugeot-Citroën's market space.

Calvet's 'intended strategy' appears thus; he expected cost efficiencies through productivity improvements to finance investment in new markets and to support continued price competitiveness.

After all, it is not clear that Peugeot-Citroën could ever have ultimately succeeded in establishing any differentiation which generates a perceived value amongst consumers of a kind that they will reward with higher prices. And so Peugeot-Citroën always had to keep a relentless focus on costs and price competitiveness.

Of course there are car makers who are more overtly lower price than Peugeot-Citroën, such as Daewoo, Kia, Hyundai, and the value-for-money marques of Volkswagen (Seat and Skoda), but it is no doubt true that Peugeot-Citroën must keep a relentless focus on costs and price competitiveness.

Cost focus and image development appear to be simply what this market requires for players to 'have a seat at the table', like a poker player's entry fee.

Peugeot-Citroën's strategy had certain limitations:

- We said that competitive advantage must be built on sustainable differences that are valued by customers and are hard for rivals to copy, yet we have seen that a Peugeot-Citroën's cost focus and image development represent a duty not a virtue. The nature of the market obliges all volume providers to concentrate on cost focus and image development as well, albeit with different personality-images. These are what are called 'threshold competences', rather than 'core competences'. So much is necessary for Peugeot-Citroën simply to avoid falling behind.
- We can see that the PEST and Porter's Five Forces are driving the successful players of the future towards globalisation. Yet Peugeot-Citroën is still not looking like a truly global player:
  - Its original strategic aim was to be No. 1 in Europe but it then started to look for new markets overseas.
  - It has avoided the joint-venture and alliances approach of many of its rivals.
  - It long failed in its attempt to establish an early large-scale presence even in its chosen overseas markets, most notably China. (More recently, it has been more successful in growing sales in its priority markets: China, Eastern Europe and Russia, and South America.)
  - It lacks even a toehold in the largest automobile market in the world, the USA.
  - A global player needs to manage its supply chain on a global basis, yet Peugeot-Citroën failed to find suppliers that can support a global play (they are predominantly, and expensively, France-based).

- – Its strategy of parallel branding was always bound to risk increasing production costs despite Peugeot-Citroën's steps for co-site manufacture, as well as administration and marketing costs. This runs counter to a relentless, even brutal focus on costs, as its intended strategy would require. The question is: if the company were, say, Peugeot only, would it now start a Citroën business? The answer is surely No, so the question for the company is now how close to that can it now get?
  - – Its resistance to Japanese entry was not about winning reciprocal access to Japan's home market, as a genuinely ambitious global player might seek. It was really about gaining some temporary commercial expediency and some local political capital.
- ■ On the positive side, investment in its people and in new technologies went with the grain of industry forces. Unless Peugeot-Citroën makes a blockbusting technological breakthrough that it can patent, however, then it is not clear how this would have led to any sort of enduring competitive advantage. Indeed, players with deeper pockets may be more likely to make the necessary – and expensive – technology-led progress.

Peugeot-Citroën: a SWOT analysis

We can summarise Peugeot-Citroën's competitive position at that time in a SWOT analysis opposite:

STRENGTHS	WEAKNESSES
• World leader in diesel technology • World leader in hydro-suspension systems • Growing experience with electric vehicles • Growing relative market shares in Europe • Growing presence in South America • Recognised brand especially in Europe • Stronghold in Europe, especially France • Improved cost efficiencies • Some iconic models, e.g. Citroen 2CV, Citroen DS, Peugeot 205 GTi	• Parallel brands rather than a suite of complementary brands • Relatively long speed to market and product development times combined with similar models to maintain • Weak in China, elsewhere in Asia and in the US, and no distribution infrastructure • Intended and realised strategies are not always identical • Relatively few genuinely global characteristics yet it is a global market • High concentration of French manufacture and French suppliers
OPPORTUNITIES	THREATS
• Overall, economic forces are for a growing market – most people have yet to own their first car • Car making will always have high political clout given its role in the economy • New markets are active in encouraging car-makers' incoming production • Environmental pressures are leading to openings for eco-friendly, personal transport solutions, e.g. California • Has the potential to supply diesel engines to other car manufacturers	• Truly low-cost producers in the Far East and in Eastern Europe are gaining market share • Free trade movements and new channels (especially the Internet) are facilitating the advance of low cost producers • Strong indigenous car makers would retaliate strongly to new entrants in to US, especially French! • European focus creates vulnerability to Europe-specific economic downturns – it lost money in 1993 • Other rivals have deeper pockets, are more genuinely global or have better suite of brands

• Potential expansion opportunities in other forms of transport (e.g. motor scooters, boats, bicycles, buses, taxis), and in leisure/fun pursuits (e.g. equipment for water sports, winter sports, outdoor activities, clothing and accessories) • Calvet's retirement might make Peugeot–Citroën more willing to form alliances	• Has the car as we have known it had its day? • Failure to break into the large markets (USA, Japan, China, India) will constrain its scope to be a volume producer/seller

MOVING FROM ANALYSIS TO ACTIONABLE OPTIONS FOR THE FUTURE

One good way of using market analyses to help form a business plan is to identify some main action-options and then imagine what would happen if each option were played out. This entails imagining different scenarios.

So, on the basis of these analyses, based on how the market was about 20 years ago, you might have devised a couple of possible scenarios.

Scenario 1: pursue a broad global strategy

Peugeot-Citroën seems less well-placed by comparison to many of its rivals to manage a genuinely global strategy and so an analyst might well have assumed a scenario in which it will ultimately fail to achieve any sort of meaningful volume in the US, Japan, China or India.

This would leave it to concentrate on France, Western Europe and South America. An analyst might have continued this scenario by imagining that Peugeot-Citroën is now a far smaller player than those who did succeed in exploiting the US, Japan, China and India. As a result of such relatively constricted sales, and despite rationalising away relatively uneconomic production facilities, Peugeot-Citroën is not able, in this scenario, to generate sufficient cost economies to support competitive pricing against its more successfully globalised rivals.

These rivals, including the new, very powerful players originating from Korea and Malaysia, could be envisaged as later turning their attentions to Africa and South America, obliging Peugeot-Citroën to retreat to its strongholds in France and Western Europe.

In order to defend these core markets from larger competitors, Peugeot-Citroën realised that although there is a niche in Europe for French *joie de vivre*, the company is not strong enough to exploit it with its two parallel brands plus the competition from Renault. Indeed, commentators have long expected further rationalisation.

Indeed, there has been recurring speculation that, in order to protect some core of a French automobile industry for local socio-economic and political reasons, the French government might broker a merger between Renault and Peugeot-Citroën on the basis that the combined entity would produce and market a single range of cars, albeit with different marques. They would project an image of Gallic flair into the European market.

As Peugeot-Citroën was losing car sales during the 1990s onwards, it concentrated on supplying other car manufacturers with diesel engines. In fact this is proving to be a major business for the company particularly as the US market looks like it could be opening up to diesel technology. Other markets have seen the growth of public transport with buses and trains increasingly using the engines made by Peugeot-Citroën's expanded diesel operations.

Peugeot-Citroën also built on its reputation as a 'design-house' because its design flair was underpinned by practical expertise. As a result, Peugeot-Citroen has a large and growing business providing design input into the cars made by larger rivals, especially smaller cars run by hydrogen fuel cells.

Since the major manufacturers have such similar cost structures, it is now only design touches and image-associations that differentiate cars effectively for buyers, so Peugeot-Citroën is able to command high revenues for its design inputs.

What would really help this scenario for Peugeot-Citroën, would be that US car manufacturers overcome their traditional reticence at working with a French company, and focus on the fact that the major future for cars is 'light and small'. They need expertise on how to build attractive small, yet tough, cars.

Of course this is just a scenario. The main themes that emerge from this scenario are:

■ Peugeot-Citroën's threshold competences are not strong enough, by comparison with its rivals, to deliver on even a narrower global strategy that the company was then pursuing.

■ Indeed, a more limited global strategy is not really viable since it will be overwhelmed by genuinely global players.

■ Peugeot-Citroën's strongholds of France and Western Europe look defendable, but only if there is rationalisation of model range within the company, and over-capacity is taken out by consolidation, perhaps involving a merger between Peugeot-Citroën and Renault.

■ Peugeot-Citroën's strengths in diesel technology, new small car design, and new fuels must be nurtured and leveraged as an important potential source of future revenues.

■ An increase in alliances and collaborations remains crucial to the company's future, although it must be canny as to how it maximises its position relative to the rivalry that will be intense between the truly global players that will emerge.

■ The reality is that it will be a struggle for Peugeot-Citroën to continue as a volume provider and so it must seek out new market space.

Scenario 2: being very French

Let us now imagine a different scenario at the other extreme. If Peugeot-Citroën cannot succeed with a global strategy under one scenario, could it change the rules of the game, the basis of engagement?

Imagine that Peugeot-Citroën were to use the 'alternative foreign policy' of its French Government as a basis to present an alternative identity that is as much informed by simply not being American, as anything else.

Continue with the scenario: This proves very popular in the emerging markets of the Far East, the Middle East and South America. In fact, this gives Peugeot-Citroën a head start in these markets since local governments are willing to allow Peugeot-Citroën exclusive access on favourable terms. Neither Ford nor General Motors, let's suppose, gets even a look-in.

Of course, the foreign policy activities of the French government would continue to help open doors, but the company has worked hard on lobbying its government on the basis of protecting a core French business from foreign attack, and projecting French images overseas into geopolitically highly important spheres.

However, in order to exploit these markets and as part of encouraging local governments to give them generous concessions, Peugeot-Citroën has also worked hard at forming partnerships with local or regional manufacturers. Moreover, it has collaborated closely with local transport companies, especially the railways, and with Internet providers (a core expertise in India, for example) in order to give Peugeot-Citroën an effective distribution capability.

In this way, Peugeot-Citroën is able to claim that it is contributing towards developing the local infrastructure, generating local wealth through employment, and transferring logistical and engineering skills to local people.

Take the scenario further: these emerging markets would also be very keen to avoid the social and environmental costs that they had observed in the developed world, and here Peugeot-Citroën's leading expertise in small cars that are diesel-powered can really help. As alternative fuels become commercially viable – and the company continues to be active in their research and development – so the successor to diesel is ready to keep Peugeot-Citroën ahead.

The combination of a very overtly individualistic foreign policy by the French government in tandem with a locally collaborative approach by Peugeot-Citroën and its specific product expertise, could prove enduringly popular in the emerging markets.

Imagine it succeeding in projecting French political influence into around a third of the world's population, providing a basis for further commercial gain by other French companies, and making Peugeot-Citroën the largest volume seller of cars in the world – although not the most profitable (because margins are lower since local spending power is constrained).

Having established high barriers to entry in the emerging markets, Peugeot-Citroën could also concentrate on selling cars in France (where it was No. 1) and Europe (including Russia), and diesel engines to car makers who now focus on the developed world.

Of course this scenario is extreme, but the main themes to stimulate the company's strategic thinking are:

■ Protecting itself against the threats and positioning itself to exploit the opportunities are likely to mean that Peugeot-Citroën should seek active political influence. What reasons could the company give to encourage the French Government to want to support it in this way?

■ In other words, in this imagined future, business success in the markets that Peugeot-Citroën is targeting will be as much an issue of politics as it is of commerce.

■ While cost efficiencies are very important, the real key to unlocking Peugeot-Citroën's future is in gaining first-mover advantage into the emerging markets and building high barriers to entry against rivals.

■ Small cars and new fuel technologies, where the company is strong, are going to be very important in the future – whether in the developed markets or in the emerging ones.

■ Developing collaborative relationships with carefully chosen partners (chosen not just for their technical acumen but also for their political capital) will be a necessary core competence going forward.

■ Developing production capabilities in low-cost areas of the world can form a platform for taking low-priced exports into traditional developed markets. It is harder to justify maintaining production in first world countries.

The common themes from the two scenarios and a suggested way forward

The two scenarios are at the extremes: a global strategy that struggles and a global strategy that succeeds. Any common themes are strong pointers to at least some of the actions that Peugeot-Citroën should have been encouraged to take at the time:

■ Trying to achieve differentiation
  – Continue its work on diesel and new-fuel technologies;
  – Be sure to have particular expertise and product flair for small cars.

■ Trying to gain market presence
  – Cultivate governmental action to support efforts to enter emerging markets – China, India, Eastern Europe (including Russia) and South America look especially promising;
  – Work on developing alliances and collaborations;
  – Where markets are hard to enter directly (e.g. the US and Japan) then 'enter by proxy' by finding a partner to whom it would sell diesel engines strictly for cars being sold in the US and Japan;

- – Develop distribution capabilities in key European markets;
- – Consider stretching to new markets (e.g. diesel engines for buses, truck, trains).
- ■ Trying to continue price competitiveness
  - – Shift production and sources of supply to lower-cost countries (could support attempts to gain market presence, but could impair its much-needed relationship with the French government, and with French car buyers);
  - – Particularly if Peugeot-Citroën were to broaden the geographic spread of its value chain, the company would need to develop core skills in managing a complex and extended value chain, and build sophisticated HQ-subsidiary relationships;
  - – If economic conditions become really tough, then consolidate the product range (even if the two marques are preserved);
  - – There are still too many volume-players, so further consolidation is likely, and therefore the company should seek out a merger while it is succeeding and not wait for a 'forced sale' since a downturn would likely hurt Peugeot-Citroën more than any of its likely partners. The bases for choosing a partner would be the thrusts in the company's strategy: it strengthens Peugeot-Citroën's work at differentiation, it helps open up the emerging markets, and it affords further scope for cost economies. Most likely, Peugeot-Citroën should look first at a European partner. Is it sustainable for France to support Peugeot-Citroën *and* Renault? Volvo appears to have a complementary product range? And what of underpinning the Franco-German axis by merging Peugeot-Citroën with Volkswagen?! Or perhaps drop the Citroën brand and take Peugeot to BMW?)

As it turned out, Peugeot-Citroën concentrated on maintaining a low-cost base supported by expanded demand in new markets with rein-vestment in maintained price competitiveness and differentiation.

CAUTIONARY REMINDER

Please remember that this whole chapter is for illustrative purposes only. It gives one example of how the PEST, Five Forces and SWOT analyses can be applied to a business and an industry that we all probably know something about. It also shows how these different analytical approaches illuminate different aspects of a business and can be (indeed, *must* be) used cumulatively to form a comprehensive picture of 'current reality' to set against the vision[1].

The analyses – PEST, Porter's Five Forces and SWOT – are not standalone and discrete, rather they inform one another through links of logic and practical fact. For example, political and legislative forces are working with technological ones to drive Peugeot-Citroën (as well as other car-makers) to produce cars of greater fuel efficiency and lower CO_2 emissions. However, so intense is competitor rivalry that the strength that Peugeot-Citroën has in diesel engines has to be set against the threat of being overtaken by new technologies that address environmental concerns more effectively as being developed by rivals with bigger R&D budgets.

The analyses, worked in concert in this kind of way, then start to point to key headline actions such as maintaining an ever lower cost base so as to support continued funding of R&D, developing a strong sense of brand uniqueness to protect against competitors – especially new marques from the Far East, and the entry into new markets in emerging economies.

In this way, a narrative is built up that points the way for more detailed business planning. It is not, therefore, that you should copy this Peugeot-Citroën illustration, rather you should mimic how the inter-action of your PEST, Porter Five-Forces and SWOT analyses as applied to your own market and business generate a narrative of insights on which you can base a set of coherent actions to achieve your vision[2].

Key takeaway from Chapter 7

1   Don't be afraid to seek out the wisdom of others: a borrowed torch can light your path just as easily as your own.

Notes and References

1   On a Web page headed 'Vision', Peugeot-Citroën states:
    'As part of its long-term growth strategy, PSA Peugeot Citroën has identified three key ideas that underpin its contribution to sustainable development:

- pursue useful technological innovations, whose design and implementation reflect the skills of the workforce,
- meet all economic, social and environmental responsibilities,
- maintain relations, based on ethical values and trust-based dialogue, with all partners.'

See: www.sustainability.psa-peugeot-citroen.com/vision/index.htm

2   Under the new and invigorating leadership of Jacques Calvet, in the 1980s 58,000 jobs were cut from a total of 218,000 and a focus on economies of scale saw the company's number of production models greatly reduced. After losing a total of $1.5 billion between 1980 and 1984, Peugeot-Citroën, reported a profit of more than $1 billion for 1987. It grew to become Europe's second-largest volume car producer (after Volkswagen). Production and sales were centred on Europe. Although the company did later try to expand into new markets in Russia and Latin America, it lagged behind rivals. More recently, Peugeot-Citroën has continued to have a colourful life. After making a profit of 885 million euros in 2007, Peugeot-Citroën posted a net loss of 343 million euros in 2008. Soon after, the French government offered a huge bailout loan of 3 billion euros to the company, inviting the close scrutiny of the EU authorities, and the Chief Executive, Christian Streiff, was ousted in March 2009, with the board saying that a change in leadership was needed to 'unlock the group's potential' because of the 'extraordinary difficulties' posed by the economic downturn.

Chapter 8

The Process of Successful Business Planning: Some Soul-searching

'You have to leave the city of your comfort and go into the wilderness of your intuition. What you'll discover will be wonderful. What you'll discover is yourself.' – Alan Alda

WHO, ME?

By this stage, you have articulated a vision for your business and you have a close, insightful and action-generative grasp of current reality.

This means that you have created the conditions for a strenuous dialectic between these two poles – vision and current reality – that will generate the energy and creativity we illustrated with a tensioned rubber band in Chapter 3.

It is this energy and creativity that will produce the remaining stages in the process of successful business planning and, crucially, the activities that will make the plan happen.

So far, so wonderful.

But who is the 'you' that has done all this? If you are going to complete the remaining stages of business planning and ultimately produce a plan that you can actually deliver, then you are going to have to have a deep and honest understanding of who you are.

Consider the following. In fact, do more: *answer* the following:

- What are you good at?
- What motivates you?
- What is important to you?
- What do you want from life?
- What interests you?
- What bores you?
- What is your attitude to risk?
- Can you talk to strangers? In 1-2-1s? In groups?
- Can you write and deliver presentations excellently?
- What is your leadership style?
- What are your flaws?
- Do you accept – invite – criticism and challenge?
- How confident are you?
- How do you behave when you are asked an important question that you do not know the answer to?
- How do you juggle your business, personal, and social lives?
- How quickly can you learn new skills?
- What are you like with numbers? With design? With selling? With people? With multi-tasking? With organising? With paperwork? With communicating? With generating new ideas? With coming up with solutions? With giving direction? With taking direction?
- Do you usually finish what you set out to do and the tasks you have set yourself?
- Are you a details person, or big picture?
- Are you a quick-thinker or a reflector?
- What are you like under pressure?
- What do you do when things go wrong? And when you make a mistake?
- What do you do with under-performing staff? With excellently performing staff?
- What has the greater influence on what happens – you or circumstances?
- Do you change your mind or mostly stick to your guns?
- What are your values?
- What keeps you awake at night?

Please answer these questions honestly; there is no point in self-delusion – indeed, it would be dangerous. Engaging in successful business planning does not require god-like omni-competence, but it does require good self-knowledge. You can always find people who have the skills your business needs when you do not have these yourself, or you can learn them – but you do have to know what you need.

Do what you are best at and let your people do the same. Some say that Pelé was the greatest soccer player who ever lived. Every sensible football coach kept him as an outfield player – no one would ever have put Pelé in goal, no matter how many HR experts might have said he has a 'development need' in that area.

Now that you have your vision and a deep understanding of current reality, you can answer perhaps the most important question of all: are you up to it?

The journey of your business, as with every business, is arduous and unending. Can you meet the demands? Be honest.

If, after all that you have worked through in this book so far, you want to give this business planning and delivery your mightiest effort, then I applaud your courage and will to succeed. So let's press on!

THE TRUE SPIRIT OF YOUR BUSINESS

You already know a lot about your business, but what about its values? If your business were an individual, how would you characterise its personality? Its ethos?

What is your business's culture? Is it, for example, tight and bureaucratic? Or loose and free-form? Is it coherent or fragmented? How much autonomy is there? Is decision-making and power centralised or distributed? How do things get done in the business? Is it good at making change happen or set in its ways? What stories are told? What are the signs and symbols?

For example, some years ago Barclays Bank tried to project a personality of 'bigness' through a concerted advertising campaign that entailed well-known personalities extolling how big Barclays Bank is.

The self-image being nurtured and communicated was of a colossus bestriding the world, achieving its financial purposes and those of its customers by dint of sheer size.

Now, while customers did welcome the benefits that come from being with a large bank, there was also a considerable view that customers especially valued a bank that they could relate to, that also seemed small and accessible, and which values personal relationships.

A personality that values bigness can lead to swagger, which is not naturally a customer-friendly stance. The Barclays campaign seemed to customers to emphasise the extreme and unwelcome imbalance of power between the bank and its customers (cf. Porter's Five Forces), and to analysts it seemed to downplay the strategic importance of being not so much large as fast when responding to a hectic, Internet-speed, globalising financial world[1].

Barclays Bank subsequently changed its advertising.

An understanding of the personality of your business can help you judge whether actions fit, or seem contrary. How would your customers, employees and other stakeholders react? This is an important question to ask throughout the process of business planning.

Alongside this question is also one from the perspective of your business's personality: 'Do these actions flow from my business's internal character?'

In effect: is your business being true to itself?

Shakespeare was right to exhort individuals 'to thine own self be true'[2] but this also holds for organisations and your own business as well. After all, unless your business is true to itself, how can it be true to others?

Your business needs to act in ways consistent with its character (unless you wish to change this – a very demanding task) and, in this way, it will develop what René Char calls its 'legitimate strangeness'[3]. Aligning your business's character or 'legitimate strangeness' with the vision and purposes that you set, and then pursuing this mission with a coherent and pertinent set of actions, is what the process of business planning is all about.

Business planning creates patterns of sense-making. Values inspire actions that drive your business towards its vision and so we come back to the notion of 'teleological' discussed in Chapter 1. This is both the thrill and significance of the business journey, and the most important relationship is between how you and your business stands in relation to where it is headed. Future purposes give present meaning.

Ask yourself – and answer – the following questions:

- What behaviours fit your business? (And which do not?)
- How are these different from your business's competitors?
- How will your business project this difference into the marketplace?
- How does this difference compare with how your business is actually perceived?
- What relationships will it be important for your business to form and sustain in order to reinforce and amplify this difference?
- What organisational structure, resources, processes and procedures are needed to reinforce and amplify this difference?

A view about the business's personality and a deliberate working-through of these questions might have meant that Barclays would not have embarked on its ill-advised (in my view) proclamation of 'bigness'.

By the same token, a view about your business's personality and a deliberate working through of these questions can create distinctive patterns of sense-making that have real traction in your marketplace.

Consider another example. You may well have heard of Lucozade, an energy drink now produced by GlaxoSmithKline. The history of this product goes back over 80 years. It was developed in 1927 by a Newcastle chemist to help his son recover from jaundice and was then bought by Beecham in the 1930s. It came in a tall glass bottle wrapped in yellow-orange cellophane with a label proclaiming that, 'Lucozade aids recovery'. In later TV advertising, an ill, bed-ridden boy would wanly reach out for a drink of Lucozade, and immediately after swallowing a few mouthfuls there was a beaming exchange of smiles between him and his caring mother.

So the perceived 'personality' of the Lucozade business was about helping unwell people – specifically children – get better. It was used when you were ill. Its world was on a continuum with GPs, nurses, visits to the surgery, medicine, chemists, and having time off school, being stuck in bed and getting fussed over. It was a good thing when you did not need to drink the product, since it meant you had returned to full health.

This perceived 'personality' was at odds with the true mission of the business, which was to be associated with health, not with sickness. By the 1970s, the business was as unwell as one of its consumers and it needed a genuine, more thoroughgoing coherence between its true personality, its behaviours and how it was perceived.

Now we recognise Lucozade – and its variants – as being a *health* drink (not an *ill* drink). It is about boosting sporting performance. The web of relationships that the business has now cultivated, through sponsorship and advertising, is with athletics and sport. The product is now associated with the changing-room and sports locker, not with the pharmacy and medicine cupboard.

The business's behaviours better fit its personality which, as a result, is now more effectively projected into the marketplace, and its relationships are more tellingly arranged to sustain this distinctiveness. This clarity, this authenticity, will help the business decide which future behaviours to rule in and also which to rule out: in short, to engage more coherently in the process of successful business planning.

Yes, Lucozade is still an energy drink just as it was when it was first developed, but its personality and, as a consequence, how the business engages with the marketplace, has been more coherently worked out[4].

WHAT BUSINESS ARE YOU REALLY IN?

This may seem to be a simple question: if you are a florist, you are in the business of selling flowers; if you are a DIY retailer, you are in the business of selling (among other things) hand-held power tools. So far, so obvious it would seem.

Yet, in fact, this question is the flip side of the root-cause analysis prompted by the questions 'Why do my customers buy from me? What is important to them?' which we posed in Chapter 6.

In fact, probably few customers actually want flowers and no customers want, say, a power drill. So it would be a strange business to be in with few or no customers!

As Theodore Levitt so aptly said: 'People don't want to buy a quarter-inch drill. They want a quarter-inch hole!'[5] And they want a hole perhaps to fill with a fixing for a book-shelf or a radiator or a hanging basket or whatever.

So, if anything, in this regard the DIY retailer is in the business of helping people to fix things, and I recall working with a florist who saw herself as being in the business of bringing joy into people's relationships.

Understood in this way, the retailer of power-drills will count as his/her competitors not just retailers of other implements that can make holes, but also sellers of glue and strong adhesives, as their products also meet the underlying root need of the customer for a fixing solution.

For the 'bringer of joy into people's relationships', the competitors are more disparate, depending on the underlying situation. For loving couples, perhaps perfumiers are competitors. For a visit to a friend's house for dinner, a wine merchant might be the competitor. For a trip to see a recovering relative in hospital, the greengrocer selling fruit could be a rival. It all depends on what problem the customer is trying to solve.

Understanding all this at the same time as understanding the personality of your business will really inform how your business can best engage with your marketplace. If you see yourself in the film business, as it could be said Kodak did, when your customers actually want pictures you will lose out to digital technologies – not just in cameras, but also mobile phones[6].

Wells Fargo, an American business, used to run stagecoaches through the Wild West. When the railways penetrated into their territories, Wells Fargo did not seek to compete with ever faster horses. No, Wells Fargo used the railways with enthusiasm. This was because they knew they were not in the stagecoach business but in the business of transporting parcels and documents.

In fact, they knew they were not even in this business, but rather in the business of conveying important and valuable information; this meant that Wells Fargo embraced the Internet revolution and is now a major provider of online banking services[7].

When the iconic Harley-Davidson thought it was in the motor-cycle business, it struggled through the early 1980s against Japanese competition. When it more properly understood its identity – 'personality' – as being in the experience business, its fortunes began to transform. Harley Davidson created patterns of sense-making that more coherently aligned its personality with its vision and actions, thereby projecting its 'legitimate strangeness' more tellingly into its marketplace.

Harley-Davidson is associated with strong themes in American culture: individuality, freedom, the pioneer spirit. You might be a conforming executive during the week, but at the weekend, on a Harley, you can swap your grey pinstripe suit for leathers with attitude, and live the dream of being Davy Crockett, Jim Bowie and John Wayne all rolled into one.

It is the buyer's perspective that determines what business you are really in. As the founder of Revlon, Charles Revson, said: 'In the factory, we make cosmetics; in the drugstore, we sell hope.'

Understanding, at a deep level, what business you are truly in, reaches both outwards to your customers' real root needs, and also inwards into your business's authentic personality. The coherent, systematic and deliberate working out of this momentous conjunction into your business's vision and also into how your business projects itself into the marketplace captures the essence of successful business planning.

Key takeaways from Chapter 8

1 Know yourself honestly: this includes being aware of your strengths and flaws, as well as what you stand for.

2 Understand and develop your business's 'legitimate strangeness' by using the answers to these key questions as your action guide:

   a. What behaviours fit your business? (And which do not?)

   b. How are these different from those of your business's competitors?

   c. How will your business project this difference into the marketplace?

   d. How does this difference compare with how your business is actually perceived?

   e. What relationships will it be important for my business to form and sustain in order to reinforce and amplify this difference?

   f. What organisational structure, resources, processes and procedures are needed to reinforce and amplify this difference?

3 By reaching inwards into your business's authentic personality and outwards to your customers' root needs, you will be able to understand what business you are really in.

Notes and References

1   Compare the Lloyds Banking Group's projection of its personality through the symbol of a thoroughbred horse.

2   *Hamlet*, Act 1 Scene 3; spoken by Polonius to his son, Laertes.

3   *'Développez votre étrangeté légitime'* from René Char's *Partage formel*, quoted by Michel Foucault in Foucault, M., *Language, Counter-Memory, Practice,* p.7, Ithaca: Cornell University Press, 1977.

4   For a much more comprehensive discussion of this perspective and approach, see Cummings, S., and Wilson, D., eds., *Images of Strategy*, Oxford: Blackwell, 2003, especially Chapter 2 'Strategy as Ethos' by Stephen Cummings.

5   Levitt, T. 'Marketing Myopia', *Harvard Business Review*, July-August, 1960, **38** (4), pp. 45-56.

6   Of course Kodak is a major seller of digital cameras now.

7   'Wells Fargo & Co. said it expects to post a record $3 billion (£2.05 billion) first-quarter profit, causing its shares to soar and providing a welcome jolt to the broader stock market and a still-troubled banking sector' – Reuters 9th April 2009. Incidentally, Wells Fargo still uses the imagery of a stagecoach and horses – see www.wellsfargo.com

Chapter 9
The Number of the Counting

'Perfect numbers, like perfect men, are very rare.' –
René Descartes

ACCOUNTING FOR THE NUMBERS

I recall an exchange between teacher and student:

> *Student*: What was the title of the book again, please?
>
> *Teacher*: 'Accounting for Bankers'
>
> *Student*: But Mr Smythe, there is *no* accounting for bankers!
>
> *General laughter*

And so, in a brief moderately witty exchange, both the activity of accounting and the profession of banking were the joint target of gentle humour. Some of you may well think they got off lightly, for the preoccupation with financial figure-work can seem to be a very other-worldly concern.

Yes, you are aware that your business has to produce annual accounts and folk like bankers do indeed ask to see these and also copies of financial projections such as cash-flow forecasts, but all that seems very strange and business people in the real world, like your-self, simply cannot, well, account for them. Sure, you go through the motions to keep them happy – after all, they may well have something you need – but you cannot help feeling that all these numbers are not really part of the true business of business.

I would say you are half right.

You are right to keep bankers – and similar folk – happy. But you are wrong, very wrong, to think counting the numbers has nothing to do with you.

Absolutely, numbers do not make a business, people do; but numbers are a very sincere form of feedback that, properly understood, can help you understand what is going on in your business. Numbers will help you to distinguish between signs of success and signs of failure, and – very importantly – they will help to generate vital actions for your business. Numbers will illuminate the workings of your business like a microscope opens up the detailed workings of the exceedingly small, and like a telescope reveals the nature of the far-away.

With an effort that is miniscule in relation to the size of the benefit, you can use numbers very effectively as an integral part of successful business planning.

THE INS-AND-OUTS OF CASH

If a reliable meteorologist were to proclaim that 'Tonight, I forecast that it will get dark', then you will likely shrug with a dismissive air, utterly underwhelmed, 'So what?'

However, if the reliable meteorologist were to proclaim: 'Tonight, I forecast that it will rain', then you will have received some useful, actionable information. Let us suppose you are due to be out tonight and, on the basis of this information, you decide to take your umbrella, which you would otherwise have left at home.

Until you heard what the meteorologist said, you would not know whether to leave your umbrella at home or bring it with you. You would prefer to leave it at home, but this preference is less than your preference for keeping dry. So you want information that modifies your behaviours. As for it getting dark tonight, that is a given and is no news at all.

So, where a forecast affects your behaviours, it is useful and such forecasts can be made on the basis of judgements about current data – combined with a view as to the forces that influence the phenomena to which the data relates.

It is the same in business. Forecasts that review current facts plus the forces that affect them will be useful when they guide future behaviours. The thinking runs something like: 'Based on what we know now, and given how certain trends are likely to unfold, we can form a view as to which of a range of possible outcomes will probably occur in the future. We can prepare accordingly'.

We do this all the time. It can be as straightforward as acting on the weather forecast to trying to foresee how someone you know – or do not know – might react to a forthcoming situation. You will try to second-guess their reaction (or list the main possible reactions) and so act accordingly – even if it is only to be prepared for several possible reactions.

What is important in ordinary life is also vital in business life. Through an understanding of current reality – the facts that apply and the forces at work – you can extrapolate a likely future (or a range of probable futures) and so devise appropriate actions in advance.

Cash is often described as the life-blood of the business, so information about how it will flow in the future is also information about the status of the future health of the business. This is why an essential tool of successful business planning is the cash-flow forecast.

Essentially, the cash-flow forecast is a view of the amounts and timings of future cash received and cash paid away by the business. It is the *timing* of the movement of cash that is the crucial unit of analysis.

For example, suppose you make widgets at a cost of £10 per widget and your price of the widgets is £12 per widget. A customer comes along and orders 30 widgets and agrees to pay you £12 for each one. It will cost you 30 x £10 = £300 to make all the widgets, but you will receive 30 x £12 = £360, and you are delighted to have made £60 profit.

Let us suppose that you incur the costs of making the widgets in January and you send the goods, with an invoice, to the customer. You reflect back on January as a good month when you made £60 profit.

However, now suppose your customer is very tardy in settling your invoice and does not pay you until April. From a profit perspective, it looks like your business made a profit of £60 in January. However, from a cash-flow perspective, your business paid away £300 in January (to meet the bills that represent the costs of making the widgets, such as raw materials, wages, etc.), and received £360 in April. The cash-flow perspective looks at when cash is actually paid away and actually received.

So, if you were to prepare a cash-flow forecast back in December, and you know that your customer is likely to place an order with you in January which you will meet that month, then you will forecast a cash outflow of £300 in January. And, if you also know that your customer can take three months to pay, then you will forecast a cash inflow of £360 in April.

This is important. Suppose another customer places an order for 5 widgets in February. You need cash in February to pay the bills that represent the costs of making the 5 widgets – namely, £50. If your earlier customer had paid the £360 he owes you very promptly, you could have used some of that cash to pay the £50. But you do not have any of the £360 and so you do not have the £50 – unless you borrow it or can use cash that you have saved from past transactions.

It is no use to you that you have made a profit of £60 in January, which was before you received the order for 5 widgets. *You can only pay your bills with cash, not with profits.*

If you cannot find the £50 to pay the costs of making the 5 widgets (and let us suppose that your customer will not pay you any of the £60 he has agreed as being the total purchase price in advance), then you may have to say 'no' to what is otherwise a profitable piece of business. This seems perverse, but it illustrates the importance to your business of cash flow.

Now imagine a worse scenario. In February a tax bill arrives for £100, and the impatient taxman wants his money immediately. Alas, it does not matter that you have £360 due to you and reckoned to arrive in April: the taxman wants his £100 now. Suppose also that no one will lend this £100 to you, the taxman will not give you any extra time, and your customer who owes you £360 will not give you any of the money before April. Your business could collapse.

This is why even profitable businesses can go to the wall: it is because they run out of cash. These businesses cannot meet the bills *when they fall due* – and no one is prepared to give them more time or advance them the money.

I have spent quite a lot of time on this not because it is complicated – it is not – and not because you do not understand what a cash-flow forecast is – you undoubtedly do – but because it is *so important*.

Cash, like blood, must keep flowing, and a priority task for you is to forecast, monitor and manage your business's cash flow. Inattention to the flow of cash can bring ruin.

So what does a cash-flow forecast look like? It starts by listing every item of incoming cash and paid-away cash on a month-by-month basis, with the resultant net position being carried forward to the next month's calculation.

A spreadsheet is the ideal way of working through the arithmetic and presenting the results, as in the bare example below:

CASHFLOW FORECAST FOR WIDGETS LIMITED - for the period January to December *[year]*							
£000s	Jan	Feb	Mch	Apr	May	Jun	Jly
CASH RECEIVED							
Sales - Widgets							
Sales - Thingamebobs							
Sales - Whatchamecallits							
Storage rental							
Interest received							
New loan							
Total Cash Received							
CASH PAID AWAY							
Raw materials							
Stock							
Wages							
Bonuses							
Rent							
Rates							
Repairs & maintenance							
Office supplies and stationery							
Printing							
Postage							
Telephone							
Electricity							
Water							
Petrol/Diesel							
Travel							
Accommodation							
Insurance							
Tax							
VAT							
Advertising							
Entertainment							
Membership fees							
Newspapers and journals							
Accountant fees							
Legal fees							
Consultancy fees							
Loan repayments							
Bank charges							
Dividend							
Drawings							
Purchase of new asset							
Total Cash Paid Away							
Net Cash Inflow/Outflow							
Cash Position - brought forward							
Cash Position - to carry forward							

Having listed all the appropriate items, the next step is to forecast the amounts involved and when, realistically, you expect to pay cash away, and when your business will receive it. In the example we have been discussing, you may wish that your customer paid you earlier than April; indeed, you may well be *entitled* to the cash before April, but if the fact remains that your best view is that you will *actually* not get paid until April, then it is in April when you should record the cash as arriving in your forecast spreadsheet.

By the same token, you might dearly wish to delay payment of an item, but if you cannot do this, then you have to record when, realistically, you expect to have to pay away the cash.

Experience will help you complete the forecast as can your advisors. You will then have a really useable view as to how cash flows in and out of your business. If there are likely to be any pinch-points, then these will become apparent and you can plan some remedial or preventative action in good time.

Remember also, that the cash you receive in a particular month may well be quite unrelated to the cash you pay away for, say raw materials in that same month. The cash income might well relate to a job of work involving raw materials that you paid cash away for several months ago. By the same token, the cash outgoings on raw materials may well relate to a job of work, the cash income for which your business may not receive for some months hence. This is one key point of difference between a cash-flow forecast and a forecast profit and loss.

An illustrative example of Widgets Ltd's cash-flow forecast plus bulleted comments are opposite:

Notice the following key points:

■ The separate sources of cash inflow are identified and forecast – this makes sense if you wish to consider each source separately when, for example, they are driven by different and separate factors.
■ Borrowing money, whether from a bank in the form of a loan or from an investor (perhaps yourself!) in the form of additional equity, counts as a source of cash. In this case it looks like it is used to fund most of the purchase (£30,000) of a new asset perhaps a piece of machinery, or a vehicle.

CASHFLOW FORECAST FOR WIDGETS LIMITED - for the period January to December [year]

£000s	Jan	Feb	Mch	Apr	May	Jun	Jly
CASH RECEIVED							
Sales - Widgets	117,820	122,153	132,889	114,872	152,548	88,740	147,47
Sales - Thingamebobs	38,769	37,845	21,870	41,853	53,649	33,176	32,00
Sales - Whatchamecallits	49,768	57,625	58,974	56,712	79,213	55,497	71,8(
Storage rental	1,250	1,250	1,250	1,250	1,250	1,250	1,2
Interest received							
New loan					30,000		
Total Cash Received	207,607	218,873	214,983	214,687	316,660	178,663	25
CASH PAID AWAY							
Raw materials	53,459	68,847	71,223	39,887	33,295	49,882	
Stock	17,112	28,704	22,342	30,537	24,789	23,664	
Wages	37,076	38,214	36,987	37,655	37,142	32,878	
Bonuses				93,749			
Rent	2,110	2,110	2,110	2,110	2,110	2,110	
Rates	1,200	0	0	1,200	1,200	1,200	
Repairs & maintenance	464	388	397	211	416	376	
Office supplies and stationery	73	82	74	67	28	92	
Printing	202	187	98	189	211	497	
Postage	323	298	362	310	276	518	
Telephone	877	923	879	981	842	1,027	
Electricity	675	709	644	682	691	753	
Water	211	0	0	211	211	211	2
Petrol/Diesel	187	176	192	172	178	223	1
Travel	167	156	118	116	1,849	121	1
Accommodation	553	762	661	584	1,213	636	5
Insurance	1,812	1,812	1,812	1,812	1,812	1,812	1,8
Tax				31,207			
PAYE/NI	14,112	15,011	13,879	42,185	12,231	11,879	12,0(
VAT	69,112	0	0	67,829	0	0	68,0
Advertising	424	376	364	412	399	348	7
Entertainment	88	102	75	82	93	77	
Membership fees	0	0	0	675	0	0	
Newspapers and journals	37	34	39	38	39	38	
Accountant fees	0	0	0	2,800	0	0	
Legal fees	1,250	0	0	0	0	1,760	
Consultancy fees	1,100	1,100	1,100	1,100	1,100	550	
Loan repayments	0	0	0	0	0	627	
Bank charges	0	0	0	0	38	43	
Dividend	0	0	0	0	2,200	0	
Drawings	21,000	21,000	21,000	21,000	21,000	21,000	2
Purchase of new asset	0	0	0	0	31,000	0	
Total Cash Paid Away	223,624	180,991	174,356	377,801	174,463	152,322	22
Net Cash Inflow/Outflow	-16,017	37,882	40,627	-163,114	142,197	26,341	29
Cash Position - brought forward	-17,988	-34,005	3,877	44,504	-118,610	23,587	49,9
Cash Position - to carry forward	-34,005	3,877	44,504	-118,610	23,587	49,928	79,42

- All the main items of expenditure are listed and a view taken as to when cash will be paid away in respect of each of them.
- Subtracting the total of cash paid away from the total of cash received each month gives the net cash inflow/outflow position.
- By combining this net position with the net result from the previous month will determine whether or not there is actually a need in the month for additional cash or not.
- In January, for example, there is a net cash outflow of £16,017 which, combined with the carried-forward net cash outflow of £17,988 from the previous month of December, means that there is a total need for cash in January of £34,005.
- True, there is more than this amount of net cash forecast to be received in February, but that is too late. The point of the cash-flow forecast is that needs for cash are identified when they arise, and for Widgets Ltd to meet the January net cash need, monies will have to be borrowed. By completing the cash-flow forecast in advance, Widgets Ltd can seek an overdraft facility from their bank in good time to cover the temporary need for cash. But what size of overdraft should Widgets Ltd ask for – and for how long?
- Well, an overdraft facility of say £35,000 would certainly cover the January need for cash, allowing Widgets Ltd to borrow the shortfall in cash from their bank. However, this cash-flow forecast suggests that Widgets Ltd will need a lot more cash in April when the accumulated cash shortfall rises to £118,610. It would be embarrassing for Widgets Ltd to ask for an overdraft facility from their bank of £35,000 to cover the January position only to come back again a couple of months or so later for an overdraft facility of more than three times as much. The bank would naturally want to know whether the directors running Widgets Ltd have got a handle on how their business is going. Will a need for, say, an overdraft facility of £120,000 become a need for one of £250,000 in a few months' time? the bank will wonder. Banks hate open-ended commitments and uncertainty. In fact, this cash-flow forecast suggests that April is a temporary blip, and cash flow is so positive in each of the succeeding months that no overdraft is needed at all after April. It is clear that this unusual need arises from the one-off payment of bonuses (£93,749), with a coinciding quarterly VAT payment not helping matters.

■ So, the cash-flow forecast gives credibility to the business acumen of the directors running Widgets Ltd. Of course, none of the figures is likely to turn out to be exactly right, but if the assumptions on which they are based are testingly scrutinised, the shape of the cash-flow forecast is likely to be right and its pattern borne out by subsequent reality. Being able to signal such credibility is what encourages others to back your business, be they lenders or investors – and winning backers is often needed to give you the wherewithal to fulfil the goals of your business plan.

■ One more point, bear in mind that this cash-flow forecast – like most – is based on a time unit of analysis of a month. You may need to consider how cash flows within your business *within* the month. For example, in an extreme case, you can imagine that if all your cash were to be paid away at the beginning of the month and if all your cash were to be received at the end of the month, then your business would have a substantial, albeit temporary, need for cash in the middle of the month while inflows are awaited. This is an extreme case, but you should consider whether anything approaching this pattern of cash flow applies to your business, even only sometimes, in order that you can make provision for it in good time and avoid embarrassment[1].

So, a cash-flow forecast is an essential part of business planning, illuminating how the business's life-blood will flow month by month. Any need for a temporary blood transfusion – an injection of cash (such as a bank overdraft) – can be foreseen and set up in advance. Moreover, monitoring *actual* cash flow against *forecast* cash flow can highlight other important business issues sooner rather than later. For example, perhaps an expected cash inflow was less than forecast because a customer took longer to pay than anticipated. Was this a simple oversight or is it a sign that your customer is struggling financially? You need to investigate and, thanks to monitoring your business's actual cash flow against the forecast cash flow that you so diligently prepared, you will be prompted to do so at an early stage.

Or perhaps you had an unexpectedly large cash outflow in a particular month. Was this the result of the new recruit in your business's accounts department paying an invoice with more alacrity than is customary? Or perhaps a customer has placed a larger-than-expected order and your business's operations team has ordered some extra raw materials as a result? Or perhaps a supplier has increased its prices?

By being alerted to the situation, you can investigate and take action – action which, although necessary, might have remained untaken without the benefit of the cash-flow forecast and you using it. In the first case, a simple explanation of procedures to the new recruit and a modification to the induction training plan for the future might be all that is needed. In the second case, some customer tender loving care might be in order: some contact with the customer to thank them for the order and to understand whether this is a one-off or the start of a trend for which you would need to gear up your business accordingly. In the third example, you might decide it is time to shop around.

LOOKING AHEAD WITH THE REAR-VIEW MIRROR: HISTORIC ACCOUNTS

You probably are fully aware that every year your accountant prepares your business's Report and Accounts typically comprising a balance sheet and a profit and loss (P&L) statement. For a limited company, these accounts have to be filed with Companies House within prescribed deadlines.

It can all seem like a tedious piece of bureaucracy which, to cap it all, is also a fairly hefty cost to your business.

What is more, the figures relate to a trading year that finished several months ago and so, it seems to you perhaps, they are of very little use in the here and now as you grapple with the pressing business issues of the moment.

Yet, properly understood, even these historic accounts can be of immense practical use and can provide highly actionable information about your business. True, unlike your cash-flow forecast, they look back to past times rather than look forward to the future, but I shall show you how to look at your historic accounts so as to glean insights into the deeper workings of your business.

Armed with these insights, you can take actions that are important to your business. This active use of your business's historic accounts is an essential part of successful business planning, and I shall use a real-life example to show how[2].

Using the balance sheet to maintain an even keel

The balance sheet of a business is a statement at a point in time of all the things which the business owns and is owed (called assets), and all of the things which the business owes to others (called liabilities).

So, for example, any stock or machinery owned by the business would count as assets, whereas any loans that the business has taken out would be classed as liabilities. Monies owed to the business by its customers – or trade debtors – are assets; and monies that the business owes to its suppliers – or trade creditors – are liabilities. Share capital and retained profits are all viewed as money owed to the owners of the business – the shareholders – and so are classed as liabilities. What counts as assets and liabilities in the business's balance sheet is always from the business's point of view, as if it were an individual in its own right (which, in the case of a limited company, it straightforwardly is).

In a business's annual accounts, the balance sheet is a statement of assets and liabilities as at the date of the business's year end. It is as though the ebb and flow of normal trade is halted for a moment and all that the business is owed, owns and owes is totted up.

Lifting the main figures, as in our illustrative example of Realcase Ltd, can look something like the figure overleaf:

What do we notice so far?

- These accounts, while prepared by Realcase Ltd's accountant, are in fact unaudited. The accountant will, therefore, have relied upon information from the company – most particularly from the company's directors – in order to construct the balance sheet. The accountant will not have independently verified any of the information. Prospective investors and lenders will almost certainly want to see *audited* accounts.
- There are three years of balance sheet figures. As we shall see, this enhances the usability of the information hugely as we shall be able to identify some key trends. Trended information is the most action-generative.
- Total assets always equal total liabilities in a balance sheet – hence its name.
- There are different classes of assets, such as 'current assets' and 'fixed assets'. Let us review these briefly in turn:

BALANCE SHEET ANALYSIS FOR REALCASE LTD

Balance Sheet - £s	Year ending: 31/12/200X (Unaudited)	Year ending: 31/12/200Y (Unaudited)	Year ending: 31/12/200Z (Unaudited)
ASSETS			
Current Assets			
Cash (at bank & petty cash)	**£326,012**	**£111,869**	**£0**
Marketable investments			
Debtors (totalled):	**£884,968**	**£1,260,061**	**£1,547,485**
Prepayments	*£11,596*	*£10,997*	*£19,421*
Trade Debtors	*£873,372*	*£1,249,064*	*£1,528,064*
Stock (totalled):	**£283,350**	**£481,351**	**£564,871**
Stock	*£235,461*	*£387,816*	*£453,727*
Work-in-Progress	*£47,889*	*£93,535*	*£111,144*
Total Current Assets	£1,494,330	£1,853,281	£2,112,356
Intangible assets			
Goodwill			
Patents etc			
Other			
Total Intangible Assets	£0	£0	£0
Medium-/Long-Term Assets:			
Investments (totalled):	£0	£0	£0
Property			
Other			
Total Medium-/Long-Term Assets	£0	£0	£0
Fixed Assets			
Fixed Assets (totalled):			
Land & Buildings	*£641,500*	*£569,722*	*£513,437*
Plant & Machinery	*£312,416*	*£287,447*	*£262,389*
Motor Vehicles			
Total Fixed Assets	£953,916	£857,169	£775,826
TOTAL ASSETS	£2,448,246	£2,710,450	£2,888,182

BALANCE SHEET ANALYSIS FOR REALCASE LTD

Balance Sheet - £s	Year ending: 31/12/200X *(Unaudited)*	Year ending: 31/12/200Y *(Unaudited)*	Year ending: 31/12/200Z *(Unaudited)*
LIABILITIES			
Current Liabilities *(Amounts due within 1 year)*			
Overdraft			£89,776
Bank Loan			
Hire Purchase	£27,432	£23,444	£19,438
Directors' Current Accounts	£77,917	£73,201	£73,201
Trade Creditors	£543,886	£837,296	£1,017,518
Taxation	£0	£5,704	£3,123
Other (e.g. accrued expenses etc)	£0	£12,295	£0
Total Current Liabilities	£649,235	£951,940	£1,203,056
Long/Medium Liabilities			
Bank Loan			
Hire Purchase	£84,041	£77,365	£70,872
Directors' Loan Accounts			
Trade Creditors			
Deferred Taxation	£13,143	£11,149	£15,037
Other (e.g. provisions etc)			
Total Long/Medium Liabilities	£97,184	£88,514	£85,909
Capital & Reserves			
Issued share capital	£10,003	£10,003	£10,003
Retained profits	£1,401,002	£1,369,171	£1,298,392
Revaluation reserve	£290,822	£290,822	£290,822
Minority interests			
Total Capital & Reserve	£1,701,827	£1,669,996	£1,599,217
TOTAL LIABILITIES	£2,448,246	£2,710,450	£2,888,182

- *Fixed assets*: items of a monetary value which have a long-term function and can be used repeatedly. These determine the scale of the firm's operations. Examples are land, buildings, equipment and machinery. Fixed assets are not only useful in the running of the firm, but can also provide collateral for securing additional loan capital.
- *Current assets*: anything owned by the business which is likely to be turned into cash before the next balance sheet date, usually within one year. Typical current assets are stock, debtors and cash.
- *Stock*: materials and goods required in order to produce for, and supply to, the customer. There are three main categories of stock: raw materials or components, work in progress and finished goods.
- *Debtors*: these are the people who owe the company money. On a balance sheet, they represent the total value of sales to customers for which money has not yet been received. The way a business manages its debtors is often a key to its liquidity. Successful credit control ensures that credit is not extended to potentially bad debtors and that late payers are chased.

■ There are different classes of liabilities, such as 'current liabilities' and 'capital'. Let us review these briefly in turn:

- *Current liabilities*: anything owed by the business which is likely to be paid in cash before the next balance sheet date, usually within one year. Typical current liabilities are creditors, overdrafts, dividends, and unpaid tax.
- *Trade creditors*: these provide business customers with time to arrange for the payment of goods they have already received. This period is one of interest-free credit, which helps the customer's cash flow at the cost of the company's. Although the typical credit period offered to customers is 30 days, often in business the average time the customers take to pay is nearer 80 days.
- *Bank overdraft*: a facility that enables a firm to borrow up to an agreed maximum for any period of time that it wishes. An overdraft is a very flexible way of raising credit in that it need not even be drawn at all and the amount borrowed may fluctuate daily.

Banks may offer overdrafts without security, though for larger sums they will take security either by a charge on all the assets of the business, or by directors' guarantees supported by directors' assets (often property) – or all of these. The actual sum borrowed through an overdraft facility at the end of the financial year is recorded as a current liability on the balance sheet.

– *Capital*: to an economist, capital is one of the factors of production, the others being land and labour (some add entrepreneurship). To the business person it means funds invested in the company, either from the shareholders (share capital) or from lenders (loan capital). Both, however, recognise that capital is stored-up wealth, which when combined with the other factors of production, can be used to make goods and services more efficiently.

– *Long-term liabilities*: debts (creditors) falling due after more than one year. These include medium- and long-term loans, debentures and (possibly) provisions for tax payments or other long-term debts.

■ In Realcase Ltd's balance sheets, we can see that its current assets comfortably exceed its current liabilities in every year. Working capital, provided typically by bank overdraft and extended payment terms from creditors, in essence, finances the organisation's day-to-day running. Dividing total current assets by total current liabilities (the current ratio) indicates whether a company has enough short-term assets to cover its short-term debt. Anything below 1 indicates negative working capital. It is highly industry specific; but very roughly, anything over 2 might mean that the company is not investing excess assets. Many believe that a ratio between 1.2 and 2.0 is about right.

When we look at various numbers in the balance sheets, we see that many of them are growing year on year (such as debtors, stock, creditors and so on). Other numbers are declining (such as fixed assets and retained profits). Is this good or bad? If you had to choose one of the three balance sheets as being the best, which one would you pick? The balance sheet for the year 200Z shows the largest value of assets. Is it also the strongest balance sheet? Understanding the strengths and weaknesses in a balance sheet requires us to look at the relationships between certain items and the trends. We need to look at the profit and loss (P&L) statement.

Profiting from P&L statements

Here are three years of P&L statements for Realcase Ltd:

PROFIT & LOSS ANALYSIS FOR REALCASE LIMITED

Profit & Loss - £s	Year ending: 31/12/200X (Unaudited)	Year ending: 31/12/200Y (Unaudited)	Year ending: 31/12/200Z (Unaudited)
Turnover (Gross Income)	£4,545,741	£4,705,793	£4,878,672
Cost of Sales	£3,279,312	£3,418,662	£3,601,128
Gross Profit	£1,266,429	£1,287,131	£1,277,544
Directors' remuneration	£155,110	£134,250	£107,300
Salaries & wages	£506,002	£526,122	£541,722
Depreciation	£109,174	£96,747	£81,343
Other costs	£483,766	£516,131	£539,291
Costs & Expenses	£1,254,052	£1,273,250	£1,269,656
Operating Profit (EBIT) or Loss	£12,377	£13,881	£7,888
Interest Income	£1,702	£6,121	£347
Interest Payable	£3,974	£7,877	£5,923
Profit Before Tax or Loss	£10,105	£12,125	£2,312
Tax (or Tax credit)	£1,233	£3,609	£788
Profit After Tax or Loss	£11,338	£8,516	£1,524
Dividends	£40,708	£40,347	£72,303
Retained Profit/Loss	£29,370	£31,831	£70,779

What do we notice?:

■ The P&L statement sets out the total income from sales in the year less all costs relating to that income including, for example, the costs of making the sales (costs of raw materials, costs of production, etc.), interest paid on any borrowings, tax, and monies paid away to shareholders in the form of dividends. Income from investments and interest income from credit balances, as well as any profit – or loss – on selling an asset (assuming this has happened in the year, of course) are also included in the P&L statement.

■ Let us review the key items in the P&L statement briefly in turn:
    – *Turnover:* this represents the total sales of the business or total gross income before deductions;

- *Gross profit*: this is the gross profit after the direct cost of sales is deducted;
- *Operating profit* or earnings before interest and tax (EBIT): this is the profit after overheads are deducted from the gross profit;
- *EBITDA*: this is the operating profit or EBIT with depreciation and amortisation added back in;
- *Profit before tax*: this is the operating profit with interest payments deducted;
- *Profit after tax*: this is the profit available for the payment of dividends to shareholders;
- *Retained earnings*: this the profit retained by the business after dividends are paid to shareholders.

■ In the P&L statements of Realcase Ltd we can see that such are the amounts of the dividends paid that there is a retained loss in every year. You can additionally see that the balance sheet figures for 'retained profits' in the years 200Z and 200Y fall, respectively, by the amount of the retained loss in the same year.

■ Notice, too, that turnover increased in the year 200Z by 3.67 per cent on the previous year. In the year 200Y, turnover increased by 3.52 per cent on the year 200X. The significance of this is that it indicates whether this business is growing or not. Yes, turnover is rising year on year, but if the rate of growth is less than the rate of inflation, the business is actually contracting in real terms. This is just one example of how using trended information from historic accounts provides insights into what is really going on inside a business. Clearly, if your business is contracting in real terms, then your action planning will be quite different from a situation in which your business is growing.

More actionable insights are available from the historic accounts once we examine the pattern of relationships between key figures.

More things in heaven and earth – and ratios

By looking at the relationships between selected figures – not just any old figures – we can gain actionable insights into what is actually going on inside Realcase's business beneath the surface:

ANALYSIS OF KEY PERFORMANCE RATIOS FOR REALCASE LTD

	Year ending: 31/12/200X *(Unaudited)*	Year ending: 31/12/200Y *(Unaudited)*	Year ending: 31/12/200Z *(Unaudited)*
Key Performance Ratios			
Net Current Assets	£845,095	£901,341	£909,300
Liquidity ratio	2.30	1.95	1.76
Acid test ratio	1.87	1.44	1.29
Creditor turnover (in days)	44	65	76
Debtor turnover (in days)	71	98	116
Stock turnover (in days)	23	37	42
Fixed asset turnover (in days)	77	66	58
Working Capital Ratio	0.19	0.19	0.19
Gross Profit Margin	27.86%	27.35%	26.19%
PBT Margin	0.22%	0.26%	0.05%
Interest Cover (using EBIT)	3.11	1.76	1.33
Interest Cover (using EBITDA)	30.59	14.04	15.07
Tangible Net Worth	£1,701,827	£1,669,996	£1,599,217
Gearing	11.13%	10.42%	15.84%
Return on Capital Employed (ROCE)	0.69%	0.79%	0.47%

sometimes called Return on Net Assets (RONA)

What do we notice?

- We can group the key areas of performance into three:
  - *Liquidity ratios*: these measure the solvency of the business and its ability to meet short-term debts;
  - *Performance ratios*: these analyse the efficiency of the business in terms of its use of resources in generating sales and profits;
  - *Gearing ratios*: these measure the proportion of the capital of the business which has come from external sources, and must be repaid with interest.
- Examining these three main areas in turn starts with liquidity ratios. The ability to meet short-term debts is the same as the business's ability to meet current liabilities. This ability is a function of the business's current assets. If current assets exceed current liabilities then – in theory – the business is able to meet short-term debts as and when they fall due. Why the caveat 'in theory'? Well, remember what comprises current assets: stock, for example, is a constituent of current assets, but Realcase would be most unlikely to be able

to pay a supplier's bill with some partly-made – or even fully-made – widgets. For this reason, it is often a good idea to look at the relationship between cash and near-cash items (such as debtors) to understand how liquid a business is – sometimes called the acid test ratio:

- In Realcase's situation, not only do current assets exceed current liabilities (the current ratio, calculated by current assets ÷ current liabilities) is greater than 1 in every year), but also the near-cash assets (understood to mean the total of cash, marketable investments, if any, such as shares in quoted public limited companies, and debtors) are in excess of current liabilities (the acid test ratio, calculated by near-cash assets ÷ current liabilities, is greater than 1 in every year as well). Although these ratios are 'worsening' year-on-year, this could be taken as a sign that Realcase is making its assets work harder. In fact, however, because we know what else is going in the business, we shall see that Realcase is haemorrhaging cash because it is retaining losses (by paying out dividends).

■ We can also look at Realcase's performance in terms of how well it is managing its working capital cycle. The working capital cycle is simply the process by which the 'grace period' – between ordering raw materials and components from a supplier and then paying for them – can give the business time to make and then sell the finished goods to a customer and collect payment. Naturally, from the business's point of view, the ideal is that the period between making goods and receiving money from a customer for them is always shorter than the period between ordering supplies and having to pay for them. Supermarkets usually operate like this. Ship-builders, on the other hand, tend to operate with the opposite cycle. In practice, a business often finds that the cycle varies from supplier to supplier and from customer to customer. Some suppliers press for payment more quickly than others who give more leeway (or whose accounts department is more disorganised!), and some customers pay more quickly than others. Understanding the timings of your business's working capital cycle is extremely important – as we have seen when we discussed the cash-flow forecast. It is of the same importance as understanding your body's circulatory system and the flow of blood. In the case of a business, we look at the relationships between creditors and sales, stock and sales, and debtors and sales to get a handle on how well a business is managing its working capital cycle:

– In Realcase's situation there are clear trends. Notice that 'creditor turnover' is lengthening year by year: 44 days, 65 days, and 76 days. (Creditor turnover – in days – is calculated thus: [trade creditors ÷ turnover] x 365 days.) The result is that Realcase is taking longer and longer, on average, to pay its suppliers. This means that the grace period is getting longer for Realcase, giving the business more time to collect money from its customers before it has to pay money to its creditors. What action is suggested by this? Realcase will want to manage its relationships with its suppliers carefully in order to maintain this position, since a lack of attentiveness could lead creditors to apply pressure for earlier payment – especially if they become strapped for cash and look to rein in their customers (you!) and seek payment sooner. The key point about your business's working capital cycle is that it is *sustainable* and *predictable*, and this, necessarily, means for *all* parties: your business, your creditors, and your customers. And this is why I am always so keen to stress that **the key to business success is the quality with which the business manages its relationships with stakeholders**.

– Notice that 'debtor turnover' is lengthening year on year even more so than creditor turnover: 71 days, 98 days, and 116 days. (Debtor turnover – in days – is calculated thus: [trade debtors ÷ turnover] x 365 days.) This means that in year 200Z, Realcase Ltd is having to wait, on average, nearly four months to get paid by its customers! Some root-cause analysis is necessary here (poor practices in the accounts department? struggling customer(s)? a bad debt? or whatever) so that Realcase can take the necessary remedial action. In short, despite taking longer to pay its trade creditors, Realcase's grace period is actually contracting because its customers are taking even longer to pay Realcase. Remedying this by seeking faster payments from debtors will, as a flip-side of the coin, be damaging to the working capital cycle of

Realcase's customers, and so once again, the skill at managing key relationships is highlighted as an essential business competence.

- Notice that 'stock turnover' is also lengthening year on year: 23 days, 37 days, and 42 days. (Stock turnover – in days – is calculated thus: [stock ÷ turnover] x 365 days[3].) It is almost taking twice as long in the year 200Z as in the year 200X. Of course, we have seen that the whole working capital cycle is lengthening, but such a slowdown in stock turnover could be a sign that there is obsolete stock which cannot be sold – perhaps bespoke stock brought in anticipation of an order that never materialised. Again, a root-cause analysis is necessary before appropriate actions can be planned and executed.

- The other two key performance measures, the fixed asset turnover (calculated in days as [fixed assets ÷ turnover] x 365), and the working capital ratio (calculated as net current assets ÷ turnover) are less significant in reviewing what is going on with Realcase. The fixed asset turnover figure is falling year on year because the value of fixed assets is reducing owing to depreciation and turnover is rising, modestly, year on year. Generally speaking, asset turnover figures are useful for determining the amount of sales generated from each £ of assets. Businesses with low profit margins tend to have a high asset turnover; those with high profit margins have a low asset turnover. They can also be indicators as to how well a company is managing its working capital.

■ How strong is Realcase's trading performance? We can consider the key relationships between figures in its P&L statement:

- In each of the three years, for every pound that Realcase earns in sales, it makes a gross profit of around 26p or 27p. This is the company's gross profit margin (calculated as: gross profit ÷ turnover expressed as a percentage). The gross margin is not an exact estimate of a business's pricing strategy but it does give a good indication of financial health. Without an adequate gross margin, a business will be unable to pay its operating costs and other expenses and build for the future. A gross profit margin of greater than 50 per cent would mean a mark-up of over 100 per cent of the cost. In general, a business's gross profit margin should be stable. It should not fluctuate much from one period to another, unless the industry it is in has been undergoing drastic changes which will affect the costs of goods sold or pricing policies. Realcase's gross profit margin is indeed pretty stable;

- The profit before tax margin (calculated as: profit before tax ÷ turnover expressed as a percentage) is, in Realcase's trading performance, negligible in each of the three years, being 0.22 per cent, 0.26 per cent, and 0.05 per cent respectively. In other words, for every pound that Realcase earns from sales, around a quarter of a penny – is kept as pre-tax profit in the years 200X and 200Y; and much less than even that tiny amount in the year 200Z. It is obvious that profit margins are far, far too fine. What should your business be achieving? It is very industry specific. A profit before tax margin of, say, 25 per cent would be comparatively high, and would suggest that your business either has exceptional products which customers are willing to pay a substantial premium for, or your business really does not have much competition and so can charge what it wishes. In cut-throat pricing industries such as certain retailing sectors (e.g. home computers, petrol), you would expect the profit margin to be much lower because of heavy competition.

- Interest cover (calculated as: EBIT [or EBITDA] ÷ interest payable) shows what margin there is in profits to cover the interest payments on any borrowings. It is significant in that lenders often (although not always) stipulate a minimum amount of interest cover (say, 2½ times) in the loan agreement which obliges the business borrower to monitor this figure very carefully. To fall beneath the stipulated threshold could be construed as a default by the borrower within the terms of the loan, entitling the lender to seek immediate repayment of the entire loan. The lender could, at their sole discretion, waive the breach and continue the loan on the same terms as before; but the borrower is taking a risk on the lender deciding in this way. We do not know whether Realcase has an interest cover clause in its loan agreement (notice that there is an HP arrangement in place, as recorded under the liabilities within the balance sheet) nor, if there is, what the threshold is. If there were an interest cover clause and if it were set at 2½ times, then Realcase would be compliant in year 200X, but in breach of this clause in each of years 200Y and 200Z. The appropriate action would be to discuss the situation with the lender and explain what the business is doing to safeguard the lender's position and reduce its risk. Please note, once again, how the quality of the relationship with a key stakeholder is crucial to the success or failure of this (and any) business. It looks like the lender and Realcase came to an agreement after the 200Y figures, but will the lender be so accommodating given that the P&L statement for the year 200Z shows a deteriorated position? It is a priority issue for Realcase.

- Imagine you are an investor with spare funds that you are looking to put into a proposition to generate a satisfactory return. You have innumerable options. You could put your money in National Savings or in Premium Bonds and suppose this would give you a return of, say, 3 per cent. You regard this as a risk-free investment since you are putting your spare funds with the government. You might look at banks and building societies which, in your view, are less assured than the government, but not by much. For the greater risk, you might want to see a return of, say, between 3.5 and 4 per cent. What if Realcase approached you and asked you to invest your spare funds with them? What would be an appropriate rate of return for your risk in this situation? Might it be three times as risky as a bank? four times? five times? Suppose you determine that, although you are prepared to take risks with your spare funds, if you were to invest in Realcase, you would want a return of, say, 15 per cent. How is Realcase actually doing? Well, if you look at Realcase's return on capital employed (ROCE – sometimes called return on net assets, RONA – calculated as: operating profit [EBIT] ÷ [total assets – current liabilities]), you can see that in not one year does it reach even 1 per cent (respectively 0.69 per cent, 0.79 per cent and 0.47 per cent)! Sure, if you became a shareholder, the return you receive from the dividend that is paid to you might, given past practice, suggest a return much greater than this, but that is only because such dividends, as we have already observed, are being paid out of *retained* profits. Present shortfalls are being made up by past surpluses. Realcase is living off its past successes. Realcase is running down its wealth in order to make dividend payments to its shareholders. If this trend continues, there will come a time when it will have diminished its wealth so much that will have reached a point of no return and will have reduced its capacity to generate new wealth in the first place. It is rather like using up savings to meet running costs and then moving on to selling possessions. It is OK in the short term, but what happens when the cupboard becomes bare? With a ROCE such as Realcase's, you, as an investor, would get a better and more sustainable rate of return from relatively risk-free government savings. There is an additional important point to make here. As things stand at present, any case that the directors of Realcase might themselves make about whether to invest in the business could be defeated by the low ROCE that Realcase is currently capable of. Why invest £1,000 of Realcase's money in the business, when it can get many times the return in a bank account? Indeed, the balance sheet for the year 200Z shows that the company has an overdraft and so it would be better for Realcase to use its £1,000 to reduce this borrowing and so avoid some of the interest it is paying out. The ROCE is an important ratio for companies deciding whether or not to initiate a new project. The basis of this ratio is that if a company is going to start a project they expect to earn a return on it; ROCE is the return they would receive. Simply put, if ROCE is above the rate that the company borrows at then the project should be accepted; if not it should be rejected. And, as we have seen, it is also a benchmark for an investor to compare returns with other investment opportunities.

■ We have considered Realcase's liquidity and performance ratios. It now remains to look at Realcase's gearing which is the relationship between the company's reliance on borrowings and its reliance on shareholders' funds:

  – Realcase's gearing (calculated as: total of all borrowings [overdraft, bank loans, HP, borrowing from directors and the like] ÷ tangible net worth [total capital and reserves minus any intangible assets]) reduces and then rises year on year: 11.13 per cent, 10.42 per cent, and 15.84 per cent. In short, Realcase relies mostly (more than six times as much) on shareholders' funds to finance its business rather than on borrowings from outsiders. This relationship is important. For example, broadly speaking, a bank has two main perspectives when considering whether or not to lend money to a business: first, how the size of the repayments can be accommodated by the business's cash flow, and secondly, how the size of the proposed borrowing stands in relation to the balance sheet. Gearing of 10-20 per cent would not on its own give a bank concern. A bank wants the cushion of the owners of the business having a substantially larger stake in the business than it has itself. Another reason why gearing is important is what it implies for the business's earnings. If a business borrows, say £100,000 over a 10-year period at 10 per cent interest from a bank, then the business's repayments could be calculated thus: (£100,000 + 10% interest) ÷ 10 years; which equals £110,000 ÷ 10 years; which comes to £11,000 per year. This means that the business must generate a profit of at least £11,000 every year for ten years in order to afford to make the repayments on the loan. If, after all the appropriate deductions, there is £15,000 of profit left, then this means that £11,000 will go to repay the loan leaving just £4,000 available to shareholders. Now suppose that the business has a very successful year and makes a profit of £30,000. The lender will still get its £11,000, but the amount available to the shareholders is now all of the rest: £19,000. When a business is very profitable, what it has to give back to lenders is relatively fixed (especially so if the interest rate is fixed), but what it gives back to shareholders can be much more fluid, depending upon what the business decides to pay in dividends (with anything left over kept in the business as retained profits which also belong to shareholders). If, on the other hand, the £100,000 were to come from shareholders in the form of share capital, then there is no pre-established amount that must be given back and so there is not a minimum profit that the business must make in quite the same way as when the funds were borrowed from, say, a bank.

- So, in a nutshell, what would we summarise as being the main observations to make about Realcase based on its three years of historic accounts (balance sheets and P&Ls)?

- Strengths are:
  - The business is liquid – the short-term obligations of the company can be comfortably met by cash and near-cash assets (current assets exceed current liabilities).
  - The business has relatively low gearing – borrowing commitments are low compared with the amount of shareholders' funds.
  - There is a past history of profitable trading (note the significant retained profits).
- Weaknesses are:
  - The lengthening period for collecting cash from customers requires investigation and action.
  - Above all, profit margins are far, far too low; the overall return is much less than an ordinary bank savings account, and is insufficient to fund recent dividend pay-outs – hence losses being carried forward. As a result, the business will find it almost impossible, as things stand, to make any kind of case for investment and is on a downward trajectory to ultimate ruin.

■ Based on this analysis, we can readily deduce two actionable priorities for Realcase: the working capital cycle (to keep cash flowing) and profitability (to make a return for a sustainable future).

In this way, therefore, do please note that an informed consideration of historic accounts can indeed generate pertinent action plans to take a business forward. In short, the numbers of a business, both forward-looking and rear-view, are truly an essential part of successful business planning.

Finally, it is possible to think in terms of a hierarchy of inter-connected financial ratios, as shown in Figure 9.1 opposite.

PLANNING THE DOING: ACTIONS SPEAK LOUDER THAN NUMBERS

It looks like Realcase has been a successful company in the past, but now it is struggling. For Realcase, perhaps used to years of uninterrupted growth, the change in its trading performance can be as chilly and as unwelcome as a change from mild weather to an Arctic blast.

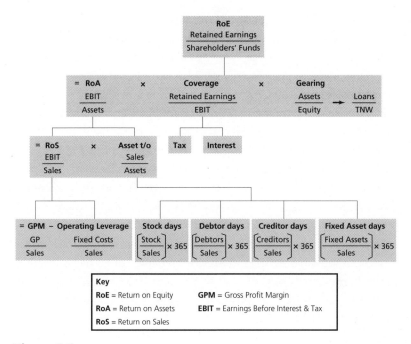

Figure 9.1

When things are going well, deficiencies in a business can persist but the pace of general growth, perhaps buoyed by benign industry conditions, sweeps the business along, ever onwards and, it seems, ever upwards. Yet, just as physical unfitness will come out eventually in some medical condition or other, so too will a less than well-run business show its flaws in the end.

In the tougher, less forgiving times that Realcase now finds itself in, its directors and managers must be right on top of every aspect of their business, building on every strength and eliminating every weakness. It requires especially strong skills – we have already talked about the crucial importance of relationship management skills with key stakeholders.

These will be crucial in tackling Realcase's under-performance priorities: the working capital cycle, and profit margins.

Priority: Realcase's working capital cycle

Relationship skills are highly relevant for tackling Realcase's working capital issues. Creative engagement with its customers will be necessary if payment is to be received more quickly than is currently the case.

Then payments terms can be enforced and invoices sent promptly. At the same time, Realcase should look to manage its stock levels more closely. It does not necessarily mean that customer service is jeopardised. How much of Realcase's stock is an extra 10 per cent on a 'just in case' basis?

If Realcase can improve its working capital cycle, the effects can be more impactful than might be expected.

We can see that in year 200Z, Realcase turned over £4,878,672 with debtors taking an average of 116 days to pay.

As a result no less than £1,547,485, of cash is tied up in amounts owed to the business. How much of that cash could the business get hold of?

Well, Realcase states in its invoices that customers should pay within a not unreasonable 30 days. This improvement of 86 days, if it had applied throughout the year 200Z would have clawed back the princely sum of £1,149,495 for the business! (Calculated as: [86 days ÷ 365] x £4,878,672 = £1,149,495.)

This is much more than the amount of the overdraft of £89,776 stated in the balance and no overdraft would be needed. If Realcase is paying 12 per cent interest on this overdraft, and if the borrowed sum is fairly constant throughout the year, this means that Realcase would be paying £10,773 a year in interest costs. Improving average debtor days from 116 days to 30 days would save on this interest cost of £10,773, which would have increased profit before tax more than four-fold!

What is more, suppose Realcase had put the remaining sum of £1,059,719 (£1,149,495 minus £89,776) in an interest-bearing deposit account earning a return of, say, 4 per cent per annum (p.a.). This would have generated a further £42,389 (£1,059,719 x 4%) in income. Combining this with the benefit of not having to pay £10,773 in overdraft interest, the overall boost to profit before tax would be £53,162! Pre-tax profit in the year 200Z would have been, not £2,312 but £55,474!

Although the profit before tax margin would still have been a paltry 1.14 per cent, compared with an actual 0.05 per cent, this is a substantial improvement just from working at getting customers to pay when they should. Might it be possible to share some of this improvement by offering incentives to customers who pay promptly or even early?

For each single day that Realcase improves its working capital cycle (e.g. getting paid a day earlier than currently), no less than £13,366 cash is retrieved (calculated as: [1 day ÷ 365] x £4,878,672 = £13,366) at a borrowing cost at 12 per cent p.a. of £1,604 p.a.

Priority: Realcase's profit margins

How does Realcase – indeed, how does any business – increase its profits?

There is no magic to this. There are, essentially, just two ways by which a business can increase its profit.

And given that profit is what is left over after costs are deducted from income, then clearly, profit can be increased either by raising income or by reducing costs, or both.

Unpacking this a little further, we quickly see that income, being the product of sales volume x price, can be raised either by increasing prices or by selling more, or both.

So there we have it: a business can raise its profits by a) increasing sales; b) reducing costs; and/or c) raising prices.

The knee-jerk reaction of too many businesses – and a reaction that Realcase must avoid by careful business planning – is to implement ill-considered cuts in costs. Of course, efficiency is important, but there are cases where a business has imposed 10 per cent cuts in all forms of spending – including staffing – only to find that they lose their best people and that customers melt away. Or they cut training or spend on external advice, and then do not have the skills and knowledge to keep the business going. Or they reduce marketing, and the supply of new customers dries up. Or investment is cancelled. Perhaps the purchase of a replacement van is put off, which simply swaps a large one-off expense for a steady stream of ever greater maintenance and fuel bills with the existing vehicle.

As in physiology, it is not just the weight of the human body that is important but the proportions between fat and muscle. Healthy weight loss is about losing fat, not muscle.

It is the same for a business. It is not just the totality of the cost base that is important but the proportions of 'good costs' and 'bad costs'. Good costs are those that will bring in greater savings elsewhere, or extra business, and thus income, or are simply what it takes to have a seat at the table in the business's chosen market (i.e. keeping what you have got).

Good costs are muscle. After all, if your costs were zero, what do you think your income would be? Yes, zero!

Bad costs are like fat. These are the inefficiencies in Realcase's (and your!) business. Inefficiencies most notably accumulated during benign trading conditions when the business was perhaps driven for indiscriminate growth: the legacy customs, the tortuous processes, the re-work, the ex gratia payments to complaining customers.

Bad costs are also the missed opportunities, the foregone revenues, like under-pricing ...

We have said that a business can raise its profits by a) increasing sales; b) reducing costs; and/or c) raising prices.

But what are the dynamics here? Not all ways are equal.

Consider a simple statement of Realcase's profit in year 200Z:

Sales:	£4,878,672
Cost of sales:	£3,601,128
Gross profit:	£1,277,544
Operating costs:	£1,269,656
Operating profit:	£ 7,888

Now, let's look at what happens when each of the three ways by which profits can be raised are tried. Suppose a 10 per cent improvement in each case:

	Original scenario	10% more sales	10% off all costs[4]	10% price rise
Sales:	£4,878,672	£5,366,539	£4,878,672	£5,366,539
Cost of sales:	£3,601,128	£3,962,241	£3,241,015	£3,601,128
Gross profit:	£1,277,544	£1,404,298	£1,637,657	£1,765,411
Operating costs:	£1,269,656	£1,269,656	£1,142,690	£1,269,656
Operating profit:	£ 7,888	£ 134,642	£ 494,967	£ 495,755
Uplift in profit:		1,607%	6,175%	6,185%

So an increase in prices has the most directly impactful effect on profit as the benefits of a price rise go straight to the bottom line.

Assuming, that is, sale volumes are unchanged despite the higher prices. Whether or not this is a realistic assumption will depend upon the assessment by the directors of Realcase Ltd of the strength of their relationships with their customers. What value do their customers place on the goods and services that Realcase provides? Again, please note the importance of relationships in yet another business issue.

The directors of Realcase Ltd may feel that keeping sales at the same volume despite a 10 per cent across-the-board increase is an unrealistic assumption. So what could be possible?

Consider what a mixed approach of, say, just 3 per cent improvement in each case could achieve (3 per cent more sales, 3 per cent off all costs, 3 per cent price rise):

	3% mixed approach
Sales:	£5,025,032
Cost of sales:	£3,493,094
Gross profit:	£1,531,938
Operating costs:	£1,231,566
Operating profit:	£ 300,372
Uplift in profit:	3,708%

So, if the directors of Realcase Ltd judge that it would be unrealistic to maintain sales in the face of a 10 per cent across-the-board price increase, then it might plan instead to combine a little price rise, with a modest effort to boost sales volume and with a modest cutting of costs. Good relationships with customers can help see the price increase through and also identify opportunities for cross-sales and up-sales that can give a further boost to income.

The arithmetic is such that improving these three elements by just 3 per cent each (3 per cent more sales, 3 per cent off all costs, 3 per cent price rise) – eminently doable, one would think – can turn what was an operating profit of just £7,888 into an operating profit of no less than £300,372!

This gives an operating profit margin of almost 6 per cent (£300,372 ÷ £5,025,032 = 5.98 per cent). The directors of Realcase Ltd might want better, but it is huge progress on the actual performance in the year 200Z and a massive leap in tackling Realcase's tip-top priority of improving its profit margins.

Priority: Realcase's profit margins – some more on top-line income

We have seen how raising prices to boost the top line can significantly raise Realcase's bottom line. Let us spend a bit more time on the top line.

Where does top line revenue come from? It is a function of the number of customers a business has, the number of times they buy, and the price they pay when they do:

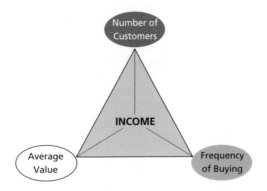

Figure 9.2

So consider the figures for Realcase Ltd:

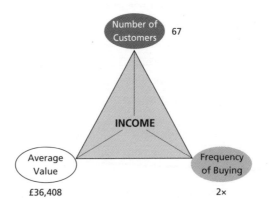

Figure 9.3

On the averages, Realcase Ltd has 67 customers who buy twice a year and spend £36,408 each time they do. This means that Realcase's gross income (turnover) is (as we have seen for the year 200Z):

$$67 \times £36,408 \times 2 = £4,878,672$$

Now suppose Realcase could brainstorm some ideas that, upon implementation, were able to increase the number of its customers by 3 per cent, the average value by just, say, 3 per cent, and the frequency of buying by 10 per cent:

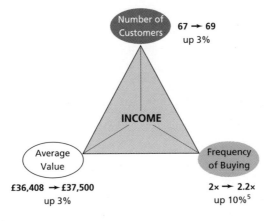

Figure 9.4

So what is the gross income now after these seemingly modest improvements in the components of revenue?

$$69 \times £37,500 \times 2.2 = £5,692,500$$

This is an increase of £813,828 or no less than 16.7 per cent!

So part of Realcase's action planning is to work out steps by which it can acquire 3 per cent more customers, raise revenue by 3 per cent, and increase the frequency of buying by 10 per cent. The arithmetic – as it is for *all* businesses – is that the combined effect is to increase gross revenue by 16.7 per cent.

Just as every business needs first to understand, and then actively to manage, its cost levers, so too must every business be very active in managing its income levers. All this is integral to successful business planning.

Managing the business's numbers is integral to successful business planning

The directors of Realcase Ltd might have said that they are far too busy firefighting to save the business to be able to luxuriate in some nebulous business planning. That, they might have said, is something for when the worst is over, right?

WRONG!

When times are precarious, uncertain and tough, your business is too important just to wing it. Such times demand more from you – and more so than benign conditions – than just a string of seat-of-the-pants decisions.

If you see issues in your business like those in Realcase, you will be understandably anxious. But it is no good flapping about in the fog. What is needed is an overall sense of direction combined with flexibility.

To survive – and win – you need to make thoughtful choices, have a sense of the strategic possibilities of your market, and understand the strategic capabilities needed to exploit them.

Such understanding will then guide specific actions: instead of an across-the-board approach to cutting costs, an intelligent mix of stopping extraneous activities and keeping the things that feed relevant strategic capabilities is the way forward. But which is which? This can only be answered in the context of a proper business plan.

It is too easy, in the heat of day-to-day battle, to look at only what is immediately in front of you. Winners will consider a broad range of options and be open to new possibilities. Resources are scarce and their deployment cannot be based on priorities that reflect the last issue that you confronted.

Cut costs? OK, but not so as to damage long-term competitiveness or customer service. Raise prices? OK, but not so as to see all your customers melt away. Re-trench and focus? OK, but not so as to overlook new opportunities. Love your customers? OK, but not so as to withhold cross-sales from them and to take all the 'sur-costs' (e.g. fuel, 'green', etc.) yourself without sharing them. Cancel that investment in IT? OK, but not so as to restrict strategic capabilities that will be crucial in the long term.

In these times of ever-increasing complexity and ever more opaque ambiguity, never has good business planning combined with flexibility combined with constant attention been more important.

Good business planning is about asking: 'What would have to be true to make the proposed action successful?'

For example, suppose you are considering cutting your customer service team in order to save costs. For this to succeed, you would have to believe that few customers would seek alternative providers at a time when your competitors would be desperate to have them. Is that plausible?

On the other hand, cutting stationery, travel and accommodation costs, but diverting the savings to spend more on customer service could be the way to take advantage of competitors who do decide to cut their customer service teams.

Or what about increasing your prices by 3 per cent? How many customers – customers with whom you sustained a good relationship for many years – would have to leave you for an unknown alternative for this action not to work? Is that likely? In tough times when they need to rely on their suppliers and relationships count?

It is essential that you keep even closer to your market to inform the quality of your business planning.

So what is meant by successful business planning? It is a coherent and systematic response to a challenge. It requires a careful diagnosis of the forces at work, a deep understanding of what matters in the market, and an honest awareness of the business's capabilities for taking relevant action.

Successful business planning, as it turned out for Realcase Ltd, is the only way to know how best:

- to keep cash flowing;
- to separate good costs from bad costs and take action accordingly;
- to stop underpricing and work out the best mix in a mixed approach;
- to grow the top line in a sustainable way;
- to come through a downturn in performance and get back to a path of growth.

The tactics for returning to good health, like the tactics for flourishing, require good business planning. Sure, a business plan without tactics is empty, but tactics without a business plan are blind.

Key takeaways from Chapter 9

1   Understand the numbers of your business and their trends – both future-looking (cash-flow forecast) and rear-view (historic accounts) – to generate actionable insights about the key levers in your business, and also to compare your business's performance with that of your competitors.

2   Cash is the life-blood of your business and you need to manage it accordingly.

3   The skill you and your team show at managing relationships with your business's key stakeholders will determine whether your business succeeds or fails.

4   Relatively modest and sensible actions about pricing, costs, sales, customer numbers and frequency of customer buying can have a disproportionately positive impact on your business's performance.

5   Price rises go straight to your bottom line; a 3 per cent uplift in customer numbers combined with a 3 per cent uplift in the value of every transaction combined with a 10 per cent uplift in the number of customer transactions, will grow your business's top-line income by no less than 16.7 per cent.

6   Know your costs: distinguishing between good costs and bad costs:
    a.   Good costs are those which support the capabilities the business needs in order to achieve its strategic objectives.
    b.   There is no magic formula for finding bad costs – only detailed scrutiny.

7   People are not the most important part of your business: people who *perform* are!

8   All customers are equal but some are more equal than others. Don't just count your customers, *weigh* them! Know your most profitable customers and *love* them!

Handy list of key financial performance ratios:

1   Net current assets = working capital = current assets – current liabilities

2   Liquidity ratio = current assets ÷ current liabilities

3   Acid Test ratio = (current assets – stock) ÷ current liabilities

4   Creditor turnover = (trade creditors ÷ turnover) x 365 in days

5   Debtor turnover = (debtors ÷ turnover) x 365 in days

6   Stock turnover = (stock ÷ turnover) x 365 in days[3]

7   Fixed asset turnover = (fixed assets ÷ turnover) x 365 in days

8   Gross profit margin = gross profit ÷ turnover

9   PBT margin = profit before tax ÷ turnover

10   Interest cover (using EBIT) = operating profit ÷ interest payable

11   Interest cover (using EBITDA) = (operating profit + depreciation + amortisation) ÷ interest payable

12   Tangible net worth (TNW) = total capital and reserve – intangible assets

13   Gearing = all borrowings (short-/medium-/long-term, including overdraft/loans/HP etc) ÷ TNW

14   Return on capital employed (ROCE) = EBIT ÷ (total assets – current liabilities)

Notes and References

1   If your cash flows are very unpredictable and large, then you may well need to prepare your spreadsheet on a week-by-week basis rather than on the more typical month-by-month basis. Indeed, banks that trade heavily on the inter-bank market or banks who lend to those that do, monitor their cash flows on a daily basis. Funds will have been advanced in the morning in the expectation that they will come back by the close of business that same day. As a result, the lender can be carrying a very substantial intra-day risk during a single trading day while they await the expected cash inflow. This is monitored very carefully counter-party by counter-party. Just as a lender sets a limit on a customer's overdraft facility, so in this scenario the lender would restrict its cash exposure on an individual basis to within what is called a 'daylight limit'.

2   'Realcase Ltd' is a made-up name but it does reflect a real-life business that I have worked with. The numbers cited in Realcase Ltd's balance sheet and profit and loss statement are disguised to respect my client's confidentiality, but they do illustrate genuine business issues.

3   Instead of the formula used in the main text, you may come across an alternative way of calculating stock turnover which, technically, could be regarded as more accurate: (average value of stock

÷ cost of sales) x 365 days. You may not know the average value of stock, so the year-end figure, as cited in the balance sheet, can be used instead. For Realcase, using (year-end value of stock ÷ cost of sales) x 365 days, the stock turnover figures come out as (result according to formula used in the main text in parentheses): 32 days in year 200X (23 days); 51 days in year 200Y (37 days); and 57 days in year 200Z (42 days). Notice that the trend is similar in both methods of calculation. Whichever method you use, the most important thing is that you ask yourself whether the figure is what you would expect in your business as it can vary through the year. After all, if demand for your goods is seasonal, then holding 40 days' worth of stock during peak periods may not be enough, and too much during the quiet times when demand is low. If the level of stock turnover is not what you would expect, then you will need to understand the root causes and implement a remedial action plan. If the trend shows a change (lengthening or shortening), then you should also ask yourself why this is and, again, whether it is what you would want for your business. The theoretical ideal is that you keep stock as close to zero as possible *without delaying sales*. Stock reflects not knowing; it is a 'just-in-case' phenomenon. How close to zero can you get in your business?

4   In practice it is usually more difficult to reduce cost of sales than operating costs, and it is more likely that a business would be able to reduce just its operating costs and not its cost of sales. But this illustration assumes both types of costs can be reduced, as it does not detract from the main point.

5   What this signifies is not so much that each customer is now buying 2.2 times a year but, rather, that 1 in 10 customers are buying one more time each year (i.e. 3 times). 2.2 is the simple average figure.

Chapter 10
Pulling It Together: The Business Plan

'The discipline of writing something down is the first step toward making it happen.' – Lee Iacocca

A BRIEF RECAP

First, let us recap as to where we have got to. By now, you have undertaken a pretty thorough exploration of the tension, between your vision and current reality.

You have created a vision that represents an ambition for your business that matters to you and that will spur you on, through thick and thin.

You also have a deep, insightful and action-generating understanding of the key external forces affecting your business, whether these are macro-forces such as political, economic, social and technological – or industry-related such as Porter's Five Forces.

You are rounding off your understanding of current reality by looking unsparingly at yourself (and your team), and at your business in terms of its capabilities and competencies, its ethos and personality, and its financial performance.

All this is now coming together to generate an appreciation of the opportunities for, and the threats against, your business. Your gleanings are not academic, as you are already noticing how goals and sub-goals, and especially some important actions, are beginning to suggest themselves.

Capturing what you have been doing so far pictorially may well look and feel something like this:

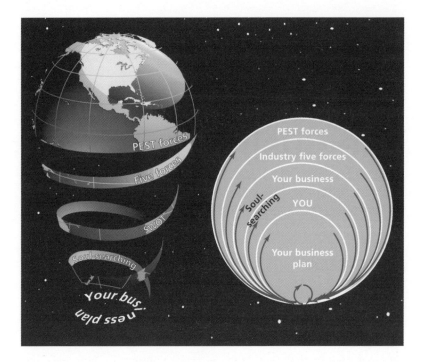

You have been pursuing a logical yet iterative process. It feels like it is naturally sequential, but in practice you will move back and forth through the key stages of the process of successful business planning. Each stage illuminates, and is illuminated by, the next, (and the one after that, and so on). Remember, as we said in Chapter 2, expect the process of business planning to resemble not so much the one-directional laying of tracks progressively towards a specific station, but more like the interactive craft process of a potter and clay. The potter's hands shape the clay, but the peculiarities of the clay will also influence the movement of the potter's hands. The end result is the product of the iterative interaction between potter and clay.

You will note something about, for example, a social force that will constitute an opportunity for your business. You record it in your SWOT analysis. Then, later on in your planning, you might recognise a capability or feature of your business that could either augment or diminish that previously noted opportunity. Or perhaps the findings from some customer research you commissioned or from some analysis of your competitors have thrown up some interesting data. You will amend your SWOT analysis accordingly. You can expect to move back and forth through the various stages as you explicitly or tacitly begin to form hypotheses about your business and the possibilities open to it, and then revise them, reinforce them or jettison them in the light of subsequent deliberations.

You are doing two things at once: you are working out how to compete successfully in known market space, and you are also seeking out ways in which to push out the boundaries and create brand new market space. No wonder you can expect to work through the key stages of successful business planning in an iterative way, moving back and forth between different stages, sometimes sequentially and logically, sometimes hopping about and intuitively.

In today's ambiguous, complex and uncertain world, it is old-fashioned and out of place to think of business planning as an engineering process: first you set the goal, then you plan how you get there, and finally you implement the actions. No, do not be fooled into thinking that such a simple sequence describes what you can expect when you actually undertake business planning yourself.

This means that as you undertake successful business planning, you can expect to hypothesise, test, revise, learn, shape, re-shape and develop the contents of your business planning. It is, therefore, most definitely not a once-a-year activity, but continuous. You will progress not just by an engineer's charts, but also by an explorer's feel. You will look out for logical fits, and also sense-making patterns.

And yet, amongst this flow you will inevitably have to stand still and take stock. In fact, it is essential if all your planning is going to have any traction on the real world and actually make a difference. This is where the rubber hits the road.

It is necessary to give all this planning tangible form. It is time to get down to business. A good plan today is better than a perfect plan tomorrow.

'The time has come', the Walrus said, 'to talk of many things'

By now, you have a mass of material – perhaps you are blinded by the blizzard of information you have accumulated. Every business plan is different, but before committing pen to paper (or, more likely, tapping the keyboard's keys) try pulling all the key pieces of information into five main groupings:

1 **What?** This question (in fact, lots of 'what?' questions) refers to the opportunity that your business is organised to make the most of. What is your business setting out to achieve? What is the success your business plan is holding out the prospect of? What business are you in? What are you going to sell and to whom? What will be the timescale to success? Remember, different is not always better, but better is always different! And remember, too, that successes can be surprising. Who would have thought that a hard drive in a box – albeit a very pretty box – would revolutionise the music business? And yet that is what Apple's mobile digital device, iPod[1] has done. But be realistic: is there really a demand for a better tea-strainer?

2 **Whence?** This question is asking about the situation from which the business hopes to spring. What forces, outside the business's control (such as PEST and Porter's Five Forces), affect the business? And to what degree? What are the relevant trends? Which forces will propel the business forward? Which forces will hold it back? What are the market dynamics? Is the market growing? At what rate?

3 **Who?** This question is about the people who will make this happen. This is a crucial area. Many businesses with great ideas have failed to find backing because their people have been unconvincing. And the reverse has happened: businesses with fairly so-so ideas and businesses in precarious positions have won support because backers have been drawn to the quality of the people. Who are the key individuals in the business? What will they do and how are they qualified and experienced to do it? What is their attitude and motivation? Who is in their network? Who are the key stake-holders (investors, owners, regulators, advisers, even other parts of the Group if the business is part of a larger organisation) and what is the quality of the business's relationships with them? Who are the business's suppliers and how are relationships with them? Who are the business's competitors and how good are they? How will competitors respond to your business? Who are the business's customers? Will they change over time (in number or by type)?

Are customers easy or difficult to get? Why will they buy from the business and not from any alternative? Will customers stay with the business? Could customers be lured away by imitators?

4 **How?** This question invites the business to describe the actions it will take to move towards, and achieve, the success it has set for itself. It is the future narrative of the business, the *drama*. What will happen and when? Why is the proposed sequence of actions the most effective – more effective than potential alternative courses? What sort of journey is the business expected to take? How will resources be deployed? What is the logic, the pattern, to this?[2] In my experience, it is easy to have the business idea, the difficulty comes in the pertinent and coherent assembling of what is needed to make the idea actually happen – and then making it happen. Remember something I said in Chapter 1? 'A plan stands or falls not by the quality with which it is written or by the quality of its research and insight but by the quality of its implementation.'

5 **How much?** Every business is about risk and reward, how much funding is needed for what reward? What could impede – or, indeed, totally block – progress? What counter-measures might be taken? What risk analysis has been done? A convincing business plan does not gloss over any vulnerabilities. It acknowledges them openly, and then talks about what steps will be taken to reduce the likelihood of them arising, and the steps that would be taken to combat them if they did arise. What do the numbers and ratios say? What is/are the business's price/s? What margins can be achieved? Why? How will progress be monitored? How will problems be picked up? What is the exit route if all goes wrong? Are the proposed rewards timely? And equitable? How will investors get their money back?

Grouping your material – or rather, the pertinent portions of your material – into these five main areas is a good way of imposing a logical structure on what could be a mass of disparate information. Once done, you are ready to begin writing the business plan itself.

GETTING DOWN TO IT: WRITING THE BUSINESS PLAN

The first thing to consider is who the intended audience for your business plan is. This could be a potential investor, whether a friend, business angel or venture capital firm, or the corporate centre in a large company, or some other financial backer, such as a bank or grant-giving organisation.

Or your business plan could be for a potential buyer of the business or someone (an individual or other business) that is looking to join up with your business as a partner, perhaps in a joint venture.

Whoever the intended audience, you will wish to slant the business plan accordingly, but it will be substantially similar whoever the readership is.

In fact, it is no less an important audience if the business plan is just for internal purposes, to help the leadership team and the workforce understand what the business is trying to achieve and how it will achieve it.

The communication of the finished business plan document is something we shall come back to. For now, we shall concentrate on composing its contents.

Each business plan is unique so any suggested template should be taken as exactly that: a suggestion. Please feel free to amend my own suggested template, especially in the light of your experience of actually writing your business plan, but I think you will end up with a business plan document structured as suggested – or at least thereabouts. There is also some discretion as to the order of in which you present the component parts.

The parts of the business plan are cited below, and then some more is said about each one:

1 Title page
2 Table of contents
3 Introduction
4 Executive summary
5 The business
6 The people
7 The markets
8 The environment
9 Marketing
10 Operations
11 Risks and counter-measures
12 Financials
13 References and sources
14 Appendices

Title page

This is self-explanatory. It will look something like this[3]:

Realcase Ltd

3-year business plan

Realcase Ltd
Enterprise Business Park
Anytown
Anyshire
AB 1 2CD

Tel no: 0123 456 7891

Month Year

Table of contents

This is self-explanatory: it will set out your chosen version of the 14 parts listed above. Make sure the pagination ties up!

Introduction

This is a brief statement of the purpose of the business plan document and might read something like this:

'This business plan has been prepared to assist in raising the funds necessary for Realcase Ltd to become the leading manufacturer of Widgets in the South West of England.

'As part of its ambitious expansion plans, Realcase Ltd is looking to Money Bank for a loan of £125,000 to modernise the factory and invest in new equipment, together with working capital facilities of a steady £85,000 rising to a temporary peak of £120,000, in order to support a forecast uplift in trading.'

So, whatever the particular circumstances of your own business plan, the introduction is brief, simply stating what the existence of the business plan is aiming to achieve.

Executive summary

This section is most easily written *last*, when the rest of the business plan has been composed. You will be clearer about what to say when the whole of the business plan has been written.

It is important to take care with the executive summary because it is the first thing the intended audience will read and, as with meeting people, first impressions count. So take time with it and be prepared to write and re-write it several times to get it just right.

The executive summary gives the reader a good account of the key points from each of the component parts of the document and a real sense of the journey that the business has set for itself. Yet it should be concise – up to a couple of pages, but no more.

There are some similarities between an executive summary and the edited highlights of a football match. Of course, the highlights include showing any goals, but they also have to show other points of interest and dramas within the match. The highlights have to give an impression of the whole encounter, but in mini-form.

Yes, an impression of an exciting contest has to be given, but calling it the greatest match that has ever been played would be just hyperbole, and scoffed at as such. Similarly, your executive summary has to convey the importance and, to be sure, the excitement of what lies ahead, but hype would simply undermine your plan's whole credibility – and your own. Another sporting analogy: as in golf, you do not aim to get a hole in one, just to get the ball close enough to hole it next time. So the executive summary does all the important work, with further information available to complete the story.

The goal of a well-crafted executive summary is two-fold: to give the reader a really good grasp of the business opportunity and how it will be realised, and to arouse his or her interest to want to find out more – and turn the page.

The business

You might well think that this part will likely begin with a brief history of the business and how it got to where it is today, but instead, I suggest you start by describing for the reader what business you are really in (see Chapter 8) and then state your business's vision. What do you want your business to become?

Then talk about some of the key goals that reflect the vision (they might be about a quantified amount of growth, or profitability, or market share, or return on investment, or numbers of impacted lives, or new markets entered and conquered) and the values that will guide the business's actions along the way. Be ambitious and captivating, yet realistic and statesmanlike.

Then you can talk about how the business got to where it is today.

Then it should move onto your business's current condition – your SWOT analysis is highly relevant here.

There should be a description of the business's activities in terms of the products and services it provides and where they are provided and to whom (e.g. consumers or other organisations). All this data can be broken down in more detail such as percentages of turnover and profits that come from each main product or service group and from which geographical markets. Consider discussing your Boston Matrix – see the Notes and References to Chapter 6.

In discussing your business's products and services, it is vital to talk about what makes your offering distinctive. If you have the protection of any trademarks or patents or a strong reputation, then this should be stated. Do bear in mind, through, that your business's strong reputation with your mum, while undoubtedly gratifying, would not count for business plan purposes. If you make any claim, it must be evidenced in ways that would convince a dispassionate – even sceptical – readership. All the especially relevant competencies of your business to sustain an advantageous position should be carefully set out, and the reasons why such an advantage should endure explained in detail.

By the same token, if there are any weaknesses in your business relevant to the goals that have been set, then this information should not be withheld or understated. However, in discussing it, it is imperative that the actions you have in place to remedy the weakness are properly described.

There should be information as to how the business is structured, both legally and organisationally.

It is also appropriate to include in this section details about your business's operational set-up. Write down information about your offices and any factories (whether freehold or leasehold, their size and condition, and their fitness for future needs). If your plan requires your business to invest in new premises, you should discuss in detail how this process will work from start to finish, and what impacts it is likely to have on your business. If you say you are moving premises to a location 500 miles away, do not also say there will be no impact on your business!

Similarly, discuss the equipment that your business uses. Note that in Realcase Ltd's introduction they refer to the need to modernise the factory and invest in new equipment. Clearly, this part of their business plan document will carry a particular emphasis. One would expect a detailed discussion about why modernisation and new equipment are needed, at what costs and with what benefits. It might be that current conditions are not up to the job of meeting future demand and so more capacity is needed. Or perhaps modernisation and new equipment is a route for the business to reduce operating costs and so grow profit margins: you will recall from our analysis in Chapter 9 that improving margins was a top priority for Realcase Ltd.

And here is a glimpse of the essence of a winning business plan: coherence. The underlying issues confronting the business are identified, and the resultant actions pertinently address them. It all hangs together in a coherent narrative: the stage and the drama.

Do not forget to discuss your business's personality and ethos. We talked about how important these aspects are in Chapter 8, and so it is also important to cover them in your business plan document. Set out what your business stands for: its values and culture. Then show how these values and your business's personality are seamlessly projected in the activities that your business plan sets out – and how they might be ruling out possible alternative activities.

The people

You might not choose to put the CVs of each of the key people within the business here, but something of that sort of information should be incorporated.

It is important to describe how the individuals have relevant experience and capabilities for the activities that the business has set itself and for the specific roles you say each one has – including yourself. This is a vital section to get right, because outside backers are especially interested in understanding the people they are supporting with money. Yes, part of the judgement will be about professional and business ability, but backers are also very interested in how motivated and energetic the people are, how flexible they are, and how hardworking and resilient.

If there are any relevant skill gaps, these should be identified openly and, once again, the remedial actions closely described. But the main bases should be covered: one of the key problems for smaller businesses is that they have some, but not all of the necessary business skills available to them. For a business to stand a chance of succeeding, it needs to be good at sales, marketing, product development, operations, human resources, finances and tax, change and project management, technology, customer service, leadership and people management, and, of course, strategy and business planning.

If there are key outside advisers, then the details should be provided, especially if there is, for example, a business mentor giving advice to the management team who is particularly expert or well-connected. I know of instances when banks have provided overdraft facilities to businesses which they were initially reluctant to do until they became aware of the fact that the business was using an experienced and talented professional adviser to help it.

And do not forget the wider workforce. Talk about the numbers and locations, and their motivation and skill levels. If your business outsources and/or offshores any of its activities, or has plans to do so, then these should be carefully discussed.

The markets

This is your opportunity to convey all the insights you gleaned when working through your analysis of Porter's Five Forces. This is an important section in your business plan document.

To recap, you will discuss here the structure of the industry in which your business participates. Following Porter, this means providing an analysis of your business's customers, suppliers, and the threats from new entrants, from potential substitute products/services, and from competitors. In particular, you should discuss the key trends and how the structural features could change over time – to both the advantage and disadvantage of your business. You should also bring out the opportunities and threats that these market features present to your business, not least whether the industry is growing and at what rate.

Refer back to Chapter 5 (page 37) to remind yourself of the sub-issues thrown up by a Porter Five Forces analysis and especially to Chapter 6 (page 49) to see again the questions about the components of the industry's structure that you should be addressing in this part of your business plan. And, in particular, pick up on the causal links since these will demonstrate the coherence of your business plan to the reader.

Your readership will be especially keen to understand the customers – current and potential – of your business and your business's competitors. What is so appealing about your business' products and services to your customers? Why will they buy from you? And go on buying from you? If your business is going to be so successful in winning business from customers, what is to stop your competitors becoming no less successful? Or even more so? Is the market growing? If so, at what rate? What share do/will you have? And your competitors? How will your business be better than your competitors' businesses?

These core customer and competitor issues are ones that the audience of your business plan document must be made to understand by your thorough, incisive and insightful discussion of them.

The environment

This part of the business plan is your opportunity to convey all the insights you gleaned when working through your analysis of Pest forces – see Chapter 5.

Be sure to talk about the relationships between these forces and the purposes and activities of your business. Some forces will help them, others will hinder them. Which ones? In what ways? What actions can your business take to amplify the benefits and reduce the problems? · All this must be set out in this part of your plan.

Marketing

Your plan document has already said a lot about your business's customers, and whether you intend to penetrate existing markets and/or seek new ones (consider discussing your Ansoff Grid – see the Notes and References to Chapter 6). This part of the plan talks about how you business will reach them. How will you price, promote and place your products or services. This is what is called the marketing mix.

When talking about your products or services, of course you will describe them (without jargon and in layman's terms), but you need to point out their features in ways that make clear what problems among your customers your business is solving. The results from customer research that might have (should have!) been undertaken are properly set out here to back up your claims about customer demand for your product or service into the future. Issues of branding should be covered here, as well as aftersales care and how any relevant legislation (such as safety) is fully addressed.

It is also appropriate to talk about any competing products/services, whether actual or potential: their reputation, the demand for these alternatives (both currently and projected), their strengths and weaknesses relative to your own offering; in fact, the whole marketing mix of your rivals' competing products and services.

As for price, your plan should discuss the trade-off between price and market share. What are the relevant elasticities of demand and supply? You need to explain why you have chosen the price-point you have. It will have something to do with the value your product or service adds to your customer, the costs of production, and what price levels competing products or services are pitched at. For example, if you reduced your price by, say, 10 per cent, what would this do to demand levels? And to profitability? Will your business offer discounts? Under what circumstances? Is there a seasonal factor? Remember, too, that there is a complicated psychology associated with pricing. Sometimes a low price can be taken as a signal of low quality – and the reverse can hold as well. These psychological factors need to be understood, insofar as they pertain to your own product or service, and fully explored in your plan. Compare also your pricing with that of each of your competitors. Discuss the extent to which pricing is part of the customer's buying decision.

'Place' is about how your product or service gets to your customers. You should set out your distribution channels. If these involve third parties, you will have to explain who they are, the terms of your business relationship, and the prospects going forward. Every business needs a Web presence these days: what is yours? How does it work? Has your business optimised your website for hits? The facts and figures need to be set out.

Is your business wholesale or retail? How does value move along the supply and distribution chain? (This includes talking about mark-ups between parties.) If your business serves overseas markets, or intends to do so, how is this (to be) accomplished? By setting up an overseas subsidiary? Through a partnership? Or simply by exporting? A thorough discussion is necessary, including the reasons why the chosen route is preferred over the alternatives.

'Promotion' covers, as you would expect, how you get awareness for your products or services. This includes advertising, sponsorships, brochures, trade fairs, direct mailing, networking, and the sales force. You should talk about how much is to be spent on each, with what expected return. And you must give the reasons *why* you expect the returns that you do.

Put yourself in your customer's shoes – the audience for your business plan will – and ask yourself: 'Will I hear about this product or service? Will it meet my needs? Will I be able to buy it easily? Will I find the price to be good value? Will I come back? Will I recommend the product or service to others? What is in your plan to ensure that your business's customers answer 'yes' to each and every question? And how do you know the actions set out in your business plan will have those effects?

Answer all these questions convincingly, and you have the makings of a successful business plan.

Operations

Your plan has already talked about the premises within which you make your products or services and the kit you use to make them. In this part of your business plan you should discuss the processes and procedures through which your business functions.

This includes your business's procedures to control stocks and debtors, to produce and use management information across your business, to ensure consistent quality, to manage 360-degree relationships effectively, to make decisions, and to recruit, manage and reward your people. Every business is reliant on IT; your business's IT should be discussed here, and whether any upgrades are needed.

Risks and counter-measures

Amongst the bittersweet lot of the business person is a certain amount of schizophrenia; certainly the ability to hold perspectives on the world that, if not in conflict, are at least in tension with each other.

You are naturally enthusiastic about the prospects for your business and you want your enthusiasm to infect others. You well understand that a can-do attitude is one of the prerequisites for success.

In this part of your business plan, you are displaying a 'can't-do' attitude. Here, every silver lining has a cloud, and you have to describe all the risks to your business and all the things that could happen to push your business plan off the rails. It is a pessimist's idyll: you need to talk about all the things that could go wrong. However, recognising the threats to the successful implementation of your plan and the jeopardies to the success your business has set for itself is a mark of potential maturity. Actual maturity is shown when you can describe, soberly and with telling effect, what you would do were any of these undesirable – and undesired – happenings actually to arise. Think of risks in terms of likelihood and impact. Obviously, likely risks with high impact deserve closest attention.

It might help you to consider risks and then convey them in your business plan by using a 3-by-3 grid:

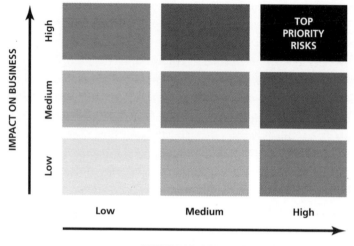

Figure 10.1

You can write-up the main risks identified in the relevant sub-box in the 3-by-3 grid. Completing such a grid for a simple task, such as me changing a light bulb, could look something like this[4]:

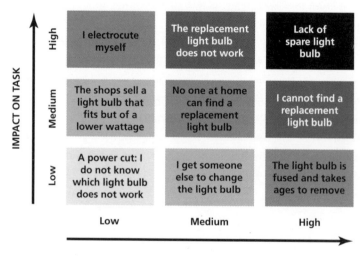

Figure 10.2

You will very probably have more than one risk per sub-box in your business plan's 3-by-3 grid, and you should discuss the avoidance actions (e.g. actively monitor stock of spare light bulbs) and counter-measures (e.g. take a light bulb from a less important light, or use a torch) for each of the most important risks.

It is certain that your business will have setbacks. Can you antici-pate any of these and prepare some counter-measures in advance? An honest attempt to do so, frankly written up in your business plan, will strengthen your plan and impress its readership.

This section will enable the readership to form a crucial judgement: are the actual capabilities of the business, and the external forces at work, the right ones for exploiting the opportunity to give the right return?

Financials

From Chapter 9 you know all about cash-flow forecasts and historic accounts. The fruits of this understanding should be displayed in this section.

It is probably best to put the full versions in the appendices, so it is the main highlights that are wanted here.

You will recall from Realcase Ltd's introduction that they are seeking 'a loan of £125,000 to modernise the factory and invest in new equip-ment, together with working capital facilities of a steady £85,000 rising to a temporary peak of £120,000, in order to support a forecast uplift in trading'. Hence, in their business plan, it is necessary for the company to set out clearly what the £125,000 will be spent on, how much the modernisation will cost, what the benefits will be, and how a fully satisfactory return on the spend can be proved.

The repayments on the loan will feature in the cash-flow forecast, which should also demonstrate how the need for the varying over-draft comes about, how long it lasts, and how a prospective lender is rewarded (what interest rate is assumed and what fees are expected) and protected (what collateral can be offered as security. In the example of Realcase Ltd, it is likely that the bank would want personal guaran-tees from the directors – interpreted as a sign of personal commit-ment – and supporting tangible security which could be assets of the company and/or assets of the guarantors.)

For a potential investor, they will want to understand how much they are in for, how long they are in for, when they will get their money back, and what they will get in return (i.e. size of equity stake). And 'understand' does not just mean 'be provided with the answers': they will want to challenge and stress-test the answers to check that the assumptions upon which they rely are well-founded.

It is often a good technique to portray the answers to these questions graphically. First, it makes a more lasting impression and, secondly, the quirks of psychology are such that graphs seem to have an authority which mere text does not always have – especially when it comes to matters of finance: provided, of course, that the claims are credible and backed up by sound reasoning arising from reliable data. Know your assumptions and produce the reasoning and evidence to support the main ones.

So, for example, you want to talk about how long your business takes to achieve profitability (usually most apparent with a start-up or new venture), then a graph something like the one below can help to get the message across:

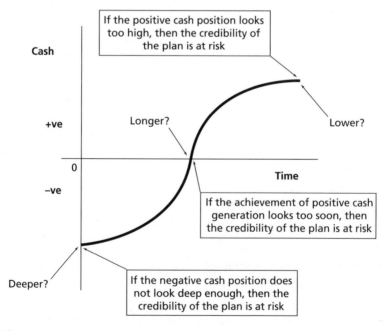

Figure 10.3

Investors are going to be most interested in the return they can expect to receive on the funds they provide. Again, you can depict the answer graphically (subject to the same caveats as above):

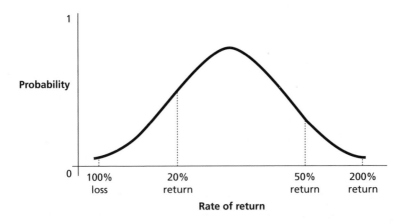

Figure 10.4

This, non-linear graph shows that it is unlikely that an investor would lose all his or her money; but it is also very unlikely that an investor would achieve spectacular returns of around 200 per cent. The graph claims to show that the most likely return is somewhere between, say, 20 and 40 per cent. Is this backed up by evidence and argument in the business plan? It is essential that it is. An investor is always wary that putative probabilities are too confident and promised rates of return are too high. You will need to confront such understandable scepticism with a carefully reasoned argument. On the other hand, with so many claims on their funds and on their time, only the most attractive propositions will win their backing.

Your cash-flow forecast will be examined for its claimed volumes of sales income and its cash-generative power. Your P&L forecast will be examined for the profitability your business is likely to achieve. Given that, for Realcase Ltd, profitability is such a long-standing issue, it can be expected that margins will be under especially close scrutiny.

As always, your readership will be interrogating the financials of your business plan to understand how many sales must be achieved as a minimum for a profit to begin to be earned. This is known as the breakeven figure.

It can be calculated by the formula:

Breakeven quantity = fixed cost ÷ (sales price − variable cost)

So, let us suppose that Realcase Ltd has fixed costs of £80,000 at whatever level of widgets it produces[5].

Assume that the company sells its widgets for £10 each and incurs variable production costs of £6 per widget.

This gives the following figures:

Number of widgets								
produced (000s)	10	20	30	40	50	60	70	80
Value of widgets sold (£000s)	100	200	300	400	500	600	700	800
Variable costs of widgets								
produced (£000s)	60	120	180	240	300	360	420	480
Fixed costs (£000s)	80	80	80	80	80	80	80	80
TOTAL COSTS (£000s)	140	200	260	320	380	440	500	560

Notice that at a level at which just 10,000 widgets are produced and sold, sales revenues amount to £100,000, but this figure is exceeded by total costs of £140,000, making a loss of £40,000. So, what level of production or sales does Realcase have to achieve before it stops making losses and starts making profits?

Using the formula gives the following figures:

Breakeven quantity = £80,000 ÷ (£10 − £6)

= £80,000 ÷ £4

= **20,000**

In other words, Realcase Ltd has to sell at least 20,000 widgets in order to start making profits. And this is exactly what the above table of figures shows.

Depicting this information graphically would give your business plan document an air of authority − as well as convey important information:

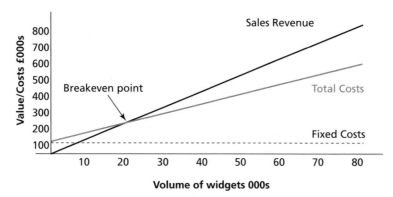

Figure 10.5

Everything to the left of the breakeven point between the sales revenue line and total costs line represents losses, and everything to the right of the breakeven point between the same two lines represents profits. (The difference between the fixed costs line and the total costs line is variable costs.)

By playing with different pricing scenarios, sales volumes and cost levels, it is possible to work out a variety of breakeven points. In your business plan, you will have to justify the combination of figures that you actually use. Also, if you have a range of products with quite different income and cost profiles, then you will have to calculate different breakeven points for each main product grouping.

Calculating the breakeven figures is important, as potential backers of your business (and you yourself) will want to know how far short of forecast sales would actual performance have to fall before the business starts to incur losses. The greater the distance, the greater the margin of comfort.

Because improving the business's margins is such a crucial priority for Realcase Ltd, their business plan will give this whole area a lot of attention[6]. You would also expect their business plan to give especially detailed analysis of their working capital cycle, how it operates, and what they will do to improve it. There could be discussion of a new set of procedures to collect sums due from debtors more quickly (such as a phone call on the day after an unpaid invoice is due, a letter after one week, and so on). In the case of your own business plan, the balance of emphasis will reflect the issues that are relevant to your situation.

In discussing the financials of your business in the plan, it is important to describe all the key dependencies. For example, Realcase Ltd is talking about its expectations of an uplift in demand. Of course, this should be quantified, so in this example, the company might say something like, 'we are forecasting growth in sales next year of 37 per cent (compared with year 200Z) and of a further 41 per cent in the year after'. An example of a dependency would be something like 'achieving these rates of growth depends upon the recruitment of an experienced national sales force of 25 individuals by the end of September this year'.

A reader will have wondered how these unusually high rates of growth in sales will be achieved when, looking at past results, sales actually fell in real terms (that is, after taking the rate of inflation into account). The reader now knows the plan envisages the recruitment of a sizeable sales force. Let us assume for a moment that the business plan has already set out convincing evidence that the customer demand for these rising volumes of sales is out there. The reader will then wonder how plausible it is that the dependency can be achieved.

It is therefore essential that the business plan not only describes all the key dependencies but also produces evidence that the dependencies are assured. So, in this example, Realcase Ltd might add something like: 'We know that one of our competitors has announced that they are withdrawing from our market because their parent company is having problems in unrelated businesses elsewhere and is consolidating resources. We expect, therefore, to recruit 15 sales people – who have a strong reputation – from our competitor. In addition, having spoken to specialist recruitment agencies in our chosen territories, we are told that it should be straightforward to recruit the additional 10 sales people we need, as local labour conditions are in our favour.'

Another example might be along these lines for Realcase: 'Our view that it will be difficult for new entrants to come into our market, and for our competitors to imitate our much-improved 'Widget Mark 2' product, is dependent on the fact that the supplier of the new machinery, which we seek funding to purchase will sign an agreement committing the supplier to exclusivity. That is, our supplier will not provide the same – or better – machinery to anyone else for twelve months. Negotiations have been completed, binding statements of intent exchanged, and contracts will be signed upon the lawyer's return from holiday.'

Of course, your own business plan will discuss the dependencies that pertain to your unique situation, but this is the flavour of what to cover and how.

An effective way of portraying the unfolding key financial events of your business's planned future while at the same time reinforcing the sense of narrative that you are trying to create, is to use 'flying-bricks'. Essentially, these show the nature and timing of key events and their impacts (positively or negatively) on the journey from point A to point B. These points could be, for example, the current level of sales (A) and the forecast level of sales (B).

For Realcase, it might look something like Figure 10.6 overleaf:

You can see that there is a clear path from the level of sales revenue that Realcase Ltd is starting its journey from – £4.9 million in year 200Z – to its envisioned level of £9.4 million by the end of the second year after the current year in which it is forming its business plan. A reader can see what events and actions will have what impacts. Sometimes the impacts will be negative, and acknowledging these instances shows to the reader that you understand how your business works.

The Time axis is not necessarily linear, but indicates roughly when an event might occur. Notice that the impact of the event is shown to endure, not by the length of the 'flying brick', but by the fact that the impact of the next flying brick begins where the impact of the previous one ends. The impacts are, therefore, cumulative.

The higher the flying brick, the greater the dependency on that particular event. One of the benefits of this style of pictorial representation – which can be used to describe many different paths, such as reduction in a business's cost-base, or the improvement in a business's customer satisfaction index – is that the main dependencies become immediately apparent.

It is clear that, for Realcase Ltd, the beneficial impacts of the new sales force, the launch of Widget Mark 2 and the launch of the new product called 'Ooji' are the most important for achieving the company's targeted growth in sales revenue. Accordingly, Realcase Ltd's business plan should be especially closely interrogated on these three key

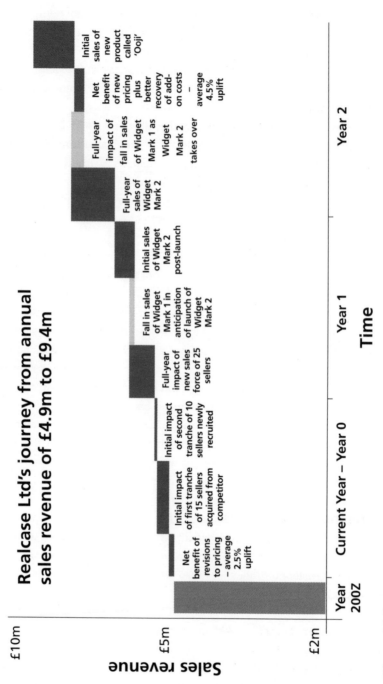

Realcase Ltd's journey from annual sales revenue of £4.9m to £9.4m

Figure 10.6

events. These events need to carry the burden of analysis and proof for much of the business plan.

The main questions that a sceptical audience will ask can be readily anticipated: how do we know the sales force can be acquired and recruited when claimed? We have seen earlier what might be said about this dependency. How do we know they will produce the level of sales stated? How do we know that the launch of Widget Mark 2 will truly take place when expected? How do we know this new version will generate the sales that are forecast? How do we know that the launch of Ooji will take place on time? How do we know it will achieve such a high level of sales so quickly – it is, after all, a brand new product? How do we know that the downsides are properly accounted for – might not the fall in the sales of Widget Mark 1 start earlier and go further than forecast? How do we know that the impacts of the planned price rises are not too optimistic: has the potential to lose sales and customers been properly taken into account?

In your own business plan, consider whether it might be effective to portray a particular journey by way of flying bricks. I personally find them very helpful indeed as the logical coherence – or lack of it – of the business's narrative is starkly exposed for close scrutiny. Whether you do or not, be sure to anticipate the questions interrogators might ask about the key dependencies upon which the realisation of your business plan is founded, and answer them in the text of your business plan document. I cannot over-state how important this is – both for the success of your business plan, and for the success of your business planning.

References and sources

In this section of your business plan, you would talk about, for example, the market research you have done and any customer surveys. Much information about PEST forces and the forces that are driving your industry and marketplace is in published documents and you should give details of the main ones you have drawn on.

If you have sought advice and input from particular individuals, such as advisers or established business bodies whether in this country or abroad, then you should give some information about them.

Appendices

In the main body of your business plan, you will discuss the main highlights from, for example, your historic accounts, cash-flow forecast, and forecast profit and loss statement, but the full versions should be kept as appendices.

It is the same with research material: refer to the main findings in the flow of your business plan and, if you do want to reproduce the raw data, then include the complete set as an appendix.

Some photographs might have their place in the main body of the business plan document, particularly if it is especially pertinent for the reader to understand the appearance of your product: for instance, you might be a fashion designer, or an established architect, or a manufacturer of a world-beating cleaning product. However, you may wish to consider putting a more extensive gallery in an appendix.

The same holds true of detailed product specifications or sales brochures. If you do decide that including these really will help the business plan, then do include them – but as appendices.

Appendices are also the place for copies of any key contracts (if they are what the business plan hinges on); details about any tangible assets which are being offered as security for a loan; articles and press clippings (again, if these are relevant); testimonials from customers or influential third parties; and so on.

Business plan checklist

Here is a simple bulleted checklist of the main items for discussion in your business plan. It is a guide only, so adapt it as you need to to suit your business's particular situation:

1 Title page
   - Name of business
   - Period that plan covers
   - Contact details of business (address, telephone and fax numbers, e-mail, website)
   - Date of business plan
2 Table of contents
   - Check that pagination ties up
3 Introduction
   - Statement of purpose of the plan document

4 Executive summary
- Write last
- Vision and key milestone goals
- Mini-version of the plan in no more than two pages covering:
  - What?
  - Whence?
  - Who?
  - How?
  - How much?

5 The business
- The business you are *really* in
- What you want the business to become
- Brief history of the business
- Current condition of the business
  - Activities: what and where and how
  - Products and services
  - SWOT
  - Competencies and capabilities
  - Personality, ethos and values

6 The people
- Organisational structure
- Details of leadership team
- Workforce
- Details of outside advisers

7 The markets
- Market structure, features and trends – Porter's Five Forces:
  - Customers
  - Competitors
  - Suppliers
  - Threat of substitutes
  - Threat of new entrants
- Make explicit links to the SWOT analysis

8 The environment
- Features and trends of the macro-forces – PEST:
  - Political
  - Economic
  - Social

- – Technological
- Make explicit links to the SWOT analysis

9 Marketing
- Ansoff Grid
- Boston Matrix
- Marketing mix of your business and your competitors' businesses
  - – Products/services
  - – Price
  - – Promotion
  - – Place

10 Operations
- Who/what/how/when to make and deliver products/services
- Who/what/how/when to administer and run the business and monitor/manage performance, especially against the plan
- IT

11 Risks and counter-measures
- Assessment of risks in terms of impact (high, medium, low) and likelihood (high, medium, low)
- Details of counter-measures, mitigations and avoidance actions
- Make explicit links to the W and T of the SWOT analysis

12 Financials
- Key points and commentary (full details in appendices)
- Details of what is being asked for (if funds being requested)
- Cash-flow forecast
- Forecast profit and loss
- Discussion of key points from historic accounts (including balance sheet)
- Particular attention to sales forecasts and details of costs
- Details of proposed major investments (e.g. purchases of equipment)
- Breakeven analysis
- Details of financial controls and management information

13 References and sources
- Key sources of information and data, both primary (e.g. research initiated by you) and secondary (e.g. data pulled from published sources whether paper- or Web-based)
- Details of individuals or bodies who have provided major help and advice

14 Appendices
- Do not pad the business plan for the sake of it – only include material, even as appendices, if it genuinely helps as reference material for the plan itself and the reason why you have composed it.
- Full sets of figures
  - Cash-flow forecasts
  - Forecast P&L statements
  - Historic reports and accounts
  - Detailed product/service specs
- Various documents
  - Evidence of patents granted, trademarks registered and copyrights secured
  - Key contracts and service-level agreements
  - Legal documents
  - Sales brochures and promotional material
  - Photographs and screenshots of Web pages
  - Full details of key research and raw data
  - Press clippings and articles
- Further information expanding on the highlights in the main body of the business plan
  - CVs of the key people
  - Details of assets being offered to secure requested loans

15 Review
- Take a break.
- Be clear what you are asking for from your business plan's audience.
- Make the whole business plan document flow as a continuous narrative.
- Get others to read the business plan and give you feedback.
- Be explicit about root causes and implications.
- Give evidence for your claims.
- 'What would have to be true for things to be as I say they are?'
- Review presentational qualities of the plan (appearance, layout, language and grammar).
- Do not flog a dead horse!

REVIEWING YOUR BUSINESS PLAN

After you have completed your first draft, pat yourself on the back, pour yourself a drink, and leave the plan alone for at least 24 hours.

Then take off your shoes, put on the shoes of your intended audience (say, a banker), and read it again. In fact, do not just read it, *interrogate* it. You will make numerous amendments, deletions, expansions, additions, re-orderings and recastings.

This is good.

You are improving the document all the time. Expect to revisit the document many times before you feel able to call it 'finished'.

In my experience, the following aspects are the main ones to be alert to:

- If you want something from your audience, have you asked for it clearly enough? We shall discuss different audiences in a later chapter but for now, again supposing for a moment that your audience is a banker, make sure that you state the amount of the loan you want, the period, the purpose, the interest rate you are prepared to pay (after all, you will have to have assumed a rate of interest in order to incorporate accurate repayment figures in your cash-flow forecast), and the security you are prepared to offer. State also whether your business needs an overdraft; if it does, again make clear the purpose, amount (this might fluctuate), the timings, the period, the interest rate you are expecting, and the security on offer.

- In all likelihood, your first draft will comprise several discrete essays. All good stuff, no doubt, but in your revisions, you will want to ensure that the different sections of your business plan come together as a coherent, flowing narrative. Make links between the sections as the logic of your plan becomes clearer in your mind. Never rely on your reader picking up on implicit logic: make all your reasoning plain and explicit.

- Do not rely solely on your own perspectives, eventually you are bound to get so close to the plan, that you will not be able to view it afresh any more. So ask a colleague, family member, friend and/or outside adviser, to read through your plan and give you their feedback. Take on board the comments that make sense to you and which you trust – but you do not have to accept everything or, indeed anything! (But you do always have to thank them for their input.)

- Keep rooting out the underlying causes and ultimate effects of the issues you discuss and the actions you intend to take. Keep digging until the spade of your enquiry hits bedrock and is turned. Make these analyses explicit to your audience. Challenge your assumptions – your audience will! – and explore alternatives. In my experience, there is too little rigour in business plans (and in business planning).

- To test the plausibility of your business plan, keep asking yourself: 'what would have to be true for things to be as I say they are?' For example, I recall listening to an enthusiastic group of entrepreneurs who had the idea for a business that, they claimed, would grow to annual turnover of £3 million within five years. Their business idea was to offer to complete simple tasks for businesses who could not do this themselves (or who baulked at the opportunity cost of doing them) but who did not want to incur the cost of giving the task to their usual adviser or provider. For example, a business might want a simple spreadsheet put together. The people in the business might be too busy or not quite skilled enough to do it themselves, but to give it to, say, the business's accountants would seem like costly overkill. This is where the entrepreneurs would step in. With access to a team of capable students, they would find one with the skills that matched the task, and the student would do the job. The entrepreneurs would offer to complete a range of different tasks by having a broad base of willing students on their books. The entrepreneurs would vet the students to check that they could produce evidence of the skills recorded against their name. The entrepreneurs would take 20 per cent of the students' earnings, and they reckoned a team of five people would be sufficient to run the whole business. Sounds plausible? But the entrepreneurs had not asked themselves what would have to be true for them to generate sales revenue of £3 million in a year. How much might a business be prepared to pay for a basic task to be completed? Let us suppose £100. The entrepreneurs would keep £20. So, to generate £3 million *for the business* (as distinct from the students), the entrepreneurs would have to do 150,000 tasks a year (£3m ÷ £20)! That is 3,000 tasks a week! It would take a lot more than a team of five people to find that volume of business (even supposing for a moment that such a volume of business actually exists), match each task to an appropriately skilled student, maintain the required database, manage the process end-to-end, and, not least, issue and track all the invoices. What would have to be true for there to be sufficient numbers of students available? Let us suppose, on average, each task takes one hour. Let us suppose also that a student declares himself or herself available to do, say, up to 10 hours of work per week. Let us additionally suppose that each student is multi-skilled enough to be able to do three different kinds of task. This means that 150,000 hours of tasks translates into 15,000 student-weeks which would need 5,000 students ([150,000 ÷ 10] ÷ 3). Notice that this assumes that the demands for an individual student do not clash. So the entrepreneurs would have to create, maintain and update a database of 5,000 students. Each name might take the equivalent of five hours to find and, say, a further five hours to verify completely and update the database. This total of 10 hours might be needed for possibly a third of the database (a student's course typically lasts three years). So, every year, the entrepreneurs are spending around 17,000 hours a year (1,700 student names × 10 hours) on the database. An individual might work 1,680 hours a year (240 working days × 7 hours per day) – call it 1,700 hours. This means that a team of 10 people are needed just to work on the database (and this ignores seasonal peaks) – which is already twice the size of the total team the entrepreneurs envisaged. Needless to say, the entrepreneurs went back to the drawing board! If I had not asked all these 'what-would-have-to-be-true-questions', a potential investor most certainly would have. The entrepreneurs had not thought their idea through and, under scrutiny, the lack of internal logic and coherence means the idea starts to fall apart. In this form, the entrepreneurs would have lost credibility with the potential investor. Better, therefore, to ask all the 'what-would-have-to-be-true-questions' yourself, *before* you deem your business plan to be complete[7].

■ Be sure your plan is clear and realistic. I find that lack of clarity and lack of realism occur depressingly often in the business plans that I read. This means being realistic about what your business can achieve and about your forecasts, but it also means you should be realistic about what you will be prepared to offer to your potential backer. Do not say you are prepared to pay a rate of interest that is a fraction of the going market rate or expect a bank to lend considerable sums of money without you offering any security. If your business plan is aimed at a would-be buyer of your business, then do not be outlandish with your asking price. If you are offering equity to a potential investor, expect to fall out with him or her if you ask for, say, £1 million of funds in exchange for just 2 per cent of your business. You would have to have substantial proof of your valuation of your business at £50 million!

■ Make sure any reader coming to your business for the first time can clearly understand, from reading your business plan document:
  – the opportunity (goals, where the business is going);
  – the customers (who provides the opportunity);
  – how your business can exploit the opportunity and serve the customers better than anyone else (the scope of the business, what it is going to do, how it is advantaged compared to competitors);
  – the rewards (the total added value created);
  – the coherence of your narrative (how do we know it will all work)[8].

■ Write clearly and simply and avoid jargon. Check spellings and layout. Poorly written business plans with a cluttered look create poor impressions whereas care with the look of your business plan makes the audience think you will take similar professional care with your business.

■ Don't flog a dead horse. The act of crystallising all your thinking into the business plan document might give rise, for the first time, to the realisation that your business is not going to work. Be honest with yourself. If your business does not have a future, then find another future for your business or find another future for yourself (sell it, do something else, beat a different path) – and be *thankful*. Be thankful that the considerable effort you have put in so far has successfully saved you from huge wasted expense and from enormous wasted time. The shards from broken dreams can cut deeply: invent new dreams and bide your time; your chance may yet come, you may find a new way. But meanwhile, keep that dead horse unflogged![9]

■ Always remember what is important: your business plan will not work out exactly as it written. What counts is that it is a compelling narrative about what could unfold when the right team pursues the right goal in the right way within a favourable context.

SOME FINAL ADVICE

From when you started the process of successful business *planning* to finally producing a good business *plan*, you can expect several weeks to elapse – especially if this is your first time. It will get easier, since the passages about the business's vision and its personality, for example, are likely to remain fairly constant, although other passages, such as those about the financials, will require more frequent revision.

But whatever the amount of time you take, it is the quality of the process that is paramount. The insights you gain, the howlers you avoid, the understanding of the levers of your business will be of enduring benefit. I have never met a business that regretted the effort.

You have completed the first step to making it happen. In the next chapter, we shall look at the second step: implementing your plan.

But before that, just some last help on how to look at the task of committing your business plan to paper.

My business clients tell me it is helpful when I have advised them to look at the exercise of composing (and presenting – on which more in Chapter 15) their business plan like this: the job of the business plan is to manage the view on the world of your intended reader. Your audience has a bundle of ideas, impressions, convictions, opinions, biases, intentions, purposes, values and prejudices all roughly assembled into *Weltanschauung*, or world view.

The task of your business plan is to move that view on the world on a bit so that it assimilates the contents of your document (the What? Whence? Who? How? and How much?) as a fully accepted additional item.

Your business plan is thus a story, a narrative, with a purpose and an internal logic and coherence which are so compelling, that your audience wants desperately to become a character in the tale. You have the stage, so make the promised drama hang together so that you shape and move on the audience's world view. We say more about this in Chapter 15.

Key takeaways from Chapter 10

1 Be thorough in your business plan while at the same time remembering its simple core: 'This is a great opportunity which can truly be effectively exploited in this way because ...'
2 Your business plan will crystallise your ideas, giving concrete form to your intangible desires.
3 Know, specifically, what you want from your audiences and put yourself in their shoes (taking your own ones off first!):
   a. for your team to give direction, to help set objectives, to monitor performance, to trigger celebration when successes are notched up and to trigger prompt remedial actions when the business strays;
   b. for your financial backers, whether investors, grant-giving agencies or banks, to win and keep their support;
   c. For your corporate centre to win and keep its support – and because they keep asking for your business plan![10]
4 Make sure that your business plan flows as a coherent narrative.
5 Get others' perspectives of others on your business plan.
6 Back up any claims you make with evidence and sound logic.
7 Don't just review your business plan – *interrogate* it: 'What would have to be true for things to be as I say they are?'
8 Your plan is the ambassador for your business: it will look and act the part.
9 Don't flog a dead horse.
10 Keep dreaming.

Notes and References

1 iPod is a trademark of Apple Inc., registered in the US and other countries.
2 'Strategy' is a word that often puts off people in business. Perhaps it has connotations of being the result of a purely cerebral activity that is somehow remote from reality. In fact, assuming a business

is not behaving totally haphazardly, every business has a strategy. Strategy might be the conscious and coherent response to a challenge, or it might be described as the deliberate and purposeful management of organisation-wide change – but it need not be explicit or even intended. Sometimes it emerges without being rooted in the plans or intentions of anyone, not even the CEO. But even here, if there is a pattern in how the organisation is deploying its resources, albeit just a *de facto* one, then *that* is its strategy.

3   Realcase Ltd has a three-year business plan, but you do not have to copy this if you believe it makes more sense for your business to have, say, a five-year plan. Whatever period you choose, I recommend that you formally refresh and re-write your business plan at least every year – or when triggered by a specific event – and review it in-depth at least quarterly. Do what works for you. Specific targets and sub-goals should be monitored, reviewed and managed much more frequently. The precise frequency will depend on the nature of your business, and it is impossible to be prescriptive. If you are a very internet-driven business, you may well be monitoring performance throughout the day – conceivably 24/7. Even a bricks-and-mortar supermarket does not wait until the end of the week to review sales and find out which shelves need re-stocking. You need to exercise your judgement on this. And remember, too, that the *process* of business planning, with all that it entails for the way you think about your business, is very necessarily a continuous activity.

4   You might not agree with where I have plotted the risks to me successfully changing a light bulb on my 3-by-3 grid. The main point is that you get the general idea. In practice, comprehensive risk identification and analysis is best done as a group in a brainstorming session. As part of the implementation of your business's risks, accountability for monitoring and managing each risk should be assigned to a named individual, and the status of the risk, together with the progress made on putting in place the avoidance action or preparing the counter-measure, should be regularly reviewed.

5   Although fixed costs are called 'fixed' because they are insensitive to the volume of goods produced – whether the company produces a thousand widgets or none, Realcase Ltd still pays, for example, the same rates on its premises – in reality, all costs are

variable given enough time. If volumes grew to such an extent that Realcase Ltd needed another factory, then it would incur an additional set of rates costs. On the other hand, if volumes fell to a low enough level for long enough so that Realcase Ltd moved into smaller premises, then its rates costs would reduce. This is how fixed costs behave: in step changes up or down, whereas variable costs tend to be a comparatively smooth, continuous line.

6   In reality, Realcase's costs are much higher than in these illustrative figures, which are why its margins are so fine. In fact, as you saw in Chapter 9, Realcase Ltd is currently operating at about its breakeven level already, and so only a tiny drop in sales volume would mean pre-tax losses. Hence you would expect a lot of discussion in the business plan about how it will improve margins (there is no safety at current levels of trading performance) through growing revenues and reducing costs by achieving greater efficiencies.

7   More robust asking of the 'what-would-have-to-be-true' question during the planning and building of the Millennium Dome, for example, might have led to a better understanding more quickly as to the number of visitors needed for this venture to make money.

8   This coherence is sometimes called 'strategic logic', but the idea of narrative flow is richer and more accessible. After all, the idea of displaying strategic logic might understandably leave you cold, but you are very well attuned to watching, say, a film or a play, or reading a novel, and then judging whether the storyline was convincing or far-fetched.

In Realcase Ltd's situation, a coherent narrative could run something like this: 'Our vision is to dominate the UK market for superior, quality widgets and related products which will be driven shortly by new regulatory requirements, by being the manufacturer of the most highly specified, most long-lasting and best-constructed widgets and related products in the marketplace, selling through relationship management processes to the B2B and public sector markets. Our initial investment in uprated machinery will enable us to manufacture widgets and other products of the required quality and so command superior prices. We can protect our position as the unique manufacturer of high-end widgets and other products (including a new product line called Oojis) by having extended exclusive contractual arrangements with the maker/supplier of the necessary machinery. We have the necessary skills in the workforce to operate the machinery and make the high-quality widgets, and we can readily acquire the necessary relationship-manager sales force who, together with our new sales and marketing director, will have the crucial contacts in the corporate and public sectors to grow the customer base. Superior prices will drive superior margins, which will fund continuous investment in product quality, product development and customer care, and give highly attractive rewards to investors.'

Pictorially, the narrative looks like this:

Figure 10.7

Your business plan has to make the narrative coherence – strategic logic – of your own business clear to your audience and, first of all, clear to yourself. This is why the process of successful business planning is such a joyously creative activity, bettered only by the challenge and stimulation of turning the business plan into reality. You are authoring, directing and playing in your own business drama.

9 It is a fact of human psychology that if we want something badly enough, we are most reluctant to give up on it. This is a strength of the human spirit. But flogging dead horses is just folly. In the early 1960s, the project of putting a man on the moon by the end of that decade seemed to many people to be no less foolish than flogging a dead horse. Telling a hopeless cause from a noble one requires wisdom. Ceasing to flog a dead horse requires common sense. Put your natural ingenuity to productive use and not to finding pointless circumventions of brute facts, as in this case:

- The tribal wisdom of the Dakota Indians, passed on from generation to generation, says that when you are riding a dead horse, the best plan is to dismount.
- In modern businesses, we find a whole range of far more advanced change strategies such as:
  i   buying a stronger whip;
  ii   appointing a committee to study the horse;
  iii   arranging to visit other countries to see how others ride dead horses;
  iv   threatening the horse with termination;
  v   lowering the standards so that dead horses can be included;
  vi   reclassifying the dead horse as 'living, impaired';
  vii   hiring outside contractors to ride the dead horse;
  viii harnessing several dead horses together to increase the speed;
  ix   doing a productivity study to see if lighter riders would improve the dead horse's performance;
  x   declaring that, as the dead horse does not have to be fed, it is less costly, carries lower overhead, and therefore contributes substantially more to the bottom line than do some other horses;
  xi   promoting the dead horse to a managerial position.

  I came across these amusing 'more advanced change strategies' as part of a set of slides presented by John Kotter, who is the Konusuke Matsushita Professor of Leadership at Harvard Business School, and an insightful writer on change and organisational transformation.

The sadness is that there are too many business people pursuing hopeless ventures. This costs them money, time, self-esteem, their sense of equilibrium, and often their relationships. This is why, should your process of business planning lead you to call it a day, I applaud your courage and wisdom. You have achieved a success!

Recognising that there is a dead horse in front of you can be the trigger for creating a fruitful paradigm shift – especially if you recognise this ahead of others.

10 Of all audiences, an internal HQ is most likely to value brevity, so you may well be able to abbreviate certain sections more so than when your audiences are external.

Chapter 11

Implementation: Making the Business Plan Happen

'You will never plough a field if you only turn it over in your mind.'
– Irish Proverb

DON'T JUST ACT: DO IT FOR REAL!

To get to this point, you have engaged in successful business planning which has given to you a sense of substantial purpose, some powerful insights into the nature and workings of your business, and a business plan document.

Well done!

Now throw all of it away. Put the business plan in the bin.

Unless you are ready to work very, very hard. The most astute business planning and the finest business plan in the world are useless until they are put into practice and implemented. Indeed, poor implementation of otherwise excellent business plans is a major reason for business underperformance. Better to have an OK business plan that is well implemented than an excellent business plan badly executed.

An important statement appeared in the very first chapter of this book and bears repeating here because it expresses something terribly important: a business plan stands or falls not by the quality with which it is written or by the quality of its research and insight but by the quality of its implementation[1]. If turning your process of business planning into the tangible form of a business plan is where rubber hits the road, implementing the plan actually turns the wheels and makes the journey.

So now the fun begins – and lots and lots of hard work.

I am convinced, though, that you are a true grafter, since the vision of what you want to achieve matters enormously to you. As we said in Chapter 3, a vision that is vividly imagined and emotively expressed will itself generate creativity and energy.

When you first committed yourself and your business to the realisation of your vision, you most likely had no idea how you were going to achieve it.

That is typical of successful people. They do not know how they are going to achieve their dreams at first, but – and this is the crucial bit – they do not allow this to put them off committing themselves to their dreams. Successful people have a high estimation of their personal efficacy: that is to say, they believe their ability to make happen what they choose to make happen – to live the life they choose, to build the business they want – is very strong. This is no self-regarding boast. It is a positive mental attitude that places their locus of control within them. Successful people are not blind to difficulties and future obstacles; it is just that they believe they will find a way, by collaborating with others in win-win relationships, to win through as and when the time comes.

This is why successful people are successful: their dreams get bigger and bigger since, as Albert Bandura says, you do not allow yourself to want what you do not think you can bring about[2]. This is why the dreams of chronic self-doubters get smaller and smaller.

So the first place to start in implementing your business plan is with yourself: your mental attitude. You need to cultivate an acute sense of your personal self-efficacy. How you do this is a hefty subject in itself and, if we meet, I would be delighted to help you. Meanwhile, until that blessed day, let me give you something to be getting on with.

AS YOU THINK, SO SHALL YOU BE

The most successful business people I have ever come across are really accomplished at managing a simple, yet hugely important cycle.

It begins with the activity of self-talk. Self-talk is the continuous dialogue that you have with yourself inside your own head. Do you recall your self-talk when you turned the page and came upon Chapter 9 about financials? Perhaps your heart sank as you steeled yourself to read on and you said to yourself something like 'I was never any good with figures' or 'I am always baffled by my accounts'.

This is self-talk.

It is insidiously powerful. Your self-talk shapes your self-image, and you perform in line with your self-image. This then in turn generates your self-talk. It's a continuous cycle:

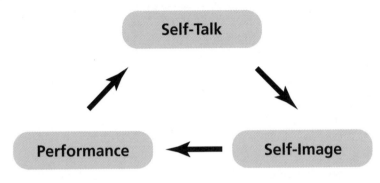

Figure 11.1

By way of example, consider my mother. She is a wonderful woman, but she is one of those people – alas all too common – who says 'I can't do numbers'.

This is her self-talk. It is negative self-talk about her prowess – or lack of it – with managing figures. And it shapes her self-image: 'Sums are just not me'.

It is deeply ingrained. So much so, that if she happens to get a sum right, she will say 'Oh, that was a fluke' or 'It was just a lucky guess'.

So even when faced with evidence to the contrary (a correctly calculated sum), my mother will explain it away in order to keep her self-image ('numbers just aren't me') intact. Moreover, can you guess what happens when she answers the next sum? Yes, she gets it wrong! It is like a self-fulfilling prophecy.

The self-talk–self-image–performance cycle is complete. 'I can't do numbers' (self-talk) creates and continually feeds my mother's self-image ('numbers just aren't me') which, in turn, ensures that reality – her performance – conforms to this self-image, and she gets the sum wrong. And then performance provokes the self-talk – 'See, I told you I was no good at sums!' The cycle is self-reinforcing and runs ever more deeply to shape the person that my mother is.

In sum, you behave like the person you think yourself to be – 'as you think, so shall you be'.

However, this self-talk–self-image–performance cycle does not have to be negative. It can be positive.

Successful business people invariably work at managing their self-talk to be positive.

This is not to say that positive self-talk does not know, say, the difference between a wrong answer to a sum and a right one. Positive self-talk is about the nature of the internal commentary that goes on.

If my mother had positive self-talk about figures, she would say when getting a sum wrong, 'OK, I got that one wrong, but I know what to do and I can get the next one right'.

This positive self-talk would then create a different self-image, 'Numbers are me', which, in turn, would generate different performance: 'See, I told you I could do this!'

Successful business people leverage the self-talk–self-image–performance cycle into a positive, self-reinforcing dynamic, not only in their lives, but also in the lives of the people in their team.

How is self-talk kept positive? Remember, this is 100 per cent under your control. My mother *could* say to herself 'I know what to do and I can get the next one right' instead of what she actually says which is 'I can't do numbers', but she does not.

Yes, it is hard. So what would help?

Do you remember the lemon in Chapter 3? Vividly imagining a possible reality in detail as though it were present can have a real affect on what is actually the case.

With vivid visualisation, you can imagine yourself competently and capably implementing your business plan.

Your self-talk then becomes a series of positive affirmations in which you express to yourself words, pictures and especially emotions and feelings as though the future potential of your business is a present accomplishment.

It is the power that comes from saying, instead of 'I'm no good with customers – I just seize up, it's dreadful', a positive affirmation such as 'I relish talking to my customers and feel great about the positive impact my products and services have on them'.

Powerfully visualising a possible future, appealing to all the senses, positively affects the present.

It is the same with the inevitable problems that will come the way of your business. Visualise the issue as if it were already solved.

In harnessing the power of vivid visualisation and in keeping positive the self-talk of themselves and their team, successful business people imagine the future as if it were already accomplished and implement their business plans effectively. They are adept at *creating memories of future events.*

SETTING OBJECTIVES

Chapter 3 examined the harnessing the power of purposes.

With so many questions to answer every day about your business, it takes future purposes to give present meaning. What might baffle you as a puzzling problem, will become solvable by reference to the business plan you have worked so hard to compose. Ask yourself: 'Does answer A or answer B or answer C most fit with what your business is trying to achieve in the business plan?' and I guarantee that such an approach will help your decision-making and problem-solving enormously.

With a business plan that is now coherent and full of actionable insights about your business, it is time to generate specific objectives. The best objectives are said to be 'SMART':

- S = specific
- M = measurable
- A = agreed
- R = realistic
- T = time-bound

There are variants on this, so pick a permutation that works for you:

- S = specific, stretching, significant
- M = measurable, milestoned, motivating, meaningful
- A = agreed, achievable, action-focused
- R = realistic, rewarding, results-focused
- T = time-bound, testing, trackable

Keeping to the initial version, it is worth expanding on what these features mean:

- **Specific**: this means that the objectives are well-defined with the responsibility for achieving the objective specifically assigned to a named individual. When the objective is to be delivered by a team, then accountability would go to the team leader who would then break down the objective into appropriate SMART sub-objectives for each member of the team. To be 'S', for example, an objective would not be 'we need to improve the business' but 'Joe Bloggs, Sales Director, is accountable for getting more customers'. Let's build on this example objective step by step through 'S', 'M', 'A', 'R', 'T'.
- **Measurable**: the adage 'what gets measured gets done' reminds us that it is important to define what counts as the objective having been successfully completed. Naturally quantifiable objectives are readily measurable and so, to be 'S' and 'M' an objective would be 'Joe Bloggs is accountable for increasing the number of customers by 15 per cent'.
- **Agreed:** Not only should the person accountable for achieving the objective know what is expected of them (sounds obvious but you would be surprised!), but that the objective is agreed with them. A sales director would struggle to agree to an objective to reduce operating costs, and would rightly suggest that such an objective would be more properly assigned to the operations director[3]. It is also about showing the 'fit' between the objectives assigned to an individual and the bigger picture of what the business overall is trying to achieve. The very best business leaders make connections between the objectives of the business as a whole, the objectives of the individual, and the deep values of the individual. As Antoine de Saint-Exupéry said: 'If you want to build a ship, don't just drum up people to collect wood ... but rather teach them to long for the endless immensity of the sea.'[4] Hence for Realcase Ltd, for example, the agreed context for an objective such as 'Joe Bloggs is accountable for increasing the number of customers by 15 per cent' is that increased numbers of customers means more revenues which fits in with the imperatives in the business plan to become the leading provider of high-end widgets and related products in the UK. At the

same time, increasing the number of customers means that yet more lives are enriched by the positive impacts that Realcase Ltd's products have. Making a positive impact on people is one of Joe Bloggs' dearest values. The objective is thus 'S', 'M' and now 'A'. One more point about 'fit': the sum total outputs of all the objectives of all the individuals in the business should amount to what the business is committed to achieving as articulated by the business plan.

■ **Realistic**: Objectives should be stretching while also realistic[5]. If the objective is too cautious, then the very best that the accountable individual is capable of is less likely to be delivered and the business as a whole will under-achieve. If the objective is unrealistic given the resources (quantity and quality) available, then there is a risk that the accountable individual will lose heart and, again, sub-optimal results will be achieved. For Realcase Ltd, prior customer research and the intention to bring some exciting new products to market (such as Widget Mark 2) have led the company to judge that the objective to increase the number of customers by 15 per cent is achievable, albeit challenging. We now see that Joe Bloggs's objective is 'S', 'M', 'A', and 'R'.

■ **Time-bound**: An objective is about who is expected to do what by when. An objective that is time-bound addresses the 'when'. So for this example objective to be fully SMART, it would read something like: 'Joe Bloggs is accountable for increasing the number of customers by 15 per cent by the end of this year, progressing on a straight-line basis, compared with last year'.

Of course, this would not be the only objective that the sales director would have since the business would rightly expect – and need – more from him or her. After all, it is not just the number of customers that is important to Realcase Ltd (or to any business), but the quantity and value of the purchases that they actually make. So there need to be SMART objectives about income as well. The sales director would be responsible for a sales team, so there are bound to be objectives about leading people. This team will deal directly with existing and potential customers, so there will be objectives about customer satisfaction. The total sales effort comes at a cost, and so the sales director will have accountabilities for delivering on cost-related objectives. In fact, the sales director, just like everyone in the team, will have a portfolio of objectives that are balanced to reflect the gamut of imperatives that the business is driven to achieve. Indeed, this is often called 'the balanced scorecard'.

IMPLEMENTING YOUR BUSINESS PLAN THROUGH THE BALANCED SCORECARD

I said in Chapter 9 that numbers do not make a business, people do. But I also said that it is not people who are your business's most important asset, but *performing* people.

Surround yourself with the best people you can, and you are more than half way to achieving business success. How do you get the best from your people? There are libraries full of textbooks on motivation, building and managing teams, and, yes, getting the best from people. In my experience, the most successful businesses follow a few basic yet important principles:

1 There is a working environment of mutual respect: people feel valued, because they *are* valued.
2 This means that people have a sense of being dealt with fairly.
3 Each individual is crystal clear about:
   a. what is expected of them;
   b. how they are doing against what is expected;
   c. what the consequences of their behaviours are (for good or ill!).
4 People understand the bigger picture of what the business as a whole is striving to achieve, and how their contribution fits in.
5 Each individual believes in what the business is striving to achieve.
6 Each individual is stimulated by his or her own role, and feels there are opportunities for personal growth.

Issues of fairness and mutual respect are down to the culture of the business and the values it holds dear. Belief in the business's vision and whether individuals feel stimulated by their roles is partly down to how well communication works within the business, and partly down to issues of 'fit'. By 'fit' in this context is meant the alignment of the business with the people in it. This is why having the best people in the business is only partly about their talents, although this is important: it is also very much about a congruence between what *they* count as important and what the business counts as important.

Achieving this congruence is a necessary condition for achieving the successful implementation of your business's plan. It is about framing and re-framing the context of your people's situation so that they can engage in effective personal sense-making in order that they, too, feel they are doing the equivalent of 'putting a man on the moon' or 'longing for the for the endless immensity of the sea'.

As for the third and fourth points, this is where the balanced score-card comes in[6]. The power in the balanced scorecard lies in its ability to translate the outcome of a business planning process into meas-ures, objectives and priorities for each individual in the organisation. Thus the business's objectives can be incorporated into the individ-ual's objectives and how the individual is measured, assessed and ultimately rewarded.

Properly done, the balanced scorecard process:

■ makes clear what is expected of each individual;
■ is the vehicle by which structured feedback is delivered on how the individual is performing against what is expected;
■ is the hook upon which is hung the consequences for the behav-iours of the individual and the standard of performance achieved;
■ sets out agreed action plans for personal development;
■ is the mechanism by which the objectives at all levels within the business are aligned so that the accumulated achievement of each individual's balanced scorecard delivers the achievement of the objectives in the business's overall balanced scorecard.

The balanced scorecard can give prominence to the relevant priorities set by the business as they change from time to time.

So for Realcase Ltd, for example, adopting the balanced scorecard would not only signal the new energies that are to be committed to a new and coherent set of priorities, but would also give the leadership team a mechanism by which to pull the whole business in a common direction towards the business's top imperatives – such as improved profitability through new product development, growth in customer numbers from better relationship management and prospecting,

increased income (more sales and higher prices), judicious investment, exclusive supplier relationships, cost reduction, and better
management of the working capital cycle.

So how does the balanced scorecard process work?

Each individual has a balanced scorecard document that, while
sharing the same format as everyone else's, has content that is unique
to them (or unique to those in identical roles, although personal devel-
opmental objectives might be individualised). The document typically addresses the key aspects of the business. These are then turned
into the axes on which are plotted the individual's SMART objectives
and against which his or her performance is reviewed and ultimately
assessed. These axes, or sections, are:

- finance
- operations/internal processes
- customer
- learning (of others and of self)

The details of what SMART objectives are agreed on each axis are, of
course, very business-specific. For your own business, it is about translating the specifics of your business plan into a set of personalised
objectives for each individual in the business. What sorts of areas of
key performance ought you to consider? Taking these axes in turn:

- **Finance**: Naturally this axis is about the key financial measures
  that are important to your business and are additionally within the
  accountabilities of the individual whose balanced scorecard this is.
  For sales people, you would expect to see measures around income
  growth, product sales, customer profitability, terms of trade (which
  is cashflow-related, e.g. when payments are due from customers).
  The sales director might additionally have SMART objectives about
  the costs of his or her team, and the costs of the marketing effort.
  For, say, the operations director, there would likely be SMART objectives about costs and, given that Realcase Ltd is purchasing some
  new machinery, you would expect Return on Investment to feature.
  Because the company is set to embark upon a recruitment drive
  to build a sales team, its HR director might have SMART objectives

around the costs of the recruitment campaign and the salary costs of the people acquired.

■ **Operations/internal processes**: This will be an especially important axis for the operations director but one of the strengths of the balanced scorecard approach is that it looks at every individual's contribution in the round. Even sales people have processes, and in their case there might be SMART objectives about capturing customers' and potential customers' data into the appropriate database. Financial advisers who sell investment products have to conduct their activities in a compliant way that adheres to important regulations. Meeting the required standards would be turned into SMART objectives for such people here. More generally, you would expect objectives around process efficiencies, right-first-time levels (i.e. avoiding re-work), smoothness of process flows, managing idle time, speed of throughput, speed of response, and whatever else is appropriate to the nature of the business's operations. In Realcase Ltd's situation, for example, objectives for their commercial director might well relate to the negotiations with the supplier of the new machinery to ensure that the required exclusivity is successfully incorporated into the agreed contract. And the agreed price might feature in the Finance section of the commercial director's balanced scorecard.

■ **Customer**: There are many possible perspectives here. There could be SMART objectives about market share (perhaps broken down by key customer segments), growth in customer numbers, complaint levels, customer satisfaction scores, retention rates, delivery of service to customers (e.g. service-level agreements; customers can be internal to the business, for example, a support function such as HR might regard the frontline team as their 'customer', even though they are all colleagues in the same business), and so on. An individual answering the telephone to customers might have SMART objectives around how quickly they answer the call, how many calls they deal with fully themselves without having to hand the call on to someone else, and how they make the customer feel (perhaps assessed by his or her leader listening in during actual calls and/ or by customer feedback). Such an individual might have objectives in their Finance section around the sales opportunities they spot and the leads they pass on to the sales team. The point is that the various axes can be readily interpreted to apply to every individual in the business.

■ **Learning**: The activities needed to raise the future performance of the individual are set out here. They could include attendance on specific courses, passing certain exams, or just spending learning-time with more expert colleagues. As for more senior individuals, you would additionally expect SMART objectives about how they pass on their knowledge and skills to others, how they develop the people in their team, and how they keep their people motivated and engaged (there could be employee satisfaction scores or a focus on staff turnover rates, etc.). The HR director might have objectives about the knowledge-sharing systems that his or her department is accountable for setting up and maintaining. In addition, there could be objectives around the cost of the external training which is procured. So, once again, this illustrates how every individual in the business can use the same structured balanced scorecard with content appropriate to their individual contribution to the successful implementation of the business plan.

Before looking at an example layout of a balanced scorecard document, let us set out some key points:

■ The balanced scorecard distils the imperatives of the business plan into SMART objectives appropriate to the contribution of the individual.

■ The cumulative impact of every individual meeting all their objectives should be that the business as a whole meets, if not exceeds, its goals as set out in the business plan.

■ The balanced scorecard is *not* supposed to be a complete list of all that is expected from the individual; after all, certain requirements are simply core to doing the job (for instance, fulfilling health and safety obligations, having basic office skills such as the ability to use e-mail). The sophistication of what counts as core to the job will vary from individual to individual, or rather, from role to role.

■ Effective balanced scorecard objectives should drive behaviours that are valuable to the business.

■ The *process* that surrounds the balanced scorecard is at least as important as the balanced scorecard document itself, if not more so. The most successful businesses:

  – agree new balanced scorecards each year or when there are major events;

  – go out of their way to make sure that there is a clear line of sight between the SMART objectives in every individual's balanced scorecard and the objectives in the overall business plan – and that this is apparent for everyone. It is a cascade process;

  – understand that setting up the balanced scorecard process, since its purpose is to answer who does what by when with what reward, is necessarily inseparable from making decisions about the allocation of resources (people, equipment, time and budgets, both ongoing and investment). The axioms by which resource-allocation decisions are made and the resultant patterns that emerge represent, as said before[7], the *de facto* strategy of the business. Successful businesses check that their *de facto* strategy is the same as that intended by their business plan;

  – ensure that agreed balanced scorecards are in place for individuals *before* the new business year starts. So if a business's year runs in line with calendar years, then balanced scorecards would be in place before Christmas to get a clear start for the new year;

  – review performance against balanced scorecards regularly, usually with a formal, in-depth discussion between the individual and their line manager at least quarterly, plus informal discussions frequently in between. The opportunity is taken to revise the objectives if changed circumstances require this, and action-plans pertinent to the moment agreed;

  – understand that focus on everything is focus on nothing. Therefore, think about the number of SMART objectives that you have on each balanced scorecard. I have seen balanced scorecards with dozens of objectives and no one had any idea what they were supposed to be doing and what was important. Less is more. Think in terms of between eight and fifteen SMART objectives in total per individual; my own view is that up to ten objectives is about right;

- – use the end-of-year review to assess performance against balanced scorecard objectives, and make this assessment the basis for decisions about individual rewards (such as increments to salary, bonuses etc.). Effective businesses make the details of the links between performance and resultant pay awards explicit to every individual before the business year starts, or at least as close to the beginning of the business year as possible.

■ How well the process surrounding balanced scorecards is done is truly the most important part of using them. Great balanced scorecard documents will be worthless if they are not managed with care, attentiveness, and a shared serious commitment to performance and the behaviours required to achieve it. The quality of the debate that is generated by the design and subsequent use of the balanced scorecard is the key to success. Strategically, the balanced scorecard systematically operationalises the business plan; tactically, the balanced scorecard aligns individual activities to collective, business goals and reinforces links between behaviours and consequences. It is thus individualised and also integrative at the same time.

■ You may have heard the expression 'give a man a fish and you feed him for a day; teach a man to fish and you feed him for life'[8]. The purpose of the balanced scorecard is to show the individual *where* to fish.

Figure 11.2 opposite is an example of how a balanced scorecard could be laid out. Do please feel free to adapt its appearance to the needs of your own business. This is no more than a suggestion.

Forcing yourself to ensure that every individual in your business has his or her own balanced scorecard will oblige you to think through exactly how your business plan is going to be made to happen by the people in your business (who else?!). Necessarily, this will also compel you to make decisions about allocating resources – including investment spending.

You will need to ensure that, when you step back and take stock, the cumulative impact of the delivery on the balanced scorecards in place and the resource-allocation decisions you have made is the successful implementation of the business plan.

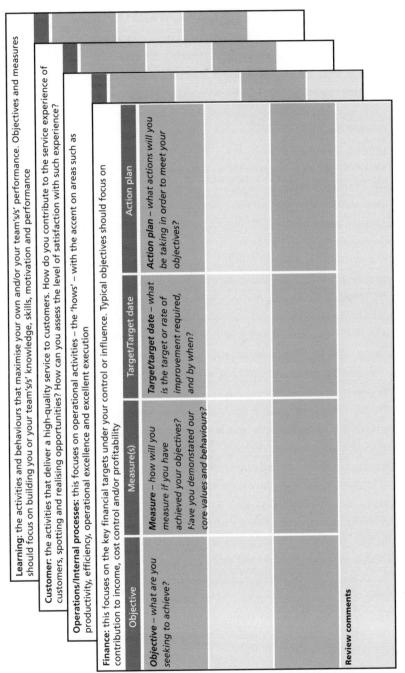

Learning: the activities and behaviours that maximise your own and/or your team's/s' performance. Objectives and measures should focus on building you or your team's/s' knowledge, skills, motivation and performance

Customer: the activities that deliver a high-quality service to customers. How do you contribute to the service experience of customers, spotting and realising opportunities? How can you assess the level of satisfaction with such experience?

Operations/Internal processes: this focuses on operational activities – the 'hows' – with the accent on areas such as productivity, efficiency, operational excellence and excellent execution

Finance: this focuses on the key financial targets under your control or influence. Typical objectives should focus on contribution to income, cost control and/or profitability

Objective	Measure(s)	Target/Target date	Action plan
Objective – what are you seeking to achieve?	*Measure – how will you measure if you have achieved your objectives? Have you demonstrated our core values and behaviours?*	*Target/target date – what is the target or rate of improvement required, and by when?*	*Action plan – what actions will you be taking in order to meet your objectives?*

Review comments

Figure 11.2

THE RHYTHM OF LIFE HAS A POWERFUL BEAT

Shakespeare spoke of the seven ages of man[9]; from 'the infant, mewling and puking in the nurse's arms', through growing up as 'the whining schoolboy, with his satchel and shining morning face, creeping like snail unwillingly to school', into adulthood with its passions, search for meaning and the acquisition of some wisdom, and finally into decline and loss of faculties 'sans teeth, sans eyes, sans taste, sans everything'.

Nothing lasts forever and both biological and artificial systems do indeed seem to follow a common life-cycle comprising various stages: newly born (or newly made), growth, maturity, and decline.

True, as time goes on, so your business can learn to do things more efficiently and effectively[10], but the relentless procession of the life-cycle asserts itself in the end.

In a world of fast-paced change, where life-cycles seem to be ever-contracting, what your business needs to do is to learn quickly and adapt. Therefore, do not rely on mere time to give your business the benefit of the experience curve. Your business needs to be more proactive in hastening the benefits of the experience curve through active learning. The benefit of experience on any one activity is lasting for an ever shorter time, so learn fast, and move on. Decline is inevitable, comes sooner and works quickly.

The life-cycle is very often illustrated by a product. Consider the videotape recorder, for example. At first, when the product was introduced to the market, it was an exciting novelty – and very expensive. Makers of videotape recorders had invested huge sums in the development of the product and, in the early stages, they were spending large amounts of money to promote the new-fangled gadget. Eventually, the product became more established, prices came down as unit costs fell (through economies of scale and, yes, experience curve effects), and less was said about what a videotape recorder could do and more was said about the extra features or qualities this or that particular model of videotape recorder had.

More and more consumers were buying videotape recorders as matter of habit, replacing their older models with newer ones as a normalised activity – perhaps even buying more than one as ever-rising numbers of households had a proliferation of televisions.

However, eventually, digital technologies were developed, and consumers started to choose disc-based recorders. The sales of videotape recorders started to decline until major retailers decided to withdraw them from their product lines. Today, some sales of videotape recorders still take place (people still have old video tapes) but eventually there will come a time when the only trade in videotape recorders will be as collectible curiosities, like antique muskets.

Your business's products and services are already on this life-cycle path. Pictorially, it looks like this:

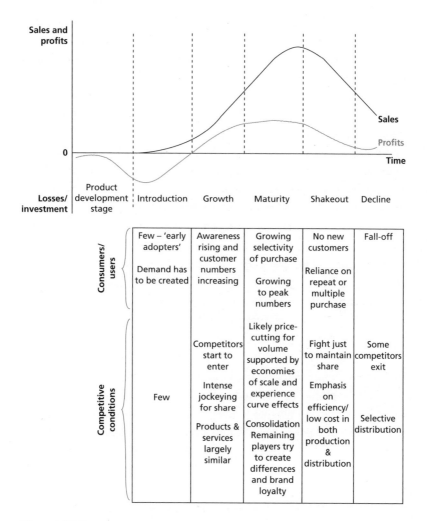

Figure 11.3

It is possible that a product can find a new lease of life after a period of decline; after all, flared trousers come into and go out of and come again into fashion over and over, and we saw in Chapter 8 how the product Lucozade was able to re-energise itself just as it claims to do for those who drink it. However, no one expects videotape recorders to make any sort of comeback – and the majority of products disappear into oblivion once the life-cycle has run its course.

Notice that different skill-sets are needed during the different stages of the product life-cycle. During the product development stage there is a particular need for innovation, creativity and design flair, plus the ability to translate the basic understandings of potential users' needs into a workable solution. During the launch stage, skills in product launch and marketing (the 'marketing mix') would be to the fore (and, in the case of videotape recorders, the ability to forge productive relationships with retailers). During maturity, marketing skills remain important, but different ones as the emphasis shifts to brand development and promotion and the ability to package value-adding add-ons to the product or service. At the same time, skills in operations rise in importance as the need to optimise efficiencies through economies of scale and the experience curve becomes increasingly pressing. Finally, as the product or service enters its dotage, good strategic thinking is necessary to decide how long to persist with the product and when to withdraw.

As the products and services that your business provides process through their life-cycles, you will need to ensure that you have the requisite skills appropriate to each stage.

The life-cycle phenomenon holds true of distribution channels as well as the products that are distributed. For example, when I bought my first computer (an Amstrad in the 1980s), I read widely and talked to lots of people (I knew very little about computers at the time), and finally made my purchase by going to a shop in order to converse with a dealer who could translate my intended uses for the computer into a make and model that was up to it. The next computer that I bought was purchased differently. I felt confident enough simply to talk to someone over the telephone and I no longer felt the need to have the computer demonstrated to me before I purchased it. Now, when I buy a computer, I feel confident enough to design my machine with specifications that I dictate online. I complete my purchases with a few mouse-clicks and the computer arrives, just as I designed it.

The way in which the product has been distributed to me has gone through a life-cycle. Is the sales distribution process in your business on a similar life-cycle? At what pace is it moving?

Notice, too, that what is true of products and people and distribution channels is also true of businesses as a whole. Your business, too, is progressing inexorably through its life-cycle. Ask yourself what stage you think your business is at. Or, if your business is broad and complex, then ask yourself what stage each of its main sub-businesses is at.

That you are interested in the process of business planning is not itself any clue as to what stage your business is at. True, a start-up business needs a business plan, but you now know that business planning is a continuous process that is essential for all businesses at every stage of their life-cycle.

You will find that other features are distinctive of the various life-cycle stages. A young business is typically small with few employees and often has a 'family' feel. Communication is comparatively straightforward and speeds of response are fairly high.

As the business grows, so pressures can intensify: there are more people to manage and leadership challenges grow. New skill-sets are needed, and in order to achieve the necessary efficiencies, increased systematisation is usually required, whether in relation to operational activities or customer management. Relationships with external stakeholders often grow in importance.

As the business sees decline approaching, then it needs to renew itself – while perhaps also managing the odd crisis or two. New products are necessary, either successor-products or completely new ones (the fruits of well-judged R&D spending). New markets are an option – perhaps new territories for offerings that are in decline in their native territory. Or perhaps nothing less than reinvention is required. For example, in the 19th century, Nokia started as a paper mill before expanding to become a rubber business as well. Of course, now the business is known for its mobile telephony products – a long way from making rubber boots.

Managing the cycle effectively time after time is hugely difficult. What a business needs to be good at during one stage of the life-cycle is not necessarily the same as what it needs to be good at during another.

This is the challenge that very pointedly confronts 'one-man-bands' as they grow: leading a young business is different from leading a mature one. Yet the magnitude of the challenge looms large for every business. This acute difficulty in managing the life-cycle effectively time after time is why so many businesses that were titans in the past have disappeared from the scene. It is also why businesses often take a portfolio approach to their activities. This does not necessarily mean that they become conglomerates (although some do), but that they view themselves rather like a garden.

When it is February or March, you will see daffodils flowering. By the end of April, they are brown, wrinkly and finishing, but blossom is starting to appear on fruit trees. Through the summer, roses bloom and by autumn, the gardener is harvesting apples and pears.

The point is that the gardener who wants to enjoy interesting plants in his or her garden throughout the year will have a variety of flowers, bushes and trees since they 'come good' at different times. Taking a longer-term perspective, the gardener will plant a mixture of annuals, biennials, perennials, new bushes and saplings to maintain variety and interest on a continuous basis.

It is the same with a business. There should be products/services or, indeed, whole sub-businesses, at varying stages of their development. Thus at any one time, while there is always a product/service (or sub-business) in decline, there is also a new product/service being launched and yet others in stages of growth and maturity.

Avoid having loose change

Change is a constant fact of life. You know that.

There is change that represents the natural cycle of life; there are forces of change which you sought to understand during your PEST and Five Forces analyses, for example, and we have seen there is change that accompanies the natural rhythm of the life-cycle. Finally, there is the change that you initiate yourself.

Your business figures in all these types of change. We have already discussed at length how to position your business in the face of the PEST forces, Porter's Five Forces, and through the key stages of the life-cycle. So let us look at your business in relation to change that you drive yourself.

Your business plan will not take care of itself; you have to make it happen.

You are well on the way when you ensure that balanced scorecards are in place for every individual. In completing this process thoughtfully and with care, you will have had to have:

■ agreed coherent sub-plans and budgets;
■ made a patterned set of decisions about deploying resources, including future investment;
■ communicated what the business as a whole is seeking to achieve, how the business will achieve it (values, keynote actions, etc.), and the expectations held of the performance and activities of every individual, with links to reward made explicit;
■ considered the skills needed to achieve the business plan and formed an action-plan to fill any gaps.

You will be organising the business not in line with the fancy theorems of precious texts on organisational design, nor at the behest of fanciful consultants who slap their flavours of the month on honest business folk without having the good grace to hang around for the consequences; rather, you will organise your business practically around *what needs to be done.*

In Realcase Ltd, there is a need for people to make widgets and related products using machines to maximise efficient use of resources. Collectively, these are called operations, and so there is an 'operations team'. Someone needs to give the team leadership and take overall accountability, so we might as well call this person the 'operations director'. In addition, there is a need in Realcase Ltd for a group of people to sell what is made to customers, so let us call these folk the 'sales team'. Similarly, they need to look to someone for leadership and to take overall accountability, so we shall call this person the 'sales director'. Perhaps this person will also be responsible for the marketing mix, and so might be called the 'sales and marketing director'. Realcase Ltd's business plan entails the recruitment of a new sales force of relationship managers. Therefore, there is a recruitment task to be done. This can be given to a 'recruitment director'. However, Realcase Ltd judges that this task, appropriately supported, can be undertaken by the 'people director', whom they call, without originality but following current parlance, the 'HR director'. The labels are not important and the roles do not exist simply because it seems that every other business has them. Rather, the labels are chosen because they are roughly indicative of what the role-holder does, and what the role-holder does is necessary for the business plan to be successfully implemented. We also noted that there is an important task for Realcase Ltd in negotiating its exclusive contract with the manufacturer of the specialist machinery it will be acquiring. Who will do this? It might be the most senior person, the CEO, or perhaps the CEO will bring in the specific expertise he or she needs and organise a small team around a 'commercial director'. As the task is eventually completed, so perhaps this team will be disbanded and the individuals – including the commercial director – reassigned to other tasks, or they leave the business. The guiding principle is, as ever, organise your business around *what needs to be done*.

The point is that organising the business around what needs to be done is the most effective way forward – and it is not rocket science. Just be sure to have the right people in the right roles, and be prepared to make changes as and when 'what needs to be done' moves on over time. Keep it simple and flexible.

And, naturally, do not forget yourself. We have never met (but perhaps we shall, one day) and so I cannot advise you specifically on your own role within your business and in making your business plan happen. You will need to judge that for yourself. So what is the best role for you to fulfil, and how best can you fulfil it, to help ensure the successful implementation of your business plan? If you 'know thyself' truly, then you will answer this question very well with neither false modesty nor false hubris, but with appropriate ambition, with a frisson of excitement, and a disposition to *serve*.

Serve? Yes, serve. You are in the service of your vision, your people and your customers. It is the leader's role to serve.

Hold fast to what and who matters, and you will succeed in avoiding loose change.

Sadly, too many change programmes in business give disappointing outcomes. This is important, because your business is starting from where it is (whether just an idea in your head or an established concern) and it needs to get to a different place (your vision made real).

This in itself is a change and, along the journey, your business will go through many changes. To make change happen successfully and avoid loose change is difficult but overcoming this difficulty starts with understanding why it is such a hard thing to do in the first place.

One reason is that there are very good business reasons *not* to change. There is an undoubted virtue in getting really good at what the business does so that it becomes ever more efficient (through experience curve effects, for example). Efficiency can mean a better customer experiences (greater speed of response, more reliability, etc.) and higher profits (through lower costs, less wastage, etc.). Practice makes perfect, and it is precisely to harness the beneficial force of this that businesses concentrate on establishing and honing their routines. Routines can deliver persistent learned practices within the business. They are a source of competence.

Routines, therefore, are very useful. It is like folding your arms. Indeed, fold your arms now. You do it instinctively without forethought. Like me, you might fold your arms with the right arm over the left, or you might be a left-arm-over-right-arm person. It is a habit and, like the habits in a business – routines – they are beneficial: they reduce uncertainty, save energy and conscious thinking time to free our attentions for other matters. Moreover they work. Indeed, our habits are perfectly attuned to our living the lives that we currently actually lead – just as a business's routines are perfectly attuned to its current level of performance.

However, there comes a time when the market moves on (the life-cycle enters the next stage) and all – or some – of these valued routines have to be jettisoned. It then becomes a virtue to discard them and replace them with new routines. No wonder this is hard! What was valuable one moment becomes rejected the next. Moreover, workers had become very adept at these old routines – as they had been exhorted to do, achieving high levels of performance as recognised and rewarded through their balanced scorecards. Now when change comes in, reaching these high levels of performance and earning the rewards that go with them can no longer be assumed. It is all very unsettling, and people's instincts are to resist the change.

Try folding your arms the other way round. So if you are like me, instead of folding your arms right-over-left as is your habit, so you will now fold them left-over-right (or the reverse). It feels weird, yes? Perhaps it took a fair amount of conscious effort to get it right, and you are very keen to return to your normal way of folding your arms.

Furthermore, consider what it takes to get good at routines. It is about following procedures over and over; it requires the ability to codify knowledge and follow it. Novelty and invention are out: what is important in following routines is the ability to replicate repeatedly. Predictability forms a tight reinforcing loop between actions and outcomes. As a consumer, this can be important to me: when , for example, I have a McDonald's quarter-pounder in London, I know it will be the same as the one I have in Bristol, or, indeed, anywhere. Consistency of delivery arouses consistency of expectation and, *voilà*, a global business. This is fine – for as long as it lasts.

When the market moves on (remember, nothing is forever), this virtue of predictable, routinised replication is not what is needed. Instead, an explorer's mind-set is necessary to find the new way that works. Imagination to invent and design new routines is required, plus high emotional intelligence to help people adapt.

So, businesses and the people within them have to be good at exploiting what is known to get to peak efficiency, and must also be good at exploring to find new ways and to replace what is known with a new 'known'. Paradoxically, a business has to be good at routines and at uncertainty. Resolving or lessening this paradox is one reason why change is so difficult for businesses to do successfully.

Because change has uncertainty at its core, it is highly situation-specific. This is why this book is not going to give you a recipe for change, as though the simple assembly of the right ingredients and a spell in the oven will, as though by magic, produce the desired result after due time.

There is no universally applicable recipe. The successful implementation of change will take much of your talents, energies and emotions, but not in any prescribed way that follows a pre-set model.

Call to mind the earlier image of the potter and the clay. We talked about this being a craft process involving interaction between potter and clay that is always 'of the moment'. My son is studying Design

Technology at school, and part of the syllabus is about understanding what are called 'resistant materials'. These are things like wood, metal and, yes, clay. The carpenter, metalworker and potter are trying to change something from what it is into something it is not yet, by bending, carving, cutting, joining and shaping the resistant material they each respectively work with. And 'respect*fully*' work with.

They work with the grain of the wood, with the metal, and with the clay.

Making change happen successfully is like these craft processes – only more so. The resistant materials in business are even less fixed than that for the carpenter, metalworker or potter. Sure, it is important to make a clear line of sight to the business plan, but as we shall see in Chapter 12, what counts as the plan will move about and evolve. It is not unassailably fixed. Actors, when they are on stage, deliver their lines as written for them by the playwright. If you know the play, then you know how the actors will behave next and what they will say. Yet when actors are in social settings in their private lives, they move about, they interact and are fluid with their situations. They form their own intentions, pursue their own interests, change their minds and follow, then suspend, and then resume following their own agendas. It is very complex. Unlike a stage-play, they are not following a pre-written script, they are writing it themselves as they go along.

This does not mean that social settings are intrinsically unpredictable. We have evolved very well in terms of being able to understand and foretell human behaviours. It is just that social settings (such as the business environment) are complex and ambiguous and, since people's sense-making is both contextual and also open-textured, the way people will see themselves in a changing situation is never certain or completed. There is indeterminacy[11].

In this context, you will have to find your own way; but already you can see that certain behavioural dispositions (not a recipe!) are going to serve you better than others when it comes to emerging from change successfully[12]:

- *A craftsman's mind-set*: When managing your business through change, you will need not so much as an engineer's mind-set as a craftsman's. An engineer can reasonably aspire to a more or less complete set of knowledge about what he or she is making in terms of the relationships between materials and forces. In a social setting, however, knowledge of the relationships is inevitably incomplete. A girder supporting an engineer's bridge, for example, will neither decide to do its assigned task, nor choose not do it (or do it poorly or excellently). Girders can fail, but not from any intention of its own. A girder will not lapse because it feels undervalued, nor will it sag because it feels unengaged through lack of communication, nor will it rebel because it feels a lack of respect. People, however, may. The craftsman's mindset interacts with the material, respects it, and appreciates the importance of context.

■ *Communication and yet more communication*: Communication is key to helping both yourself and your people avoid the natural denial or resistance loop and break free into exploration and commitment. Communication is so important because the world of people is interactive and recursive. People design and implement change – and they are also players in that change. Your role is to help people achieve congruence between:
  – context – the why of change
  – content – the what of change
  – process – the how of change
In sum: Communication is critical to making the change journey successfully – informing, educating, motivating, calling to action, giving *meaning*. But you must communicate over and over again. If you tell a group of people something once, half of them will hear it and perhaps a couple of per cent will remember it. You tell a group something three times, most will hear it and a few more per cent will remember it. There might also be someone who will actually act on it. You tell a group something six times, and most will believe it – and they might even act on it. But if you stop saying it, the people will think you do not believe it any more! This is not because people are wilful or contrary; it is just that they need bigger plates, as their plates are full. Given the natural bias towards the status quo which we have already discussed, people have to know that the change is no passing fad, but is here to stay.

■ *Generating energy*: Defence of routine is natural, since routines have been historically a source of strength and individual success. Change will only successfully take place if those affected want to change. This must mean a shake-up. The esteem in which the status quo is held has to be replaced by a disturbed discontent. As was said in Chapter 3: 'It is the same for people and for businesses. Neither will choose to move from where they are unless they are discontent with the here and now. They have to be dissatisfied with the status quo before they act to create a new status quo.' The most effective stewards of change deliberately create energy for something better by showing that things are not how they are supposed to be – just like a crookedly hanging picture generates energy in a person who simply has to go to it and straighten the picture out. The creation of this energy in the business requires communication: meticulous communication of the 'how things are supposed to be' which means where the business is headed and its vision; combined with meticulous communication of how the status quo is no longer good enough. This is not to rubbish the status quo; after all, that would be to rubbish the business's history. Businesses, like people, are what they repeatedly do. Change, therefore, represents not just the burden of learning something new, it also represents a challenge to who we are. Hence, there must be really good reasons to change. Would you be interested to change the way you fold your arms? I doubt it! Why? Because it is not important, nothing hinges on it. Honest and respectful communication can succeed in valuing what has gone before while also stressing the imperative to a different way ahead. This is sometimes called creating the 'burning platform': 'We can't rely on past successes', 'Not changing is not an option', 'There is no alternative', 'Change or die'.

■ *The lure of the vision*: Your people are energised, but which way do they channel their energies? It will be in the direction of the more dominant image. If the status quo is too comfortable or the burning platform is not properly understood or is disbelieved, people will slip back into old routines. The business will fail to adapt and the plan will remain forever just a document, never troubling the real world. But if the vision has been communicated with enough power and emotive detail that it connects with the people's own deep purposes and answers their WIIFM ('What's in it for me?') questions so that it becomes a *shared* vision, then their energies will be channelled into progressing towards the new future. Provided that the vision is not regarded as outlandish and unrealistic. This is why it is so important to communicate the early implementation steps, so that people can see that the business can quickly be on its way. It is about taking people through the key aspects of D x V x I > R (discontent x vision x implementation > resistance [or inertia]) that we discussed in Chapter 3.

■ *Support to succeed*: Offering clarity to help people adjust to change is important. This is why this chapter has discussed at such length the process and workings of balanced scorecards. Offering support to people is also important, which is why balanced scorecards include an axis about learning so that people are positively nurtured to acquire the skills necessary to succeed in the new status quo. Part of the vision has to be not just that people are successfully brought to an understanding of the change, not just that they are successfully brought to agree to or even accept the change, but that they truly know how they can flourish in the change. This is, to a significant extent, about teaching them to manage the self-talk / self-image / performance cycle that was discussed earlier in this chapter. Helping your people to manage this cycle will not only give them a crucial tool to support their flourishing in the new status quo, it will also give them (and yourself!) the confidence, resilience and flexibility to take on future change. Routines are like genes – they need to adapt to changing circumstances. After one change will inevitably come another. And be realistic: expect things to get worse before they get better, even with very well-implemented change. People need time to make the transition – *you* need time! – and it takes repeated trials before new ways of working become as routinised as the old. In people, excellence is a habit; in businesses, excellence is a matter of routine. Just be sure to celebrate progress and successes along the way. In the spirit of continuous improvement, today is the worst we shall ever be!

■ *An act of wizardry*: In using the metaphor of wizardry here, I am not thinking of some external application of magic like the wave of a wand in a *Harry Potter* book. Rather, I am thinking of the sort of wizard that we see in the *Wizard of Oz*. In this story, the Wizard had no magic power of the kind we normally think of. And yet there was a real power at work. It was the power of *expectation* that awakens a strength that is already within. In the *Wizard of Oz* story, the Lion found courage not by having courage magicked onto him, but by being given a medal – after all, all courageous creatures have medals. It was the same for the Tin Man, who found his heart after being given a ticking clock, and the Scarecrow felt he had a brain once he had been given his diploma. The Lion started to act courageously because he behaved like the person he believed himself to be. Before, he believed himself to be cowardly, and so that was how he acted. Now, he believes himself to be courageous, and so courageously is how he acts: 'as you think, so shall you be'. And this change of self-image was catalysed by the power of expectation. People grow into what is expected of them[13]. Important to the successful implementation of change is to change your expectations (of yourself and of those around you). 'I see you putting together a fantastically powerful business plan and I see you implementing it excellently'. That is my expectation of you. It is clear; it is in the present tense; and it is *true*. People understand the world by recreating it in line with their expectations. Thus, to see the world differently, to see the world anew and afresh, we need to be open to new expectations. Creating new expectations is part of the change process. Being open to new possibilities, to new ways of understanding the world, will help you and your people manage your own and their own responses to change. Creating these new expectations – these *memories of future events* – is the most powerful thing you can do to make change happen successfully in your business. You will be the potter, shaping the clay as powerfully as Pygmalion[14].

- *Story-telling*: One way to help open up people to new expectations and support a more vivid visualisation of a successfully changed situation (with them flourishing in it) is to use the power of narrative through story-telling, myths and symbols. We are well used to fables encapsulating an instructive truth. In a business setting, a story can capture a lesson about how the new practices within a business can actually work and the impacts they can have. The story might contrast the new ways with the old ways and illustrate how the person who 'stepped out' succeeded in the changed world.

They might show how new interactions can operate and how new arrangements can take root. Stories can help people make sense of the unfamiliar, generate confidence, and strengthen what is otherwise fragile. Narratives put patterns of meaning onto a changing world. They orientate the teller and the hearer, rendering the changing business more ready-to-hand. Such externalisations can help people internalise the new. It is possible to act your way into new ways of thinking[15]. Stories can create images of collective cohesion to help reposition the business in a new direction. Equally, stories as told can reveal how your people are interpreting what is going on and how they see their place in it. They can act like a gauge as to how receptive your business is for change. The communication of change, to be effective, has to be two-way. Acts with symbolic meaning can give stories an impetus. A novel behaviour or a totemic initiative can signal the change you want there to be. You might, for example, scrap a longstanding meeting format, or move yourself out of your office, or abolish a specific performance measure, or sponsor an event that reflects your business's new aspirations – the possibilities are endless. What would have symbolic power and what would be of indifferent significance depends, of course, on your business's particular context. Again, success requires a clear grasp of the future and a no less clear grasp of current reality.

■ *The power of individual example*: Leading change by example, being the change you want to see, is a very powerful way of championing it within your business. Here is an exercise that I do with my groups when I am facilitating workshops on leadership. I begin by asking everyone in the group to raise their left hand as high as they can. Then I pause for a moment, and I ask them to raise it yet higher. Arms stretch upwards just a bit further. I pause again, and then ask them to raise it higher still. More stretching but eventually, someone will stand up – perhaps even on a chair. When this starts to happen, I ask the group to put their hands down and relax. The point of the exercise is this: it takes just a few moments to illustrate the force of cultural norms. In a workshop setting there are tacitly understood behavioural norms. It just is not done to stand on furniture even to comply, with the highest possible degree of performance, to an instruction ('raise your left hand as high as you can'). Yet these behavioural or cultural norms impede progress to maximum effectiveness. We get there, but only in the end! In particular, note that when the first brave person stands up, everyone copies. This brave person takes on the challenge and stands up, and not only pushes on the boundaries of cultural norms, but also pushes out the boundaries of what is possible. Taking risks and raising performance go hand in hand. So, confidence – the confidence in knowing who we are, what we stand for and in our own personal effectiveness – can truly trigger organisational or cultural change and establish new norms. It is the power of individual example. Your role as leader in your business is to recognise that you can hasten or impede that process; you can inhibit or amplify the power of individual example. Think about this workshop illustration and ask yourself how I might have phrased the task to get the best results at the first time of asking. Perhaps a different kind of culture or context would help us get to standing on chairs more quickly?

Key takeaways from Chapter 11

1   Your business plan is just a document until you make it happen.

2   As you think, so shall you be: manage positively your self-talk / self-image / performance cycle – and help others to manage theirs positively as well.

3   People who perform are your business's most important asset: support them so that they can give you their best, and by using the balanced scorecard process (SMART objectives plus quality discussions) you can personally ensure that each individual knows:

   a.   what is expected of them;

   b.   how they are doing against what is expected;

   c.   what the consequences of their behaviours are.

4   Look at your business through the perspective of the life-cycle.

5   Use the tools and techniques to manage change, but above all, understand change as a craft process that needs:

   a.   a craftsman's mindset;

   b.   communication and yet more communication;

   c.   the generation of energy

   d.   the lure of the vision;

   e.   support to succeed;

f.   an act of wizardry;

g.   story-telling;

h.   the power of individual example.

Notes and References

1   'I am convinced that the prime management problem is 'making it happen"; from Harvey-Jones, Sir J., *Making It Happen: Reflections on Leadership*, p. 28, London: Fontana, 1989.

2   Albert Bandura has written extensively on personal efficacy: 'Perceived self-efficacy is defined as people's beliefs about their capabilities to produce designated levels of performance that exercise influence over events that affect their lives. Self-efficacy beliefs determine how people feel, think, motivate themselves and behave ... A strong sense of efficacy enhances human accomplishment and personal wellbeing in many ways. People with high assurance in their capabilities approach difficult tasks as challenges to be mastered rather than as threats to be avoided. Such an efficacious outlook fosters intrinsic interest and deep engrossment in activities. They set themselves challenging goals and maintain strong commitment to them. They heighten and sustain their efforts in the face of failure.' And 'People must, therefore, have a robust sense of efficacy to sustain the perseverant effort needed to succeed' (Bandura, A. 'Self-efficacy', in Ramachaudran, V. S. (ed.) *Encyclopaedia of Human Behaviour*, Vol. 4, pp. 71–81. New York: Academic Press, 1994. One work which sets out the main tenets of his views on efficacy is, Bandura, A., *Self-efficacy: The Exercise of Control*, New York: Freeman, 1997. It is probably easier to get hold of than the article in which he introduced the notion of self-efficacy: Bandura, A. 'Self-efficacy: Toward a unifying theory of behavioural change', *Psychological Review,* 1977. **84**, pp. 191-215.

3   Of course, it would be quite proper for the sales director to have accountability for objectives relating to the sales budget and the costs of the sales team.

4   *'Quand tu veux construire un bateau, ne commence pas par rassembler du bois ... mais reveille au sein des hommes le desir de la mer*

grande et large' from *Citadelle* (published posthumously in 1944 and as *The Wisdom of the Sands*, 1952).

5   This balanced tension between the stretch of an objective and the realism of an objective is a replica of the tension between vision and current reality, encapsulated by the metaphor of an extended rubber band, which was discussed in Chapter 3.

6   See Kaplan, R.S., and Norton, D.P., 'The Balanced Scorecard – Measures that Drive Performance', *Harvard Business Review*, Jan-Feb, 1992, reprinted in Dyson, R.G., and O'Brien, F.A. (eds.), *Strategic Development: Methods and Models*, Chichester: Wiley, 1998. The power of the balanced scorecard to drive superior business performance is not just validated by my personal experience but also by academic research: for example, one group of researchers found 'significant evidence that the BSC [balanced scorecard] contributes to the perceived organisational performance of firms deciding to implement this new control system – whether it be as a new strategic performance measurement system or as a more elaborate form of a strategic planning and control system. From a managerial point of view, these results confirm the relevance of the balanced scorecard. In that respect, the BSC represents a value-added management system to survive and prosper in today's complex and dynamic business world'. And 'These results support the hypothesis that the BSC contributes positively to an increase in the organisational performance when it is used as the main tool to translate the strategy of the firm. They are coherent with the idea of using the BSC as a framework for translating the strategy in order to achieve a clear understanding of the vision and its strategic and operational implications, to discover the major cause-and-effect links between the various strategic objectives, to develop a strategy map that reinforces the translation of the strategy, and to facilitate its communication.' (De Geuser, F., Mooraj, and S., Oyon, D. 'Does the Balanced Scorecard Add Value? Empirical Evidence on its Effect on Performance'. *European Accounting Review*, **18** (1), pp. 93-122).

However, note that the effectiveness of the balanced scorecard does depend upon knowing what are the 'the major cause-and-effect links between the various strategic objectives'. Performance measures focused on market share are all very well, for example, but it is the quality of business won that counts. The expense of recruiting lots of inactive customers can make for Pyrrhic success. Customers should be 'weighed', not merely 'counted'. Furthermore, recruiting lots of customers without having the operational infrastructure to support them is perilous in the extreme. You need to take an holistic approach to get the best from balanced scorecards.

7 Notes and References to Chapter 10, Note 1.

8 Karl Marx has an amusing variant on this: 'Catch a man a fish and you can sell it to him. Teach a man to fish, and you ruin a wonderful business opportunity'.

9 William Shakespeare, *As You Like It*, Act II, Scene 7, spoken by Jaques.

10 In a business context, you might come across the expression 'the experience curve' – often in a reference to work done by The Boston Consulting Group. This usually refers to the relationship between the cumulative experience built up in a business (or any organisation) and its unit costs. It is portrayed graphically in this way:

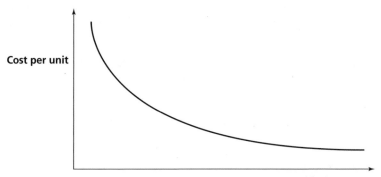

Figure 11.4

As a business continues to make more of its outputs over time ('cumulative outputs'), so the effect of the experience curve is to reduce unit costs. This is because people working to produce the outputs learn how to do it better, whether the workers themselves or the managers organising activities to achieve optimal outcomes.

If, for example, suppliers to the business also benefit from their own experience curve effects and, in addition, pass these benefits on in the form of reduced prices to their customers, then the business again benefits from reduced unit costs.

Of course costs are important to all businesses, but the relevance of the cost curve is especially acute for businesses that have chosen to compete specifically on price. For these businesses, low costs of production will figure prominently in their strategic logic.

However, all businesses can benefit from the effects of the experience curve. Indeed, some businesses exist partly because of these effects. For example, there are businesses who take on the activities of others (such as certain HR activities like payroll, or front-end telephony services) when such activities are outsourced. In my own business, I do not employ people to answer the telephone. I have outsourced this activity to an external organisation, although it appears to a caller that they are speaking to my business. Among other things, I am benefiting from that external organisation's experience curve (and economies of scale).

11 This inescapable indeterminacy is why so many change champions in business respond with the tools of apparent control. These are the project plans, the Gantt charts, the review documents that assess progress with strands of change for their 'RAG' status (red, amber, green), and the many committees and working parties. They have their place, and if you are to effect change programmes in your business you will need to use them all skilfully (or bring in those who can). Indeed, many reasons why change programmes have disappointed are because these tools and the practices that surround them were deployed sub-optimally. Perhaps the links to the overarching business plan were unclear or tenuous. Perhaps the necessary controls were absent or disciplines lax. Perhaps roles were ill-defined or the statement of requirement poorly articulated. Perhaps sponsorship of the change was insufficiently active. All these are crucial factors in implementing change successfully, and there are numerous books that will provide full details and a lot of advice to help with them. However, remember throughout that all of these tools and techniques will provide just an illusion of control. They attempt to make an engineering process out of what is really a craft process. The true path to the successful implementation of change is to combine all these tools and techniques with a bold engagement with the people aspects of change. (See also Beer, M., Eisenstat, R.A., and Spector, B., 'Why Change Programs Don't Produce Change', *Harvard Business Review*, Nov-Dec, 1990, pp. 158-166.)

12 In an interesting book about change in the National Health Service, Andrew Pettigrew talks about creating what he calls 'receptive contexts for change'. See Pettigrew, A., Ferlie, E., and McKee, L., *Shaping Strategic Change*, London: Sage, 1992, p. 273.

13 One of my favourite quotes of all time is this one: 'If I accept you as you are, I will make you worse. However, if I treat you as though you are what you are capable of becoming, I help you become that', *Goethe*.

14 Ovid's ancient story of Pygmalion is, of course, the inspiration for George Bernard Shaw's play which in turn inspired the musical and film *My Fair Lady*. In Ovid's narrative, Pygmalion was a Cypriot sculptor who carved a woman out of ivory. His statue was so realistic that Pygmalion fell in love with it. He offered the statue presents and eventually prayed to Venus, the goddess of love. She took pity on him and brought the statue to life. Pygmalion and his statue, now alive and a real woman, married. There is something about the fervency of Pygmalion's wish for the statue that awoke the life within. Leaders of change understand this Pygmalion principle very well indeed. They see the potential in people around them. This sculpts the reality. They expect great achievements and people achieve accordingly. It is the same with your families. The way you unconsciously treat the child causes them to grow into your expectation. If you find fault, see a blemish, then as a strong parent, more than likely you will create it. On the other hand, if you see a happy, well-adjusted child, then this is most likely what the child will grow up to be. The principle is that people will live up to or down to the expectation. The most successful leaders of change always see more in their people than they do in themselves. They use the Pygmalion concept positively in those around them. They expect their people to accomplish the change journey and make it happen successfully. And they see this success not only in those whom they encounter, but also in the people that they are going to interact with in turn. That is how successful people achieve success. Before they go into any situation, whether it is a meeting or a presentation or whatever, they visualise the ideal outcome that they expect. Their whole self then works to bring the reality to be what they have sculpted. It is the action of a true leader who has a passion, and who wants the best for people, to see the potential for greatness is all around. The true leader then sculpts reality to be great. I see you as a great leader. What happens if your people let you down? As a good business person – a good Pygmalion – you simply have to take the risk, and if you are not willing to take those risks you cannot be a great sculptor.

15 The 17th-century philosopher, Pascal, justified his belief in God on the basis of a wager. If God does not exist, then no harm is done in believing in him. On the other hand, if God does exist, then the potential for great harm in not believing in him, Pascal reasoned, is tremendous. Therefore, he concluded, better to believe in God.

The point about this is that Pascal believed that by taking on the form of belief in God – the rituals, the language, the texts, the stories, the myths, the symbols, the metaphors, the behaviours, the network – you could also work your way into genuine religious belief. In short, outward behaviours could lead to an internalised commitment.

Chapter 12

Implementation: Finding Failures Fascinating!

'I have not failed 10,000 times. I have successfully found 10,000 ways that will not work.' – Thomas Edison

FRUITS ARE FOUND OUT ON A LIMB

Your business does not have to be in ship-building for you to be pushing the boat out.

Business is about taking risks. This is not because business people want risks but because the most worthwhile ventures entail some risk.

Your business is a very worthwhile venture. It entails risk, therefore. Risks invite failure, otherwise they would not be risks: they would be dead certs.

So be ready for failures and setbacks. I have not read your business plan, yet I am certain that things will not work out in practice exactly as your plan sets out. For all the careful research and forethought you have put into compiling your financial forecasts, for example, the actual numbers will not be identical to your predicted numbers. As a field marshal once said, 'no plan survives contact with the enemy'[1]. You understand that this does not at all undermine the value of either your business plan or the forecasts it contains, but recognising the fact that reality will, on occasions, thumb its nose at your manoeuvrings and designs will keep you centred.

Your business encounters a setback. Let us suppose it is something like: Megabucks Ltd has said 'no' to you after your sales pitch. What happens next?

You will react to it. You might say: 'This will never work; we shall never win Megabucks Ltd as a client.' You might go on to affirm an appeal to wider 'evidence' or to a 'governing principle' to shore up the credibility of your reaction: 'Companies like Megabucks Ltd never bother with businesses the size of ours.' Naturally, after an analysis like this, the only rational conclusion is something like: 'There's no point our chasing these larger companies – we might as well stick to what we have got.'

This conclusion has consequences. At a stroke, your business is throwing away its business plan, giving up on its wondrous vision, and is staying as it is. The journey stops.

It all seems so sensible and rational. But consider what has really happened here. An approach to setbacks that works like this will inevitably mean that your business plan will *never* become reality. All businesses take risks, so all businesses are bound to suffer setbacks. If you rationalise your way into throwing in the towel at the first setback, then your business will remain a paltry lightweight – if it survives at all.

Mistakes, failures, setbacks, problems, crises, disappointments – they are all stepping stones on the path to success. Without such steps, there would just be a yawning chasm between you and your success – and you would never get there. So let's look again at our example setback.

You react to it. You might say: 'What do we have to do differently to win companies like Megabucks Ltd as a client?' You pursue the question further – perhaps you obtain feedback from Megabucks Ltd itself (a good move) – and you make a diagnosis: 'We did not win this sales pitch because we had not done sufficient prior research about the customer and so did not link our product offering closely enough to the customer's needs.' Naturally, after an analysis like this, the only rational conclusion is something like: 'Next time, when sales-pitching to a company like Megabucks Ltd, we shall be more thorough in our prior research and concentrate on spelling out the benefits of our products that are especially relevant to solving the customer's issues.'

This conclusion has consequences. Your business modifies its business plan, keeps latched on to its wondrous vision, and raises its game. The journey goes on.

The same setback, but what different consequences! In the latter scenario, the setback is treated as a positive learning opportunity. The result is that your business takes action to raise its capability, to become more accomplished in how it wins new customers and new sales. OK, your business may miss out on Megabucks Ltd – at least for the time being – but there is always Loadsadosh Ltd and Bagsamoney Ltd and a whole host of future prospective customers where your business will do a much better sales pitch: making a really positive impression, acquiring a higher standard of customer-centric competence, and ultimately winning new sales.

Two different scenarios: in what does the difference consist? It is not in the situation – the setback is the same. It is not in any external forces – these are the same. It is not in the business – it is the same business. Your business.

The difference is in the choice made after the setback occurs. In the first scenario, the business chose to respond negatively. In the second scenario, perhaps because the business understands that setbacks are the necessary stepping stones to its future success, the business chose to use the setback as a positive learning opportunity.

When responding to a setback in your business, think about the question you really, really want to ask. Do you really want to ask 'What's wrong?' or do you want to know 'What would the problem look like when it is solved?' Do you really want to ask 'Why are we under-performing?' or do you want to know 'What do we have to do differently to get those extra sales/make the customers happier/stop making mistakes, etc?' People move towards what they focus on – for good or ill. So get people – and yourself! – to focus on solutions, not the problem.

The key steps in choosing to use setbacks as positive learning opportunities are to:

- re-frame the questions about the setback to focus on *solutions*;
- find and adopt the beliefs that are *useful* to hold about the setback;
- find and assimilate the *learning* from the setback;
- resolve to *do better* next time.

Eliminate the negative, accentuate the positive

Notice how the process of response to a setback mirrors very much the self-talk / self-image / performance cycle that we discussed in Chapter 11. Like this cycle, the response to a setback can work negatively or positively:

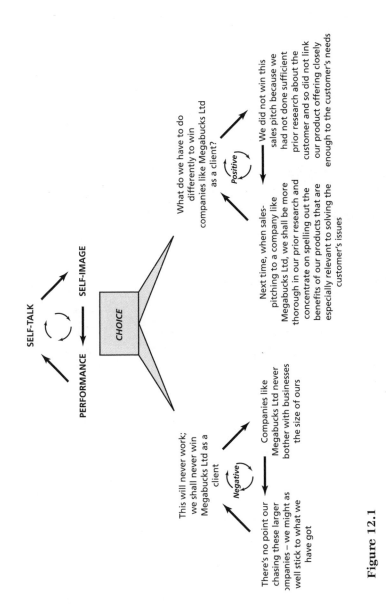

Figure 12.1

Whether the cycle works positively or negatively, whether your business responds to setbacks negatively or positively, is down to your choice[2].

You will also find this choice infectious throughout your business. So choose carefully – and reap the consequences!

Key takeaways from Chapter 12

1   Find failures fascinating!
2   Whether your business responds to setbacks negatively or positively is down to your choice.
3   How you exercise your choice will hugely influence how others in your business exercise their choice.
4   Re-frame the questions about setbacks to focus on solutions.
5   Find and adopt the beliefs that are useful to hold about setbacks.
6   Find and assimilate the learning from setbacks.

Notes and References

1   Attributed to Field Marshal Helmuth von Moltke (the elder).
2   I agree with those who believe in the unassailability of individual choice. For example: '... no matter what experimental knowledge of the previously unknown causes that determine a man's beliefs is accumulated, that which a man believes, and also that which he aims at and sets himself to achieve, will remain up to him to decide in the light of argument', in Hampshire, S., *Freedom of Mind and Other Essays*, p. 3, Oxford: Oxford University Press, 1972.

Chapter 13

Implementation: Open Focus

'Stay committed to your decisions, but stay flexible in your approach.' – Tom Robbins

THE EYE OF THE BEHOLDER

Different perceptions about the same thing can all be true.

Figure 13.1

What do you see?

If you see the profiles of two heads staring at each other, then you are right. If you see a white vase, then you are also right!

Whichever one you saw, have another look at the picture. Can you see the other image?

You are opening yourself to new perspectives and getting a more complete appreciation of reality. Perhaps you have seen this picture before. It is, of course, a picture of both: the profiles of two faces and a vase.

Different perceptions about the same thing can all be true. Communication and empathy can sensitise us to others' viewpoints and enable us to see more, to broaden our reality. Especially when situations are complex.

Practice can make perfect. We can teach ourselves to be open to new perspectives. We can become consciously aware of possible blind spots and look at things more mindfully.

Take this example. Do you see a duck or a rabbit? Or both?

Figure 13.2

My own experience when I first saw these images was that seeing both the duck and the rabbit was fairly straightforward and effortless. But it took me a little while before I could see both the two face-profiles and a vase. (My young son, James, is convinced it is a candlestick!)

This made me think: 'What else am I missing?' 'What other blind spots have I got?' 'What are other people seeing that I am not?'

Alas, far too often I meet people in business whose minds are set like concrete. It is not that they hold fast to their convictions (which in many ways would be an admirable trait); rather, they do not even listen to alternative viewpoints, let alone seek them out. They dismiss people with different perspectives as 'not being on board'. This is such a limiting constraint on their business and really jeopardises the successful implementation of your business plan – and it is self-imposed!

Seeing the world involves much more than our eyes. There is a process of filtering, of interpretation. What we see is most definitely in the eye of the beholder. In your business, it is very important to understand that we all have blind spots. That way, you will welcome the perspectives of others to give you a more complete view – *plus* you will fulfil an obligation to add to the perspectives of others and help them see beyond *their* blind spots. You will increase the chances of business success.

It is a never-ending task. My young daughter (when aged 6) taught me again about the importance of perspectives when we were on our family summer holiday one year. We were enjoying the seaside in Wales and, looking at the wetness of the sand and the action of the sea, I did the Daddy-thing and announced sagely that the sea was going out.

'Oh, no that's not right, daddy! The sea is coming *in*!' my daughter Hannah exclaimed.

I looked again and said: 'No, I don't think that's right, the sea is going out'.

'No, daddy! It's coming *in*!' And Hannah made a sweeping gesture with her outstretched arm inwards towards her body.

'It's not going out', and Hannah then made the reverse motion.

Finally it dawned on me. *From the perspective of the sea*, as it extends over the land, so it would be going out. And, from that same perspective, as it gathers in towards itself, so the sea would be coming in. Why should my viewpoint of the land prevail?

It is a question of perspective. And not for the first (or last) time, the perspective of a child's eyes had enriched my own.

PHYSICAL GROOVES LEAD TO MENTAL GROOVES

Consider the grid of nine dots below:

Draw this grid on a piece of paper and then join up the nine dots with just four lines, ensuring that each dot is on a line and that your pen always stays on the paper.

How does it work for you? Like this, perhaps?

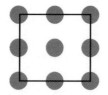

But these four lines leave one dot untouched!
Or this?

Again, one dot untouched!

So, to ensure no dot is untouched, are you ending up with something like this?

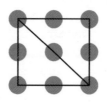

This joins up all the dots, but uses five lines!

What is your view on this puzzle? Perhaps you think there is no answer and you have been wasting your time. Or perhaps you are bored because you have seen this before and so you are alert to this sort of thing now.

Let us look at the solution:

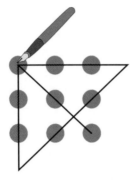

All nine dots are joined with four lines and without the pen leaving the paper.

The point is that the failed attempts were based on the assumption that the lines had to confine themselves to the parameters of the space suggested by the dots.

This is interesting. Where did such an assumption come from? It was not in the stated instruction. It was self-generated out of habit – and led to a blind spot spawned by grooved thinking. Physical grooves lead to mental grooves[1]. If the pattern of the nine dots grooved our mind into seeing a tight space, this will have precluded us from seeing the answer.

The answer, of course, lies in *thinking outside the dots*.

Many problems in business have their solutions in thinking outside the dots. I was once in an internal company meeting led by a good friend of mine[2]. The meeting was struggling to find a way to shorten the timescales of a complex project down from five weeks to only three weeks. It was a tense affair. The project delivery date could not move. The innovative juices of the team were exhausted. The pressure was palpable around the room. Heads were down and no ideas were coming forward which could solve the problem.

One person suggested that our IT colleagues should work overnight cutting and testing code. This was quickly dismissed by many around the table. But one of the team suggested that working overnight was an idea which we should not dismiss that quickly (beware premature evaluation). We decided to give the idea 10 minutes of air time.

Who could work overnight in the IT division? Blank responses.

OK, so re-frame the question (look back to Chapter 12). Who works overnight who could do the testing for us?

Still blank, but then one of the team said that her brother in America was the only person she knew who worked when she was asleep. Laughter around the table, but the remark was seized upon by another team member who suggested that we got her brother to do the testing for us. Eureka! 'Let's send the code at the end of the day to America, get them to check it overnight and get it back to us in the morning so that we could correct it and get on with the next piece of code cutting!'

The project team found a great code testing company in America – flew out the next day set it up in 24 hours, and the project was delivered three weeks later.

And that started with an idea to get our IT colleagues to work day and night for three weeks, which was dismissed very quickly as impossible. Beware premature evaluation!

If you have come upon the nine-dots problem for the first time, you may feel that I cheated you out of finding the solution. You might say that you were misled. The flawed attempts at solutions were deliberately revealed to you in such a way and in such an order that you were led astray into framing the approach to finding the solution within the confines of the nine-dot grid. But does that not happen in real life?

Do we not come by information in an order which may not be haphazard but over which we have no control? Remember, it is not just the data that shapes our views, but the *order* in which we receive the data. And this, too, can lead to blind spots.

Achieving success in solving business problems requires business people to seek out the 'seeing' of others and look at information from different perspectives, be they different perspectives of time or of viewing angle. It is about the inside and the outside. And helping others to do the same.

Even when you find the solution to your business problem, remember that every solution has unintended consequences. The world is so complex and ambiguous, that every solution put in place – even by the most broad-minded and inclusive approach – has unintended consequences. Look for these – do not let them sit in your blind spot. You may need to act.

If you have seen the nine-dots problem before, you may be feeling somewhat impatient as looking outside the dots is all pretty obvious to you. This particular groove of thinking is no longer yours – perhaps it never was.

In which case, perhaps you can join the nine dots ...

... with just *one* line.

Let us look at the solution:

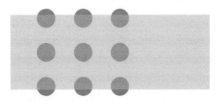

There is nothing in the framing of this problem about the *thickness* of the line! The line that joins up all nine dots might be a bit thicker than the earlier ones but it is a lot thinner than, say, the lines on a road.

So the answer to the join-the-nine-dots-with-four-lines problem required a different mental groove or habit by resisting the obvious groove and seeing an alternative pattern. But when the problem changed to join-the-nine-dots-with-one-line, even this new groove was not up to the job of finding the answer. Yet another new pattern was needed.

In business, as in life, we simply cannot have too much openness to new patterns, since we are always coming across new problems.

Novel thinking to solve one problem will simply be the groove that stops us seeing the solution to the next problem. And smugness, or the sense that we have enough novelty already, will definitely stop us solving the next problem ... or the one after that.

Perhaps the nine dots can be joined together *without any* lines.

Could folding be the answer? Why confine ourselves to operating in just two dimensions?

BEWARE PREMATURE EVALUATION[3]

Think back to the duck-rabbit picture. Imagine two people looking at it – le's call them Tom and Harry. We can imagine that when Tom asks Harry 'What do you see?' and Harry replies 'I see a duck', Tom could well say 'You're wrong – I see a rabbit'.

Clearly they are both right, but only by having both perspectives, adding the other's to their own, do they get a full appreciation of the whole. This is now a familiar point.

So imagine instead the following: Tom asks Harry 'What do you see?' and Harry replies 'I see a rabbit'. Tom says, 'That's great – so do I. We agree'.

And yet, although Tom and Harry are indeed seeing the same thing their understanding of the reality before them is incomplete. They are missing the full picture. They have agreed too soon, falling to premature evaluation.

By agreeing so readily, Tom and Harry are missing the fact that there are two images here. The full, true picture eludes both Tom and Harry. Superficial sameness of thinking, sameness of pattern, sameness of groove, means that Tom and Harry lull themselves into thinking they have got a complete understanding of the problem (or opportunity). In fact, their ways of thinking have closed down possibilities. Only alternative perspectives, different patterns set upon the data, open up further possibilities of understanding.

What would be worse would be to invoke majority opinion. Imagine their colleague Dick comes along and is asked what he sees. He replies 'I see a duck'. 'That can't be right', Tom and Harry respond in chorus, 'we see a rabbit and we agree on that'. Majority opinion founded on premature evaluation can yield a dangerous over-confidence to exclude a contrary or alternative or additional view.

If we see only a rabbit and not a duck, evaluate prematurely, and keep within self-imposed constraints, then our blind spots grow, our thinking becomes smaller, and our business becomes smaller.

Here is a sum:

$$1 + 1 = 3$$

Bad arithmetic? A printing error? Beware premature evaluation. If you want to implement your business plan successfully, cultivate a different response: 'Interesting, where is your other 1?'

The 'missing one' could be to do with customers, competitors, suppliers, stakeholders, government, or a core competence, a relationship, a conversation, a communication, a culture, a scientific breakthrough, etc., etc.

A new idea is vulnerable to a sneer or a yawn; it can be stabbed to death by a joke, or worried to death by a frown on the leader's brow. It can be suffocated by the weight of a thousand tiny, nibbling 'Ah yes buts', by being judged ahead of its time, by being given to the smothering embrace of a committee, or by a pot of jam (see page 234!).

Beware premature evaluation: it will stunt your ideas base. Bright people will fall from your business. Smug 'Yes, but' people will sit in their comfortable grooves killing off an idea which could change your world.

In the 1870s a major industrial company dismissed the telephone as having too many shortcomings to be of value. In the early 20th century, a French field marshal and top military strategist viewed aeroplanes as mere toys with no military value. In the 1920s, a substantial investor turned down the opportunity to invest in radio, believing it would have no commercial value since he could not understand why anyone would pay to send a message to no one in particular. In the 1940s, the top man at IBM could see room in the world for no more than five computers. In the 1960s a major record company turned down the chance of signing a new pop group called The Beatles, believing that their sound would not be popular and that guitar music was on the way out. In the early 1970s, Microsoft did not exist. In the early 1990s, Google did not exist – nor did Amazon. In 2001, a press release proclaimed the merger of Halifax and Bank of Scotland which created HBOS as offering 'substantial benefits for shareholders, customers and employees'. Seven years later, the top executives of HBOS were making apologies to the Treasury Select Committee for the ruinous performance of the business, and in January 2009 it ceased to be an independent entity, having been acquired by Lloyds TSB.

Blind spots and premature evaluation abound; no one – not you, not me, not anyone – is immune. Fantastic opportunities are dismissed out of hand by so-called experts; top businesses of today have come from nowhere not many years ago, and top businesses fanfared as pregnant with possibilities for generating great value have disappeared in a similar timescale.

What are we overlooking today? What are we lauding as the current bright sparks that will go up like a rocket but come down like a stick? One seer said: 'The future is already here – it's just unevenly distributed'[2]. Have you seen it? Perhaps it is sitting in one of your blind spots. Or perhaps a colleague has already seen it, but her view was prematurely evaluated away. Or perhaps you have indeed seen it – and so has the competition – but, like Tom and Harry, you do not fully recognise all that it is.

Successful people do it the other way round: they smother problems and oxygenate opportunities.

MATURITY IN BUSINESS IN THREE SECONDS

How long does it take for a child to respond to a question or a command, or a summons to food, or a tease, or a jibe or a gift?

Yes, about a nanosecond. And the response can be one of high emotion – tears, tantrums, spontaneous laughter or even the stamping of a foot, the crossing of arms and the sour look followed by the word 'Why?'

There is no gap between stimulus and .... response.

By placing a gap between stimulus and .... response we create maturity and it takes all the years from childhood to adulthood to learn the power of three seconds.

Maturity takes three seconds and in that time you are able to consider three things. They are the context of the stimulus, the content of the stimulus and the message in the stimulus.

I have found that, in business, effectiveness in communication and in influencing (which I take to be hallmarks of maturity in business) demands a constant assessment of these three elements. I can bring this to life by way of a simple example.

I once had a member of staff who could not place three seconds between stimulus and .... response. On one occasion I wished to have a quiet word with him about a particularly sensitive staff issue. I approached him at his desk and asked him if he would care to join me for a coffee. He replied that he had just had a coffee and carried on with his work.

Now what went wrong there?

When I said 'Would you like to join me for a coffee?', I meant 'I need to talk to you away from the office?'. He thought I was asking him if he was thirsty.

When he said 'I've just had one', I thought he meant 'Get lost!'

I walked off from that exchange knowing that I had failed and that he was an idiot!

Where did it go all wrong? He thought I was asking if he was thirsty. I thought I was asking him to join me for a private chat.

If he had looked at me and considered *context, content and message*, it would have been easier. He was three seconds away from true effectiveness – but so was I! If he had considered why I had walked over to him rather than ringing? If he had considered why I had chosen to ask him for coffee away from his desk? If he had noted that the content of my request was different from the message of my communication? The exchange would have worked. Take care when refusing a coffee!

On the other hand, if I had considered how he might interpret my question? If I had thought what different sort of question should I have asked to get the desired effect? Take care when offering a coffee!

This crucial three-second gap between stimulus and response works in both directions for true effectiveness in business.

Yes, please understand the context, content and message post-stimulus, but also *anticipate* context, content and message *pre*-stimulus. True effectiveness in implementing the business plan thinks about the meeting to come, the one-to-one interaction and the presentation to be delivered, and works out what needs to be said, what body language needs to exhibited, what pre-work needs to be completed *beforehand*.

FOCUS, FOCUS, FOCUS – AND THE WASP

Robert Shiller, a professor at Yale, said that 'the ability to focus attention on important things is a defining characteristic of intelligence'.

Clearly, then, wasps are not intelligent.

I would not expect wasps to be students at INSEAD – or even Harvard.

How so? (You need to ask?!) Picture the scene. The sun is beaming almost as much as you are and the friends you are with. The warmth is luxuriant and it is a happy time of relaxed chat and spontaneous chuckles as you all while away the time with a few beers.

Then a buzz. An insistent buzz. A wasp swoops in and around, skirting your hair, face and ears before narrowing the shape of its flight ever tighter around your glass of beer.

You wave it away. It works – for seven seconds. The wasp comes back. You wave it away again, trying to judge what is the fiercest wave possible that is just short of being so fierce as to antagonise the wasp into stinging you.

It works – for four seconds.

Another tactic is needed. So you pour barely a thimbleful of beer into an ashtray which you push to one side. The wasp homes in on the beery ashtray, leaving you in peace, but ignoring the riches of a whole glassful of beer.

You resume your summer pleasures, having given up a little to retain what is important – almost all your beer and your contented bearing.

This is an essential lesson about implementing your plan with business maturity. Knowing what counts as important keeps you focused on your goals, since you can then give away what does not matter. Indeed, distractions are often generated by the noise of others – including colleagues. Their petty gripes, their preoccupations with inconsequential minutiae, their arid agendas for fruitless political manoeuvrings, their myopic horizons.

To ensure such trivia do not deflect you from what counts, give such noisy people a beery ashtray – or, perhaps better (because my wife has told me 'beer' is very male), *a pot of jam.*

By the same token, and crucially for your own effectiveness, do not yourself be distracted by any pot of jam.

To ignore the lure of a pot of jam calls for an extensive hinterland of valuable skill and nous. It means that you have to have a deep understanding of both your own purposes and those of the would-be distractor.

You understand the axis of future-present. Noisy people without deep purposes, on the other hand, are by turns brow-beaten and cheated by an unremitting, unintelligible, and at best cheaply titillating here-and-now. Their responses have little purchase because there is no sense of future goal. Like pallid passengers in a small boat tossed about in open sea, without a forward point to head towards there is a general feeling of queasiness.

The forward goal sets the present course – *the problem defines the solution*. We have explored the power of purposes extensively in previous chapters. The point to hold fast here is that future goals give present meaning.

By contrast, the noise of petty concerns and small-picture preoccupations are the misplaced solutions of purposeless people desperately looking for appropriate problems to solve. They are content, therefore, with a pot of jam.

Do not be such a person. Ignore the small pot of jam. Concentrate on the whole jar.

Focusing on the implementation of your business plan enables you to inhabit a much bigger world. You focus on important things. The future *and* present are understood. The alternative is not understanding one or the other, but *neither*.

Sifting out the unimportant and focusing on what matters lies at the core of the successful implementation of your business plan.

Focus, focus, focus – and follow the owner, not the dog

Consider a dog and a park.

A dog enters a park at time 'T'. Where is it headed?

Only by following what is important – the dog owner – do we glean where the dog is ultimately headed. The dog itself repeatedly misleads us.

It turns out that the dog was ultimately headed back to the entrance from which it came.

When determining where the dog is headed, the dog is not actually what is important.

It is the dog owner that is important. Indeed, we could have jumped to a wrong conclusion (*beware premature evaluation*) by assuming that the dog owner (and therefore, ultimately, the dog) was headed along the prescribed path in the park. This would be wrong (*grooved thinking*).

In fact, the dog owner was headed to the park lake for the view and then back again. Now we know where the dog was ultimately headed.

Follow the owner, not the dog.

There are innumerable dogs in business and in life waiting to mislead us. Business is fixated with monthly or weekly or even daily figures, yet these rarely tell you what is really going on. Life is filled with screaming headlines and transitory preoccupations which, at such close examination, lose proportion.

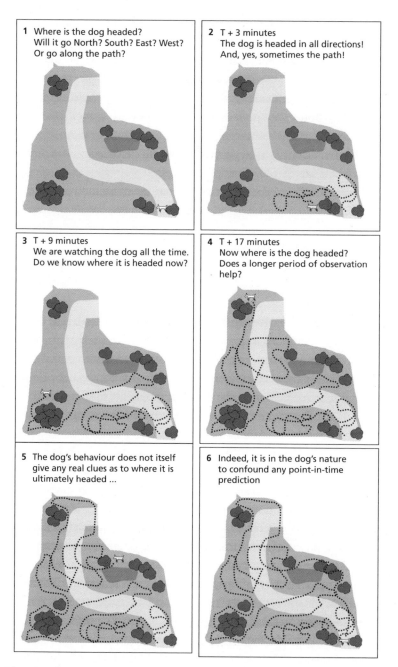

1 Where is the dog headed?
Will it go North? South? East? West?
Or go along the path?

2 T + 3 minutes
The dog is headed in all directions!
And, yes, sometimes the path!

3 T + 9 minutes
We are watching the dog all the time.
Do we know where it is headed now?

4 T + 17 minutes
Now where is the dog headed?
Does a longer period of observation
help?

5 The dog's behaviour does not itself
give any real clues as to where it is
ultimately headed ...

6 Indeed, it is in the dog's nature
to confound any point-in-time
prediction

Figure 13.3

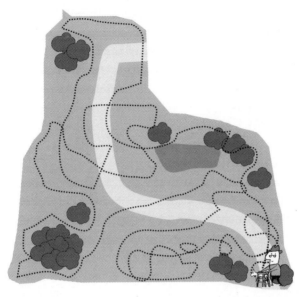

Figure 13.4

I used to monitor the monthly customer satisfaction score of the business I was working in. Over time, a pattern would emerge that started to make sense. But month by month, like a dog, it would move around all over the place. Instead, following what was really happening with the customer experience, concentrating on the relentless effort to improve what mattered to customers, spotting the key moments that told the customer whether our business could be trusted and relied upon – all this was following the dog owner. It was what was important in taking the business forward.

The dog's journey is, at best, a convoluted and often misleading proxy for the dog owner's. Like a monthly performance figure, it can provoke a spasm of ill-founded reaction.

FOCUS, FOCUS, FOCUS – AND THE BUCKET

The experiment of filling the bucket is told by Stephen Covey and, separately, by his son, Sean Covey[5]. Imagine a university professor who turned up for his class one day with an empty bucket. He then proceeded to fill it with rocks and then asked the assembled students whether the bucket was full. They said it was. The professor then poured gravel into the bucket which started to fill in the gaps between the rocks. He then asked the class if the bucket was full. 'Now it is', they said. So the professor then poured sand into the bucket, asked the students the same question and then got the same answer. So finally, the professor poured water into the bucket. At last everyone agreed that the bucket was indeed full.

The point of the story?

Well, yes, no matter how full your time is, there is always room for something else.

But more than that, what would have happened had the professor started in the reverse order; that is, not with rocks but with water? Clearly there would immediately have been no room for anything else.

The size of the objects is representative of importance.

In business, as in life, it is easy to 'play-pen' by spending too much time on relatively less important activities or issues, at the cost of elbowing aside time on more important matters. Going through your e-mail inbox can suddenly become more important than making that difficult sales call, for example – or that difficult sales call occasions the postponement of that pre-arranged tricky staff interview.

The successful implementation of your business plan requires you and your team to keep relentlessly focused on what is important. How is importance to be judged? The answer is in the context of purposes! That is, the extent to which achievement of the vision is progressed. It is all in your business plan.

Like a self-guiding missile, we move towards that which we focus on – for good or ill. Do not leave the important things until last – you will never get round to them. Your time is finite: do the most important things first (rocks); if you have some time left over, then do the second most important things (gravel); and so on. Do not start with unimportant trivia – no matter how much you enjoy doing them. You are now the servant of your vision; you must be disciplined in your focus on that.

Check how you are doing and get your people to check themselves as well. At the end of every week, make a list of the five most important issues that had to be addressed that week (your business plan will be the ultimate source of these). Then review how you spent your time in fact, and list the top five time-eating activities that week. Is there a fairly close match between where you mostly spend your time and what is most important? Remember to frame the issue properly: 'What would have to be different for me to spend more time more effectively on what is important?' No matter how well aligned this is, and in the spirit of continuous improvement, make a list of top issues for the week ahead and resolve to do even better!

FOCUS, FOCUS, FOCUS AND THE POWER OF ONE[6]

Should you or anyone in your team or any team in your business try to do it all?

Of course not. This is a sure route to being overwhelmed and defeated.

You are very busy with lots to do, an ambitious vision and an exciting yet challenging business plan. In sorting out issues and chasing opportunities, in collaborating with others on deciding the best course of action and in giving direction to outside providers, you need to cut to the chase.

Here is a very simple method to help you do that. Imagine, say, an IT expert is blinding you with technicalities on which you are supposed to base a decision. It might be about your business's website, or a piece of software that you might adopt. You need to display wisdom, but you are not feeling very wise. You need to make an informed decision, but you do not understand the data that is being put to you. Part of you is elsewhere, thinking about the meeting which you need to be at or the telephone call you should be making.

Try this: 'I know you have lots you want to tell me, but isn't it true that, of the things you have told me, one is more important than the rest?'

I have never heard the answer 'no'. Get the expert to narrow the choices to the one most important thing – and do that. If it turns out that there is time and also resources to do the next most important thing, do that next.

This is like the well-known 80/20 rule, but even more focused for busy people – like you.

KEEPING YOU BRAND NEW

I said that you are the servant of your vision – and, by implication, of your business plan also.

Servant, yes; slave, no.

You will be no good servant to your business and your business plan if you do not nurture your *whole* self.

Perhaps you are seeking investment in your business – that might be what triggered you into putting a business plan document together. Why is investment so important? Perhaps you are surprised that I should ask. 'To support the growth and development of my business,' you reply. I can believe this. Investment is a valuable engine of progress and enrichment.

You are no different. You need to invest in yourself to fuel your own growth and development. I do not solely have in mind here training yourself in new skills or acquiring new knowledge. What I mean is recognising the reality that you are a whole person who is trying to implement your business plan. Therefore, it is nurturing the whole of you that is essential in order for you to be the best servant of your vision and business that you can be. Slavery would be to forget the 'you' that is you.

If you are to raise your game for the benefit of your business, if you are to grow to be the best business maker you can, then you have to grow the whole of you, not just the portion of you that you spend in – and on – your business.

Put your business to one side for a moment. You know what is important to you in your life. Perhaps you are a mother or father and so you count your children as the most important people in your life. They deserve your time – and you deserve theirs. How good would you be for your business if you starve yourself of their company? How corrosive would be the resentment and regrets of the positive cast of mind that is essential for business success?

The appetites of human nature are broadly based. I do not doubt your commitment to your business, but you will best deliver on that commitment when you recognise that you must nurture the whole of you in order also to nurture the part of you that is driving for business success. This means that to implement your business plan successfully, you must maintain balance in your life. By 'balance' I do not mean that the various areas of your life must be given an equal number of minutes. Rather, I mean that the fundamental values that drive you are appropriately reflected in how you give yourself to the various areas of your life.

Get the balance in your life wrong for too long, and you will not succeed in implementing your business plan. But work at keeping the balance roughly right and then you will be in the best possible personal shape to implement your business plan successfully. As William J. H. Boetcker says: 'If your business keeps you so busy that you have no time for anything else, there must be something wrong, either with you or with your business.'

Here is a very practical process that will help you get the balance of your life right and so give you the surest basis to achieve business success.

1 Make a list of the key areas of your life. These might be home, work, friends, yourself, charity work or whatever.

2 Draw a cross on a piece of paper and then draw four further lines at 45 degrees in each quadrant. You should end up with something that looks like a rimless wheel with eight spokes. Each spoke should have a range of values from 1 to 10 with the outer end of each spoke being 10.

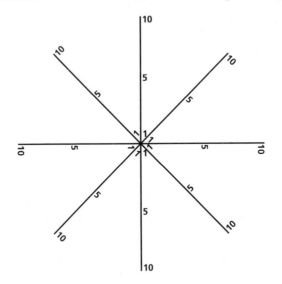

Figure 13.5

3 You now have the infrastructure of what will be a balance wheel representation of the key areas of your life. Assign the designation of a key area of your life to each one of the eight spokes[7]. Overleaf is an example and, as I had some time on my hands, I have pretti-

fied my example balance wheel by drawing in concentric circles at each of the value points along the spokes[8].

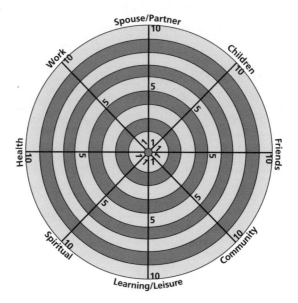

Figure 13.6

4   Score each of the key areas of the your life in terms of how much of yourself you are currently putting into each one ('investing' would be a telling word here as it is much more comprehensive than the idea that it is about merely throwing more time at a key area of your life: it is about how much of your *soul* you give): '1' is very little; '10' is a huge amount. On your life-balance wheel, plot your scores. Join the points together. Review what the resulting shape (Figure 13.7, opposite) is telling you. The likelihood is that the shape will not be round but will be skewed in the direction of a couple of areas in particular. A perfectly round shape is not necessarily what you optimally want, but ask yourself, honestly, whether the shape is as you want it to be.

5   Review your personal life-shape and question yourself as to what shape you would ideally want. Which areas of your life are you under-investing in? If you are to implement your business plan successfully, you should be investing in *all* the areas of your life as you would ideally wish; that is, as would be true to your fundamen-

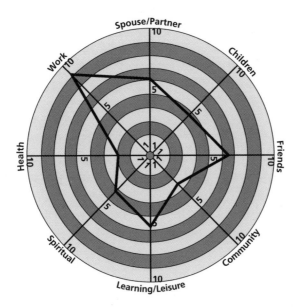

Figure 13.7

tal values. Plot your ideal ratings for each key area of your life on your life-balance wheel – you will probably have some areas to the forefront of your mind more than others. The resulting picture will highlight the priority areas of your life into which you will want to raise your level of personal investment.

6 In Figure 13.8 overleaf, the individual is saying that she/he wants to give more of herself/himself to her/his children, ease back on work and also give more to her/his health – the pale line versus the dark line. Remember: please choose the designations of the key areas of your life that matter to you. Please also plot the current levels of personal investments that are true for you, and also plot the desired level of investments that you ideally want. All of this is personal to you – there is no right or wrong here. It is no one's place to dictate a life-balance shape to you – least of all my place. What I can do, for your sake and for the sake of your vision and business plan, is to exhort you to work effortfully at getting the life-balance shape that you want, that reflects the proper outworking of your fundamental values. I know your business depends on it. And also please note that your actual life-balance shape will move about over time, so the areas for priority attention will also

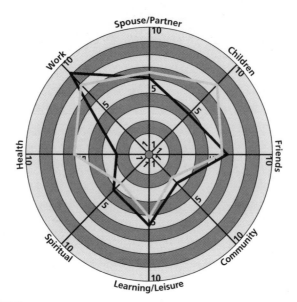

Figure 13.8

move about. Indeed, it is possible that you will re-evaluate your life and what is important to you, and so your ideal life-balance shape might change as well. All this means that it is important that you review your life-balance wheel regularly. The frequency is up to you, but in a hectic life, monthly would be sensible. No, more than 'sensible'; it would be *wise*. As you resolve to close your prioritised personal investment gaps, set yourself clear actions to make good the shortfall – you know about SMART objectives. Set yourself SMART objectives as much in your life as in your business.

And now, a crucial point.

It would be trivialised by saying it is about 'what is sauce for the goose is also sauce for the gander', but that is indeed what it is about.

In this section, 'Keeping you brand new', the argument is that if you are to improve the effectiveness with which you implement your business plan, then you need be mindful and effortful about growing the whole of you, not just the portion of you that is spend in and on your business. This is about more than monitoring the minutes you spend on each key area of your life. It is about how much of yourself you invest in each area, and that this represents a coherent outworking of your fundamental values.

If you accept the rightness of this argument, then logically, it must also hold for all the other people in your business as well. Sure, it is imperative that the business makes clear its expectations of all its employees (we discussed the role of individualised balanced scorecards in accomplishing this). At the same time, it also about creating the conditions in which people can be enabled to meet these expectations by having space to become the best *person* they can be, in order to be the best *employee* they can be. Growing the portion of the employee that is given to the business, so the argument runs, means growing the whole person. You employ the *person*, not merely the employee. It is no different from yourself[7]. (This is why recruitment is an activity that requires real skill, care and emotional intelligence.)

You need to work out what this means in practice: every business is different, every individual is different, every life-balance wheel is different.

This does not mean that every whim of every person is indulged – there are obligations to the business and the vision by which the team is bound together. It might mean, however, that pragmatic and workable compromises are made in exceptional circumstances (such as giving a parent time off to attend their child's nativity play and the time is given back by the employee another time). People of good will, with an underpinning of shared intent, can usually find a way[10].

Key takeaways from Chapter 13

1 Seek others' help to see beyond your own blind spots.
2 Help others see beyond their blind spots.
3 Physical grooves lead to mental grooves.
4 Every solution has unintended consequences.
5 'The future is already here – it's just unevenly distributed'.
6 Avoid premature evaluation.
7 $1 + 1 = 3$.
8 You are what you repeatedly do: excellence is a habit.
9 Use the three-second gap between stimulus and response.
10 Do not be a wasp: focus on what is important (future purposes give present meaning).
11 Follow the owner, not the dog.

12 Always start filling your bucket with rocks.

13 Harness the power of one.

14 Your business and business plan are so important that you need to keep your life balance wheel in good shape.

15 The life-balance wheels of your people are important too – to them, to your business, to you. Create the conditions for appropriate balance.

Notes and References

1 It was my philosophy tutor at university, Dr J.D. Kenyon, fellow of St Peter's College, Oxford (now retired), who made this sagacious remark. I am keen to credit it to him, not least because he was such a stimulating tutor to whom I owe a huge debt.

2 Cary Adams, former inspirational colleague, present good friend, and future millionaire international entrepreneur.

3 Dennis Sherwood defines premature evaluation as 'the tendency to rush to judge'. Sherwood, D. *Innovation Express*. p. 100. Oxford: Capstone Publishing, 2002. He characterises it as 'a condition, often exhibited by aggressive males, who, in a fit of over-excitement evaluate ideas far too soon, thereby killing innovation stone dead, and creating a most unsatisfying situation for everybody!' (*op. cit.* p. 83). See also Sherwood, D., *Smart Things to Know about Innovation and Creativity*. Oxford: Capstone Publishing, 2001. I have worked with Dennis Sherwood in the past; he is a very wise and insightful collaborator with an especially simple yet highly effective approach to innovation and creative thinking (see www.silverbulletmachine.com). Also, if you are interested in putting some rigour into what we have called the search for root causes and your essential quest to understand the levers in your business, then his book on systems thinking would be a real help: Sherwood, D., *Seeing the Forest for the Trees: a Manager's Guide to Applying Systems Thinking*, London: Nicholas Brealey, 2002.

4 William Gibson, quoted in *The Economist*, 4th December, 2003. As individuals, we are not naturally good at recognising novelties without distortions. We either tend towards over-optimism or to feel the prospect of losses more sharply than gains. For example, all drivers would rate their driving ability as 'above average', but they cannot all be right! And if I offered you £100 to walk in a straight line for ten yards, you would not hesitate. But if I were to repeat the offer provided that you did it on a ledge 500 feet in the air, without rails to hold on to, you would be much more circumspect. Over-optimism can lead to rash commitments, false futures and bitter disappointment, whereas oversensitivity to losses can lead to inaction, missed opportunities and bitter disappointment. The open focus of a learner's disposition is the best way of avoiding the Scylla of over-optimism and the Charybdis of oversensitivity to losses. This gives you the future as yours to make.

5   For example: Covey, Stephen. R., Merrill, A. R., and Merrill, R. R., *First Things First: To Live, to Love, to Learn, to Leave a Legacy*, New York: Simon & Schuster, 1994, and Covey, Sean, *The 7 Habits of Highly Effective Teens*, p. 114. New York: Simon & Schuster, 1998.

6   I am grateful to my friend, Chris Farmer, leader of the Corporate Coach Group (see www.corporatecoachgroup.co.uk), for discussing the power of one with me.

7   You can have more than eight spokes in your own life-balance wheel (or fewer); it really is up to you.

8   The designations of the key areas of your life are entirely personal to you. These need to be what are the key areas to *you*. What you have here is no more than an example. Please choose what is right for you.

9   Applying an argument to yourself but then refusing to apply the same argument to other people simply because they are other than you is, by and large, an epitome of moral irrationality.

10 'Finding a way' makes good business sense. Think of it like this: businesses and organisations have always competed, whether over scarce resources or for the good opinion and custom of their clients and users.

Broadly, and taking a long-term historical perspective, we may see organisations as competing through their ability to succeed through an ever-changing series of quests.

The first might be regarded as the quest for production as mass production techniques were devised that not only delivered large-scale output, but also, crucially, economic wealth for large-scale consumption. Then the quest for market share began a focus on the science of customers – how to win them, keep them and segment them. The quest for efficiency returned to a supply-side orientation as various techniques, often pioneered in Japan, became more widespread, and alternative sourcing routes (e.g. offshoring, outsourcing, etc.) began enjoying vogue status.

More recently, we are witnessing the quest for the customer experience, where a former preoccupation with needs-benefits equations has been enriched by an interest in the non-rational, emotional make-up of customers and their demand for a total experience.

The future will be different again. It will entail organisations needing to compete and succeed in the quest for meaning. For the first time, a more holistic quest challenges organisations. It includes customers' growing concerns for the environment and ethical issues, which are increasingly setting an agenda for production. However, for the first time, the interests of employees now figure.

Future success will more and more depend upon the knowledge, skills and adaptability of employees and leaders who are adept at emotional intelligence and at forming relationship networks. Such workers will demand more than just fair remuneration, decent working conditions, and a conducive work-life balance. They will want work itself to mesh into the individual employee's demand for a meaningful and fulfilling life.

Increasingly, scarce talented workers will pick their employers – and move actively from one to the other – on the basis of how well they contribute towards and enable them to live a meaningful life.

For employers to grow what their employees can provide during the hours of work, employers will have to help employees grow the whole person. This activity will be necessary for business success.

Chapter 14

Implementation: Relationships – Familiarity Breathes Content

'A growing relationship can only be nurtured by genuineness.' – Leo Buscaglia

SOFT SKILLS ARE HARDER THAN HARD SKILLS

In Chapter 9 I said that: 'the key to business success is the quality with which the business manages its relationships with stakeholders'. Indeed, it was one of the takeaways from that chapter.

Relationship management is all about building long-term relationships to ensure solid, profitable associations and thus protection against attack from outside competition. The development and breadth of these relationships is very much based on people.

Your business is the locus where a network of relationships comes together: with customers, suppliers, employees, investors, competitors, society, and governmental bodies. Indeed, as John Kay has said: 'It is the totality of these relationships which defines the individual firm and creates its distinctive identity'[1]. Value is created by developing, qualitatively, a set of relationships that others are unable to make.

Proficiency in these so-called soft skills is, therefore, crucially important for the successful implementation of your business plan, but it is also difficult to attain. Understanding why it is so difficult is the first step to overcoming the difficulty and achieving the necessary proficiency in managing your business's network of relationships, thereby winning with your business and successfully implementing your business plan.

THE PRISONER'S DILEMMA

Consider a simple scenario. Two businesses, Noughts Ltd and Crosses Ltd, are considering a joint venture. They each ponder how best they should behave with the other and they alight upon two broad behavioural dispositions.

Each company reasons that they can either be forthcoming with the other in the proposed joint venture, or they can hold back. What should they do?

Well, this might well depend on what the other one does. The reasoning could go something like this. Noughts Ltd says to itself that if Crosses Ltd holds back, then it would pay Noughts Ltd to hold back as well. But if, Noughts Ltd goes on to reason, Crosses Ltd decides to be forthcoming, then it would be better for Noughts Ltd again to hold back. So, Noughts Ltd concludes, whichever of the two behavioural dispositions Crosses Ltd chooses to adopt, it would pay them to hold back, so that is what Noughts Ltd decides to do.

However, in the privacy of its board room, Crosses Ltd is reasoning in an exactly parallel fashion. It concludes that whether Noughts Ltd chooses to be forthcoming or to hold back, it would be better for Crosses Ltd to hold back, and so that is the behavioural disposition it chooses.

So both Noughts Ltd and Crosses Ltd choose to hold back, and the joint venture quickly collapses amidst bitterness and mutual recrimination. The proposed collaborative relationship was just too difficult to form, let alone sustain, falling still-born before the powerful structuring force of self-interest. Indeed, they might well have shared the view that it was in each of their own business interests to collaborate in a joint venture, yet the unyielding logic of their own self-interest was not only as rigid as iron, it was also ironic in preventing them from reasoning their way to stay true to their real business interests. In fact, it reasoned its way to the opposite.

This illustrates a type of problem called the Prisoner's Dilemma[2]. It gets this name from a version of the problem that runs like this.

To add colour to the scenario, imagine that it is the time of Robin Hood and his battles with the Sheriff of Nottingham. Now imagine that two members of Robin Hood's gang, let us call them Mungo and Midge, are arrested by cronies of the Sheriff of Nottingham, taken to his castle and put in separate dungeons.

The Sheriff of Nottingham has no evidence against either Mungo or Midge but that does not stop him coming up with a cunning plan to bend the rules of natural justice so as to sow discord among the supporters of his foe, Robin Hood. So the Sheriff of Nottingham speaks to Mungo and Midge separately and puts this proposition to each of them.

In fact and unbeknown to the Sheriff, Mungo and Midge hardly know each other and care nothing for the radical redistributive social-ist activities of Robin and his Merrie Men: they just want to get out of jail and go home. So they listen carefully when the Sheriff of Notting-ham speaks to each of them alone:

'You can either confess or not confess. If you confess and the other one does not confess, then I shall let you go free and I shall put the other one in jail for ten years. If both of you confess, then I shall put you both in jail for seven years. Or you might choose not to confess. If you do not confess and the other one does confess, then I shall set that person free and I shall put you in jail for ten years. If you do not confess and nor does the other one, then I shall put both of you in jail for one year. It is now up to you. You have one hour to let me know your decision: do you confess or not confess?'

Mungo and Midge are in separate dungeons and they cannot confer. The options are straightforward as Mungo and Midge separately ponder them: to confess or not to confess. But the outcomes seem complicated, so to help them, they each draw a grid in the dirt on the floor of their dungeon. It looks something like Figure 14.1 overleaf.

The best outcome is for Mungo not to confess and for Midge not to confess. However, Mungo is deliberating like this. 'Should I confess or not confess. It depends on what Midge will do – but we can't talk to each other. What if Midge confesses? Well if Midge confesses and I don't confess, then I shall end up with ten years in jail. But if I do confess then I shall still end up in jail, but for a bit less – only seven years. So if Midge confesses, then the best thing I can do is to confess as well. But what if Midge does not confess? Well, if I don't confess,

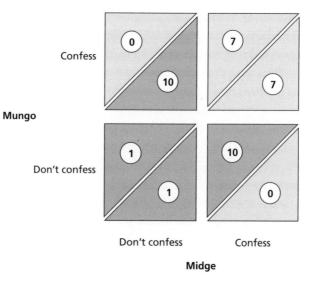

Confess

Mungo

Don't confess

Don't confess   Confess

Midge

Figure 14.1

then I shall be put in jail for a year; but if I confess I shall be set free! So once again, the best thing I can do is to confess. So, overall, whatever Midge decides to do, the best way ahead for me is to confess and so that is exactly what I shall do. I confess!'

In the next-door dungeon, Midge is reasoning in exactly the same way about Mungo and concludes: 'So, overall, whatever Mungo decides to do, the best way ahead for me is to confess and so that is exactly what I shall do. I confess!'

The sheriff of Nottingham arrives an hour later to hear Mungo confess and Midge confess, and so he proclaims: 'Right then! You both go to jail for seven years!'

And Mungo and Midge are led away wondering how they let slip the optimal outcome of just a year in jail each had both of them not confessed!

Rather as with the joint venture problem, impeccable reasoning led each of them away from the optimal outcome. Suppose now that the Sheriff of Nottingham, for his amusement, turns to Mungo and Midge and says: 'You will each be returned to your separate dungeons and you can have another chance to decide – the same rules apply.' Will another go produce a different outcome? The answer is 'no', because the logic remains exactly the same. Whatever the other chooses to do, it is better to confess and so that is what they both decide to do – again. And so, once again, they are both condemned to jail for seven years.

Now suppose that the Sheriff of Nottingham, who is not yet bored with this game, says to Mungo and Midge: 'You have had two goes at this and on both occasions you have chosen to confess and so condemned both of you to seven years in jail. This time, I shall have you returned to the same dungeon where you can have another go – the same rules apply – but this time I shall let you talk it over with each other. I could not be fairer! I shall be back in an hour to find out what each of you decides to do.'

So Mungo and Midge are led away and thrown into the same dungeon. They start to discuss their options: 'Well obviously if we both do not confess, then, instead of being in jail for seven years, we shall be in jail for just one year. So I reckon we should both choose not to confess. Agreed?' Mungo asks. 'Agreed,' Midge confirms.

They have both agreed what one of the rules of the 'game' is: it is indeed the case that if both choose not to confess, then both will go to jail for just one year. It is a lot better for each of them than both going to jail for seven years. However, that is all they have agreed on. Privately, each one is thinking 'Well, if the other one is not going to confess, and then I actually do confess, I shall be let free – which is even better than one year in jail! So I shall choose to confess!'

In fact their thinking does not stop there: 'Actually, come to think of it, the other one is going to reason in exactly the same way – I reckon they are going to choose to confess so that they can go free; in which case, I would get stuck in jail for ten years if I stick to choosing not to confess! Well I'm not going to do that: I'm going to confess!'

Yet again, and despite having the opportunity to confer on this, Mungo and Midge reason their way to deciding that each of them will confess, and the Sheriff of Nottingham, hugely enjoying it all, sends them to jail for seven years.

Even if Mungo and Midge were given yet another opportunity to confer with each other and even if they promised to each other not to confess, it would be in their interests to break their promise. No matter how many times they repeat the exercise, it is the same logic and so the same outcome.

In business, there is always lurking this Prisoner's-Dilemma-type problem. It may not be explicit; indeed, more often than not there is no conscious reasoning, but the Prisoner's Dilemma casts a shadow over all human interactions. In a competitive environment, not only is a rival business actively working towards gaining an advantage over you, but there is always the thought in a customer's mind: 'Are they trying to get one over on me?' – or in a supplier's, or a colleague's, or a regulator's.

You might think that the existence of a past and a future would imply that it would make sense to behave in ways which are not the best for either party in the short run. For Mungo and Midge, it always pays to confess; yet not doing so is in the long-term interests of them both. Alas, however, as we have seen, the creation of a long-term relationship might be a necessary condition to achieve the optimal outcome, but it is not alone sufficient. Repeated encounters do not change the logic that structures the situation and so structures the players' behaviours.

EMERGING FROM THE PRISONER'S DILEMMA

Mungo and Midge know that the best outcome is achieved by both of them not confessing – logic or communication with each other establishes that – but neither can convince the other that they can make a credible *commitment* to not confessing. This inability to make commitments is costly – they both end up imprisoned for seven years. Mungo will not commit unless Midge can and does also – it is no good retaining any flexibility or a wait-and-see approach. And it is no good having lots and lots of meetings to discuss it. The root issue of 'commitmentlessness' is unresolved, and for as long as it remains unresolved, Mungo and Midge are condemned to prolonged periods of incarceration.

This is why, in business, it is not enough for sales people, for example, to have lots and lots of contact with a customer or prospective customer. Too often, sales people believe they only have to speak to their contact over and over, and that alone will bring a positive result. Not so. Only when the sales person restructures the situation to enable – and, importantly, induce – a *commitment* to be made will a good outcome be achieved. Understanding this, and understanding how to induce the necessary commitment to be made, is the key to forming and sustaining successful business relationships and so is the key to business success.

This is why in other settings players attempt to change the pay-off. Gangsters, for example, are always fearful that they will be turned in to the police by one of their gang. A prospective 'grass' has to weigh up two scenarios. One scenario sets the likelihood and scale of the potential benefits of continued loyalty against the risk of capture by the police and the unpleasant consequences of subsequent imprisonment. The other scenario is to start grassing on the gang, thereby incurring the wrath of its members versus the benefits of more lenient treatment by the police and a reduced or waived period in prison.

Gangsters realise this, which is why they are so keen to affect the dynamics of the scenarios by changing the pay-off. Disloyalty – or grassing – will not just incur the gang's wrath, it will mean broken legs (or worse) for the grass, and much unpleasantness for the informant's family as well. Hence offers of safe houses, new identities, relocation and police protection are attempts by the law enforcement agencies to change the pay-off again.

More mundanely, this is what legal contracts are for. They are devices by which the iron logic of the Prisoner's Dilemma can be alleviated by changing the pay-off of the situation. A spoken contract between Mungo and Midge would not amount to much because there is no pay-off heavy enough to counterweigh the benefit to the individual party of reneging on the oral promise.

However, in the earlier scenario of the prospective joint venture between Noughts Ltd and Crosses Ltd, one way forward for them is to sign a legal contract that details what each party has to do to be counted as 'forthcoming'. The consequences of reneging on the contract and holding back would mean legal action and hefty fines. This financial cost outweighs any short-term gain from holding back, and so, because both parties can read the situation in the same way and weigh up the pay-offs in the same way, they each have the confidence to commit to being forthcoming. The joint venture flourishes.

Signing the contract is a credible way of removing from possibility the approach of wait-and-see, and instead committing to a specific set of actions rather than a different set. Put graphically, if we are competing in a staring contest and you cut off your eyelids, then I know you are going to win because you have removed any possible way in which you can lose! (But at what a price!)

NOT TRUSSED, BUT TRUST

In the late 1970s, the car manufacturers Rover and Honda formed a successful alliance. While it was in operation, the two companies, just like Noughts Ltd and Crosses Ltd, would have to have solved Prisoner's-Dilemma-type problems.

First, they both saw that for each of them, the benefits of the alliance working were much greater than any benefits in failure. Second, the two parties tested each other out in a ballet of move and reciprocal move. They realised that they both saw the game in the same way. Ultimately, as the two parties knew how each other would behave in unfolding circumstances, they built up a confidence in behavioural prediction: in a word, *trust*.

Once the two parties felt they had mutual trust, they had taken the alliance through to a crucial phase in its development. No legal contract can oblige parties to be 'open' in a relationship, but a basis in trust can encourage openness. I agree with the writers of a top-notch book on strategy: 'Trust is probably the most important ingredient of success and a major reason for failure if it is absent'[3].

Consequently, during the alliance, there was progress towards ever-greater joint development of products, more co-production, and cross-sourcing of components. Honda also trusted Rover's competencies, for example in four-wheel drive technology.

There is also the trust that can develop within what some writers have called 'secure defences' so that the parties to an alliance 'develop safeguards against the unintended, informal transfers of information'[4]. Feeling safe is a necessary condition for making the moves that lead to building trust. This is what lies behind the saying that good neighbours are found behind good fences. In business, the same thinking lies behind 'no obligation quotes' or 'exploratory meetings': people will more readily enter into something if they can see an easy exit. Your business needs to create these conditions with all its stakeholders, which is where the true risk/reward of business lies.

The trust in the Rover/Honda alliance extended through all levels of contact between the companies and was signalled in a 20 per cent share exchange. The trust that held the alliance together was much more important than any legal document, since no contract can force you to be flexible or co-operative. There was a joint investment of emotional energy as important as any investment of sterling and yen[5].

In your business, it is your task to structure and re-structure situations so that the pathological problems of the Prisoner's Dilemma do not arise. You need to create conditions that induce commitments to be made – by your business and by your counter-parties (customers, employees, stakeholders).

You achieve this by acting on the 'Four Cs':

- **Continuity**: People know it is a long-term, repeat game.
- **Communication**: Communication is so clear and open that people understand the benefits that flow from certain sets of behaviours rather than others.
- **Consequences**: The pay-off structure is shaped so as to encourage the behaviours that produce the optimal outcomes.
- **Commitment**: Commitments are induced because of commitments made – options are closed down.

This entails risk. You make a gesture to show commitment, how do know that you will not be taken advantage of?

The truth is that you do not know. It is a risk. Sure, you will never deal with that counter-party again (or at least only on a highly regulated transactional basis) but you will have learned that there is no basis for a *relationship* – you simply do not see the game in the same way as each other.

But the risks from *not* taking this risk are much greater. If all your relationships are wholly contractual, you will not gain enduring competitive advantage. If you can write a relationship wholly into a contract, then others can replicate or reproduce the same contract. It is the part of the relationship that cannot be written down that is the basis for distinctiveness over your rivals.

This means trust.

Trust can be induced on the basis of reputation where a positive reputation in business is gained by the provision of consistent quality in repeated trials. This can mean high quality as is found with, say, a Rolls-Royce limousine; that is, high quality in the sense of superior workmanship and expensive materials. But there are also other possibilities. Honda, for example, has a positive reputation because the quality of their cars consistently meets expectations time after time. Consistently meeting expectations is one way of showing that you both see the game in the same way.

Let us continue with our Honda example. They have a positive reputation for cars, but they also make other goods, including lawnmowers. How might they induce a prospective customer to make a commitment to buy a Honda lawnmower? A positive reputation takes time to establish, but Honda signals its commitment to produce quality lawnmowers by offering a seven-year warranty[6]. This demonstrates the company's commitment to the reliability of its product because seven years is a lengthy period. It is a credible commitment because failure to deliver under the terms of the warranty would result in legal sanctions. It is also a credible commitment because if users of Honda's lawnmowers were making claims under the warranty very often, then this would be very embarrassing – and expensive – for Honda. They could not afford the downside of lots of warranty claims.

Thus Honda has structured a situation which induces commitments from others (in this example, customers: prospective buyers of lawnmowers) by first making a credible commitment themselves. Commitments are credible when they are costly not to fulfil. Repeated credible commitments, publically made, build a reputation. A positive track record – a positive reputation – will take longest to establish in those markets where it is most valuable.

Of course, as soon as a commitment falters and a reciprocal commitment is disappointed, then the reputation is gone and Prisoner's-Dilemma logic reasserts itself. This is why positive reputations are so hard to build, so jealously guarded, and so quickly lost.

THE PRISONER'S DILEMMA AND THE EXAMPLE OF REALCASE LTD

We know that repeated encounters (lots of meetings) do not themselves break the Prisoner's Dilemma. Rather, as we have seen, the way out of the dilemma is through making a credible commitment, and this can entail closing off options so as to encourage the other party to reciprocate. The inability to make commitments condemns the prisoners to long periods of incarceration.

Similarly, in business, it is the job of managers so to structure and restructure human interactions that these pathological problems do not arise. This is through a shared picture of a long-term relationship – the parties see the game that they are playing in the same way. Each party feels protected from opportunism, and makes – and enables – the gains from making a commitment.

The ironic but crucial insight is that the benefits come only from closing down options in order to make credible commitments. This is the necessary basis for a long-term relationship enabled by parties seeing the game in the same way. Quality relationships are the appropriate response to complexity: it requires investment in the other party to evoke a reciprocal response. There is no short-cut.

How do parties come to see the game in the same way?

Think back to Realcase Ltd. The narrative of their business plan is to develop high-quality widgets that they can sell for high prices, where high quality is a combination of high craftsmanship and high specification. Realcase Ltd has a classic Prisoner's Dilemma to overcome.

Suppose you are a prospective business customer of Realcase Ltd; let us call you Might Buy Ltd. You are happy to offer a high price provided that you receive a high quality widget in return. The ideal for you would be to get high quality in return for a low price, but the worst possible outcome would be to get low quality in return for your high price. You do not want low quality, but better to pay a low price for it than a high one.

For Realcase Ltd, the ideal outcome would be to achieve a high price for low quality, but the worst outcome would be the reverse: a low price for high quality. It would be better to get a low price for low quality, but this is not their chosen business path, and what they are after is to achieve a high price for high quality. After all, Realcase Ltd reasons, if they were to deliver low quality for this high price, they would be most unlikely to get any repeat business and word would spread, losing them customers. Realcase Ltd's business plan would be in ruins.

Might Buy Ltd's and Realcase Ltd's high/low price v. high/low quality grid looks like this:

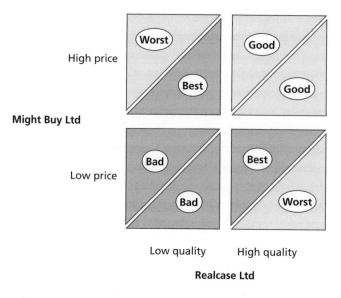

Figure 14.2

The best outcome is that Might Buy Ltd offers a high price, and gets in return from Realcase Ltd high quality; but how does the reasoning go? Might Buy Ltd thinks about what it should do: offer a low price or offer a high price. Its choice depends upon what Realcase Ltd chooses to do. If Realcase Ltd provides low quality, then it would be better for Might Buy Ltd to offer a low price. What if Realcase Ltd offers high quality? Well, Might Buy Ltd reasons, it would still be better for Might Buy Ltd to offer a low price. So, Might Buy Ltd concludes, whichever choice Realcase Ltd makes, it would pay Might Buy Ltd to offer a low price and so this is what it decides to do.

Now put yourself in Realcase Ltd's shoes. They reason in exactly the same way: whichever choice Might Buy Ltd makes, it pays Realcase Ltd to offer low quality. So we end up with low quality for a low price and neither company is content. Their businesses not only miss out on a good outcome, they are damaged as well.

Realcase Ltd needs to consider how it will alter the pay-off structure by making a commitment to induce a reciprocating commitment from Might Buy Ltd. Repeated encounters might help to communicate to the prospective customer that Realcase Ltd sees the game as a long haul and so is seeking repeat business. If Might Buy Ltd believes this, then they might be induced to commit – to take a risk. But on their own, repeated encounters (lots of telephone calls from the sales team, a blizzard of promotional brochures, a sales pitch) will not affect the logical structure of the situation.

However, Realcase Ltd wants to build a team of skilled client relationship managers – and they can help. They can communicate to clients how Realcase Ltd sees the game; they can demonstrate a keen interest in finding out how the customer sees the game; they can highlight and emphasise areas of shared views; they can use what they learn to construct pertinent situations that will work in terms of inducing reciprocating commitments; they will learn how the pay-off structure can be changed to good effect.

To change the pay-off, Realcase Ltd could provide a lengthy warranty or offer money back guarantees. These would be credible demonstrations of faith in the widgets as a product, signalling that Realcase Ltd is in for an extended game. Over time, the positive testimony of other customers can be used to evidence a good reputation with a view to generating trust and inducing prospective customers to make commitments and offer high prices.

In parallel, Might Buy Ltd could signal commitment by contracting to place an order at a high price, provided that an example widget that it takes on approval performs as specified. Realcase Ltd's easy readiness to agree to such a process would signal to Might Buy Ltd its confidence in what it produces.

Trust is beginning to be built.

'OH, MR PORTER!'

We can now understand why our discussion of Porter's Five Forces in Chapter 5 is so frequently laced with references to the importance of relationships.

On the basis of his analysis, you might well think that getting your business to be in a very powerful position relative to, say, your customers would be highly desirable. However, such an asymmetry of power makes it very difficult to create the conditions necessary to break away from the Prisoner's-Dilemma dynamic. Because the business is so powerful, it is hard to make credible commitments that induce reciprocal commitments from relatively weak customers.

This is because, from the perspective of the customer, it is not clear what promise could be made that would be too costly for a powerful supplier to break when it suited them.

This is a problem that banks have. What is the worst that an individual customer can do if he or she is unhappy with their bank? The customer can take his or her custom away and give it to a rival bank. The profits of the bank that has lost the customer would not be affected, even to three decimal places. The customer knows this. So if a bank says it really wants the best for its customer or promises to be there when the customer needs them most, the declared commitment lacks credibility because the worst cost the bank could incur by not keeping that promise – the loss of the customer to a rival bank – is no cost at all.

What about the miscreant bank's reputation? Well, for as long as the reputation of banks is low anyway, how much worse for them can it get? Perhaps the news of poor treatment will spread, and so the poorly-behaving bank will lose not just the individual customer, but lots of customers. Even if the individual invested time and energy into a campaign – which would be very unlikely – this is not how bank customers typically behave. Most customers are inert, and for as long as there persists the reputation that all banks are 'much of a muchness', the potential cost of poor customer treatment in terms of a mass loss of customers remains, in the assessment of the individual customer, much more theoretical than real.

The asymmetries of power in the banking industry are such that Prisoner's-Dilemma-type problems are so difficult to solve. You might study Porter's Five Forces analysis and think, if you were a bank yourself, that this is good. But it is a Pyrrhic victory. This is why there are external efforts to change the pay-off structure. The regulator, the Financial Services Authority (FSA), has introduced obligatory rules on banks to 'Treat Customers Fairly' and the FSA will fine banks who fail to live up to the rules. The fines increase the costs for the banks and so alter the pay-off structure, just as the police try to shift the pay-off structure when enticing informants to grass on their gangsterish bosses[7].

The difficulties posed by being so powerful in relation to any one customer for solving Prisoner's-Dilemma-type problems are the flip side of the relationship with suppliers. Huge asymmetries of power are in fact, difficult for both parties. Once again, it is about your business and your suppliers either seeing the game in the same way to form the basis of a fruitful, trusting relationship, or dealing with each other on a purely transactional basis that is closely governed by carefully drafted contracts. However, as we have already noted, no contract can oblige the parties to be open and flexible and accommodating, and if your relationships with suppliers are wholly described by contracts, your business will have failed to create anything distinctive. This is important where a business has outsourced activities that are important to its business. A Service Level Agreement (SLA) is a necessary under-pinning of the relationship, but as with any legal document, no SLA can compel such a vital supplier to go the extra mile. An SLA has to sit in the context of a trusting relationship if such value-enhancing distinctiveness is to be achieved.

This is why outsourcing any of your business's activities has to be considered with great care. It is not just about ensuring that the provider has the competencies to undertake the activities effectively and to standard; it is also, very importantly, about ensuring that your business has the competencies to build and sustain lasting and trusting relationships. Bear in mind that the longer an outsourced relationship exists, the harder it is to switch to another provider or to repatriate the activity in-house. The supplier knows this. Are you confident that your business can build the sort of relationship with the supplier that will protect you from them exploiting this to their advantage and to your disadvantage in the future in a Prisoner's Dilemma kind of way? Remember: people will move on, and the counter-parties that you got on with so well during courtship will not necessarily be the same as the ones who will be involved in the marriage after the initial honeymoon. In the beginning, you will talk to people who are incentivised (pressurised?) to get your custom. Later, when the supplier has got your custom, you will be dealing with people who will be under pressure to maximise their income. Can you, over the long term, continually structure and restructure the dealings between your business and your supplier so that the pay-off keeps the relationship positive and Prisoner's-Dilemma-free? If you do consider outsourcing, there are many factors to get right, but please do not embark on any outsourcing until you can answer this question affirmatively with great confidence.

If, on the other hand, you are a provider of outsourced services, then you can now understand the cast of mind of your prospective clients. You can begin to work out what sort of commitments you might need to make to induce a reciprocating commitment from your prospective client, given how they view the game. Changing the pay-off structure so that your client wants to commit to having a long-term relationship with your business in the face of the vulnerabilities they will feel will be the key to your business success as an 'outsourcee'.

You will recall that Realcase Ltd is on the brink of finalising an exclusive contract with the supplier of bespoke machinery that will give the business a real advantage over its rivals. The exclusivity is a source of enduring distinctiveness. However, if the distinctiveness is valuable enough, there is nothing to stop a rival to the supplier developing similar machinery and making that available to Realcase Ltd's competitors, even if Realcase's own supplier is tied to Realcase. Moreover, although the exclusive contract is useful and valuable, it will not alone be a source of all the value that could be gained unless there is a positive, committed and reciprocated relationship that surrounds it. 'Where there is a will, there is a way', and if the supplier is minded ever to drag its heels to find ways out of its contracted obligations, then it no doubt could do so. Litigation rarely ends in anything other than tears.

You can see that, just as with managing customer relationships, there is much more to managing supplier relationships that merely negotiating on the terms of trade.

Turning to other players in Porter's analysis of industry structure, let us consider competitor rivalry. It is the Prisoner-Dilemma dynamic that can drive ruinous price wars. You might be tempted to reduce your prices in the hope that your competitor will go out of business. What does your competitor do? If it keeps prices high, then it could lose market share to your business and, yes, it could ultimately go to the wall. So it decides to cut its prices and now both your business and your competitor have kept your respective market shares but you are both making lower profits.

What does your business do now? If you raise your prices, your business will become vulnerable to the very thing you were trying to inflict on your competitor. Your rival, with lower prices than you, could steal market share away from your business and *you* could go to the wall! Do you reduce your prices yet further? But your competitor will feel obliged to follow suit, thus cutting the profits of both your businesses without gaining market share, and you could *both* end up going to the wall.

In fact, in response to your first reduction in prices, your competitor might not just cuts its own prices to match; it might go even further and reduce its prices beneath yours. This might be the way in which your rival tries to signal its determination to be an aggressive competitor. However this reputation for aggressive responses is established, if a player could make its rivals believe that it would react strongly against them, then this alone could be sufficient to dissuade them from behaving precipitously. In this example, your business would be disinclined to embark on cutting prices because you would know that your rival would react aggressively, ultimately harming your business in ways that make any gains entirely elusive.

Of course, this would also be a useful reputation for your business to establish, especially if you are operating in price-sensitive markets.

However, there is no guarantee that all – or any – of your competitors will behave rationally. In such circumstances, your best protection is the quality of your relationships with your stakeholders, most especially with your customers. Your business needs to create the conditions in which the lure of lower prices will not be valued as highly as the common view of the game that your customers have with your business, and the benefits that subsequently flow from reciprocated commitments.

Hence for a business like Realcase Ltd with a dedicated team of client relationship managers, the challenge of customer retention will be a very important source of SMART objectives on the balanced scorecards of the team's individual members.

A CRISIS OF FAITH WITHIN REASON

If there is no guarantee that your competitors will behave rationally, there is certainly no guarantee that your business's suppliers or customers or staff or funders will behave rationally, especially when market conditions are difficult or when there is a crisis. Will they flee, fight or freeze? You need to know.

To keep the support of every key person, group and stakeholder when in a crisis, you have to convince them that you are on top of things. Reflect back to them some of their views on what you should do. As William J. H. Boetcker says: 'Confidence is the foundation for all business relations. The degree of confidence a man has in others, and the degree of confidence others have in him, determines a man's standing in the commercial and industrial world.'

So, stakeholder by stakeholder assess your supporting network. How will your suppliers react, one by one? How will your clients react, one by one? How will your funding partners react, one by one? Each of them will assess your reaction to the crisis and they will react accordingly. A bank will tighten its exposure to you if you do not have a crisis management plan or contingency plan – they will expect to see cost-control measures (just remember to target 'bad costs' and not 'good costs' – see Chapter 9) and evidence that you have really thought through tough 'what if?' questions like: 'What would your business do if you lost your best customer?'; 'What would your business do if sales revenue fell by 30 per cent?'; 'What would your business do if you had to lay off a quarter of your people?'. Bankers are fairly straightforward creatures.

Suppliers will expect loyalty, partnership and consideration: teamwork is everything. They will expect dialogue and discussion so that the full value chain is not put at risk – explain to them that you are squeezing trade terms with clients to pass on the benefits to them. Remember that a failure in a critical supplier line can kill your business too (and this is more than just a cash issue).

How will your clients react, and which ones when? Assess their vulnerability to downturn. Consider their business model with the same rigour that you assess your own. Consider seeking new clients as others suffer. Renegotiate longer contracts at a discount with the more resilient clients. Dump the bad ones before they dump you, owing you cash. Be intelligently brutal – this is about leveraging Prisoner-Dilemma-type dynamics in your business's favour. Your business gets a reputation for rewarding constructive customer behaviours and punishing negative ones. You are actively managing the pay-off structure.

Remember – and this is important – making commitments is not only about being cuddly and warm. It can also be about being steely and determined. The purpose is to enable the other party to make confident predictions about your future behaviours so that they themselves feel able to commit confidently to certain behaviours rather than other ones.

Look within your business as well.

Especially in crisis times, your business simply cannot afford to hang on to people who do not link directly to income generation. Signal your control of costs through some simple measures and lead by personal example (no more first class train travel, for instance). Get your people to follow the lead. They must feel that times are hard and that they can influence the business even more so than when times are good – have another look at Chapter 9, p. 136.

Meet and discuss your plans with key owners and collaborators (shareholders or business partners). How are their nerves? Are they steady? Can *you* steady them? If 'no', then seek out new partners with experience.

Network closely with competitors (I understand that this will strike you as counter-intuitive), because severe crises affect an industry, a local community. Work with them and the local business clubs and local government to seek out opportunities to reduce local business rates, for example, to alleviate pressures by means of payment holidays, shared supply agreements, combined cost management, innovative ways to combine resources for non-core activities (perhaps HR or IT support, etc.).

When times are volatile or when economic conditions are tough, people's reactions can be hard to predict. Longstanding assumptions cannot be regarded as safe. The agility of your business's management team to see change, react to change and drive value from change is the key issue, particularly if you are a small business with little to fall back on. When the wind blows, fly a kite. When the wind stops, go to a pub.

EVERYONE IS THE SAME: AN INDIVIDUAL

Prisoner's-Dilemma-type problems lurk in employer/employee and employee/employee relationships. They relate to issues of what level of pay and rewards to give to workers (compared with what rival businesses might offer), and they also include the same sort of holding back-versus-forthcoming challenges that are faced by prospective joint ventures and alliances. For example, you can imagine an employee asking her/himself: 'Why should I help so-and-so department when it would just make that team look good and distract me from my own work? I won't help them'. And, yes, you've got it, so-and-so department refuses to help the employee on the basis of exactly the same reasoning. So no one helps anyone and the business, after a period of fraughtness and struggle, implodes.

It is because the Prisoner's Dilemma features in these internal people interactions that first, I stressed in Chapter 11 the vital importance of communication with your people and of establishing clear links between behaviours and results; and secondly, I emphasised in Chapter 13 that a positive approach to the life-balance wheel is necessary not only for yourself, but also for your people.

These are the ways in which the game can be seen in the same way by employer and employee, by leader and led, by colleagues with colleagues. Collaborative relationships, founded on trust, that produce significant business outcomes and implement the business plan successfully, are thus built. You can get a lot down in a job description and even a balanced scorecard, but all these will still not capture the need for an employee to be innovative, flexible, positive in attitude and deed, and prepared to go the extra mile. These are voluntarily given commitments that it is the business's task to induce by making credible commitments itself. What if an employee lets you down? You simply have to take this risk. It is a lesser risk to your business than any alternative.

A TIP FOR PRACTICAL ACTION: BUBBLE-BURSTING

At the end of every week draw a map of your key business relationships. It might look something Figure 14.3:

You should make your relationship map relevant to you and your business.

Once you have drawn your relationship map, consider which relationships are not as you would want them to be.

By this is meant that the relationships are not as they should be for the successful implementation of your business plan. There might have been an interaction that you feel finished less than ideally, or perhaps the relationship has not received any attention lately. You may feel a conversation or a meeting is overdue or is otherwise

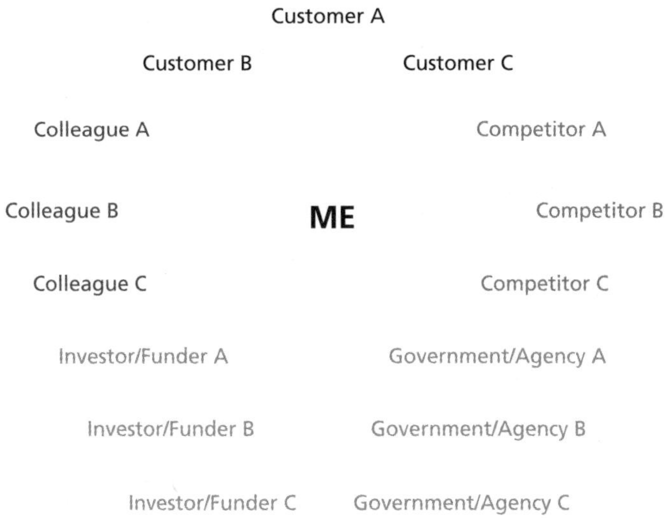

Customer A

Customer B   Customer C

Colleague A   Competitor A

Colleague B   **ME**   Competitor B

Colleague C   Competitor C

Investor/Funder A   Government/Agency A

Investor/Funder B   Government/Agency B

Investor/Funder C   Government/Agency C

Figure 14.3

needed, either from your point of view or theirs. Perhaps you are in crisis mode and you need to work at the relationship (see earlier). Or you might judge that there is a risk of Prisoner's-Dilemma type problems arising and you need to invest some of yourself into the relationship. The need might be yours or the other party's – you might have a benefit to bestow. In short, there could be lots of reasons why the relationship is not where it needs to be.

Put a ring around the counter-party where this is the case, as shown in Figure 14.4 (overleaf).

This signifies that the relationship is in a 'bubble'. If it helps, think in terms of scoring your key relationships – key to the successful implementation of your business plan – with a mark out of 10. As these are your key business relationships, you should be aiming for 10 out of 10 with every one of them. In practice, you will be continually working at them. Any score of, say, less than 8 out of 10 signifies a relationship that demands your attention as a priority.

You might end up with something like this:

The relationships that are put in a bubble – that is, the relationships which are not where they need to be – will vary from week to week. I recommend that you do this exercise every week because, in the fast-moving world of business, relationships are very dynamic.

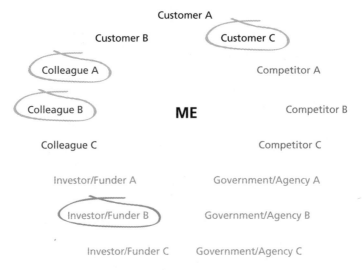

Figure 14.4

Your task in the coming week is to liberate the sub-optimal relationships (there are four in this illustrative example) from the enclosing ring that you have drawn around them: to burst the entrapping bubble.

This will require a positive action on your part – a conversation, a meeting, an act of support or help, a contribution to the other's success: 'You have to build the Emotional Bank Accounts that create a commerce between hearts'[8].

Review your relationship map a week later (who gets on the map might change), scoring each one out of 10 if that helps you make your assessment, draw bubbles around the relationships that are not where they need to be and, once again, take action to burst the bubbles. This bubble-bursting is a continual – and absolutely vital – activity for the successful implementation of your business plan[9].

Key takeaways from Chapter 14

1   Your business will create value by developing relationships that others are unable to make.

2   Understand that business success requires that your business forms and sustains winning relationships that are founded on trust. Trusting relationships require commitment. And making a commitment is necessary to induce a reciprocating commitment.

3   Do this by:
    a.   putting yourself in the other person's shoes (taking your own ones off first!);
    b.   seeking 'first to understand, then to be understood'[10];
    c.   being dependable;
    d.   communicating regularly – ideally face-to-face – so that you and your counter-party know you are both in a long-term, repeat game that you see in the same way;
    e.   communicating clearly – ideally face-to-face – so that you all know the benefits that flow from certain sets of behaviours rather than others;
    f.   re-shaping the pay-off structure so as to encourage those behaviours that produce the optimal outcomes;
    g.   recognising that making commitments is not simply synonymous with being cuddly and warm; it can mean being steely and determined. The key is making commitments that induce confidence in others to commit confidently to certain behaviours rather than others;
    h.   networking widely amongst all your stakeholders and contacts.

4   Act on the 'Four Cs' to build quality relationships:
    a.   continuity
    b.   communication
    c.   consequences
    d.   commitment

5   Managing your business successfully is about inspiring and showing confidence.

6   Burst bubbles actively.

Notes and References

1   Kay, J., *Foundations of Corporate Success*. p. 31. Oxford: Oxford University Press, 1993. I shall be drawing considerably from John Kay's discussion of the conceptual underpinnings of relationship management; his treatment is clear and insightful.

2   There is a very extensive literature on the Prisoner's Dilemma. It captures a notion in game theory, and originated with Merrill

Flood and Melvin Dresher when working at RAND Corporation in 1950. The form that we shall be discussing was created by the mathematician Albert Tucker. It was subjected to sustained experimental investigation in Axelrod, R., *The Evolution of Cooperation*, New York: Basic Books, 1984. My own thinking about the Prisoner's Dilemma has been heavily shaped by John Kay's book, *op. cit.*, pp. 31-61.

3   Johnson, G., and Scholes, K. *Exploring Corporate Strategy* 6th ed., p. 383. Harlow: Prentice Hall, 2002.

4   Hamel, G., Doz, Y., and Prahalad, C.K. 'Collaborate with Your Competitors – and Win', *Harvard Business Review*. Jan-Feb, 1989, reprinted in de Wit, R., and Meyer, R. *Strategy Synthesis: Resolving Strategy Paradoxes to Create Competitive Advantage*. London: Thomson, 1999.

5   This shared commitment was crucial. Commenting on the Rover/Honda alliance in 1992, a business thinker wrote: 'Rover's economic survival depended upon the alliance ... and its commitment has been high from the outset: this was less important from Honda's viewpoint. However, the Japanese company has shown an equal degree of commitment throughout, and the alliance has prospered.' Faulkner, D. 'Strategic Alliances: Co-operation for Competition' in Faulkner, D., and Johnson, G. *The Challenge of Strategic Management*. p. 137. London: Kogan Page, 1992.

6   See www.honda.co.uk

7   One bank, Lloyds TSB, did try to alter the dynamics of its industry as far as business customers were concerned. It reasoned that its success as a business depended on the prior success of their SME customers. To project this understanding as a credible commitment to the market, it produced a set of offers, plus a highly innovative customer diagnostic tool called RouteMap, and much marketing literature that were launched in 2001. To reinforce the message that the bank was about helping SMEs achieve success in whatever terms they define, there was even a Web portal called success4business. If SME customers could come to believe that the bank did indeed see its success as a consequence of theirs, and not as a rival to it, then the customers could come to believe that they and the bank wanted the same thing. In short, they see the

game in the same way. Sadly, however, after three years, Lloyds TSB pulled away from that set of offers, RouteMap was withdrawn, and the success4business portal no longer exists.

8   Covey, S. *The 7 Habits of Highly Effective People*. p. 239. London: Simon & Schuster, 1999.

9   So long as you engage in this activity regularly (I recommend weekly), I really do not mind if you prefer to think in terms of a different metaphor from that of bubble-bursting. Perhaps you think you are drawing walls, and so are actively wall-smashing. That is fine by me. Or perhaps you prefer to draw lines on your map to the relationships that you feel are indeed where they need to be, leaving the other, sub-optimal relationships adrift. In this case you might prefer to think in terms of bridge-building. Again, I really do not mind what you call it or what metaphor you like best: it is what works for you that counts. It is in right actions that your business will succeed, not right intentions.

10   Covey, S., *op. cit.*, habit 5.

Chapter 15
Presenting Your Business Plan

'There are three things to aim at in public speaking: first, to get into your subject, then to get your subject into yourself, and lastly, to get your subject into the heart of your audience.' – Alexander Gregg

GIVING A GOOD TALKING TO

You have developed some fantastic ideas during your hard work at business planning. By putting these ideas down on paper in a coherent business plan, you have turned your ideas into promises.

Now the time has come to turn your promises into commitments by telling other people about them.

As we learned in Chapter 14, commitments received can only be induced by commitments given. Proclaiming what you and your business are going to do – what it is aiming for, where it is headed, how it will travel there, what fruits of success it will enjoy – is a crucial step in making traction on reality more likely, on making your business plan actually happen. You are declaring, publically, your commitment to the vision and to the journey. You are making a public declaration of commitment to service, to – and make no bones about it – very hard slog. It really does have to matter to you.

It is also time to seek out reciprocating commitments. These might be a commitment of funds and advice from an investor, a commitment of a loan or overdraft from a bank, a commitment of monies or subsidies from a grant-giving agency, or a commitment of time, energy and talent from your people. (There is another possibility: perhaps you are looking to commit yourself to a new venture and so your business plan is, in this case, a sales prospectus and you are looking for another business or entrepreneur to commit to purchasing your business.)

Each audience is different, so how you tell them about your business plan has to be modified to reflect this. There is a large measure of commonality, but the differences are important. So first, *know your audience.*

This chapter will give you some advice on how to tell each different type of audience about your business plan in the most effective way. You need to think about what the audiences have in common and also how they are different.

And you need to think through something that, I would not be at all surprised, is giving you a real headache at the moment. It is perfectly natural and understandable. But we need to work together to get rid of it.

HEAD ACHES?: NOTING FACTS FASTER, THEN PLAN A WIN

If your head aches, I can understand. You have a sense of what you want to do, roughly. You know there are customers for your product, roughly. You know your business will grow big, roughly.

Yet along comes a business adviser (or similar) who then presses you with questions like: 'What will be your level of sales in three years' time?'; 'Who are your major competitors?'; 'What is your breakeven level?'; 'What will be the next product after this one?'; 'What will be your rate of customer acquisition?'; 'Where will you expand?' So many questions!

You do not have the answers. It is a cacophony of interrogation – and enough to give anyone a headache! You plead with your questioner: 'How on earth can I be expected to know the answers to these questions?'

'Look,' you go on to say, 'I know quite a few things – roughly. I have a great product which I'm sure is going to be big. It just feels right. I shall feel my way and the rest will evolve as I go along.'

'After all,' – you are warming to your theme now – 'it's like driving a car. I am concentrating on looking ahead – this is why the windscreen is so much bigger than the rear-view mirror. And, just like driving, I can successfully make progress even when it is dark. I can't see very far ahead – certainly not my end destination – but I can still make my way perfectly well looking within the rolling distance illuminated by my headlights. I don't know how many right turns I shall make in the journey, nor how many left, but I shall be able to make them as necessary when the time comes.'

'Besides,' – you feel on a roll now – 'Bill Gates didn't start Microsoft with a load of prior customer research. When Richard Branson started his business by using a public telephone box as his office, he didn't have a detailed competitor analysis tucked under his arm. Analysis leads to paralysis and I've got to keep spontaneous and adaptable. You ask about how I am going to get funding? Well, if access to capital is limited, then that just means I'll have fewer competitors. Besides, the best funding comes from customers, not external investors. So I'm focused on selling – that's *my* market research. I've got lots and lots of hard work to do. So stop giving me a headache!'

You can wrap this well-meaning but misplaced rant in the garb of academic credibility by thrusting in front of your questioner (tormentor?) a book by Amar V. Bhidé called *The Origin and Evolution of New Businesses*, and pointing to Chapter 2, 'Planning vs. Opportunistic Adaptation'[1].

I am absolutely convinced about the benefits of business planning but even so, it is right that I am open to the other 'one' that makes 1 + 1 = 3 (see Chapter 13); after all, I might be concentrating on the duck and Bhidé might be seeing a rabbit.

And that is exactly what is happening here. The title of Bhidé's Chapter 2 – 'Planning vs. Opportunistic Adaptation' – is setting up a false pair of opposites. Just as there is both the duck and the rabbit, so there is both planning and opportunistic adaptation. The one delineates the other. We are familiar enough with the process of planning to know that it by no means precludes opportunistic adaptation. Indeed, we can go further. One of the main benefits of engaging in the process of business planning is that the circumstances for opportunistic adaptation can be recognised as such only in the context of having engaged in business planning (through a process as described by this book). Future purposes give present meaning. Of course your business has to adapt opportunistically, but how are you to identify, in the maelstrom of modern business life, what is just such an opportunity to make a telling adaptation unless you have a context, an unfolding narrative that you are working towards realising?

It as though Bhidé sees 'planning' in the way we called 'old fashioned' in Chapter 10; that is, a simple linear engineering process that runs the business along a set of rails. In truth, of course, the process of business planning is a craft process. It is a non-linear, exploratory, emergent process. As we said in Chapter 8 and repeated in Chapter 10, the essence of successful business planning consists in the coherent, systematic and deliberate working out of your business's vision into the marketplace. There is no 'versus' between this and 'opportunistic adaptation'.

Let us turn to the task of relieving your headache. Once you latch on to this understanding of the process of business planning, the 'interrogation' of your business starts to make sense. The honest effort to answer the questions as best you can will necessarily bring with it a better understanding of your business and its marketplace. Of course the specific answers that you give will turn out to be wrong because, as Niels Bohr, the Nobel Prize-winning physicist said: 'Prediction is very difficult, especially if it's about the future.' But the process of business planning is no mere crystal-ball-gazing: it is about acquiring insights about your business and its context so that you can build added value.

Investors, bankers and backers are actually very sensible people. When they ask you, for example, 'What will be your level of sales next year?' and you reply '£1.2 million' (or whatever you believe the truth to be), they all know that the actual result will not be exactly £1.2 million. This is not because they do not care for accuracy or that they pathologically disbelieve everything you say, it is because they know the world works in a complicated way and that, therefore, detailed predictions will always be confounded by the natural workings (not even the quirks) of the business world.

What these people are really interested in is the processes of research, analysis and synthesis that led you to the working belief that next year's sales will be (in the order of) £1.2 million. Are the assumptions that you have made reasonable? Are you basing your view on relevant data? Are your inferences from the data logical, plausible and coherent? Have you considered what you would do if sales turned out to be, not £1.2 million, but only £¾ million? And what would be the impacts on your business if sales grew to £2 million?

The people who ask questions like these are wanting to establish whether or not you know your way around your business confidently, broad-mindedly and with good understanding.

When reviewing progress, they want to know that you are monitoring performance closely and intelligently, and especially that you take prompt action to address underperformance.

Even when their questions are about numbers, it is still you and your team they are really keen to assess. Of course the numbers have to stand up – you will not get an investment or a loan if they do not – but they are doing the equivalent of what we talked about in Chapter 13: they are asking you for a cup of coffee. Do not protest that you are not thirsty; do not complain that it is impossible to forecast what your business will achieve in the future. Do not rely on the mere hope that 'things will sort themselves out'. Consider *context, content and message*: give yourself a gap between stimulus and response (both during your encounter and beforehand!).

So see the questions for what they are: a challenge to be overcome by the proper engagement with the process of business planning. They are the currency of a business conversation between adults, not children.

Unusually talented and undoubtedly hard-working individuals like Bill Gates or Richard Branson may well have created hugely successful businesses without all of the formal activities that I have described as part and parcel of the process of business planning. But there is no doubt that, however they achieved it, they had (and still have) a wonderfully insightful understanding of their business and its context. It is the acquisition of this insightful and actionable understanding of your own business that is what you are really after. It is just that for me – and perhaps you as well – it takes the engagement with the formal activities that I have described to get there.

I am not a business archaeologist. I do not know exactly how many potentially great businesses have left their remains in the dirt of ruin and collapse for want of an honest and hard-working engagement with the process of business planning. I do not know how many enthusiastic and ambitious businesses are now just fossilised bones, desiccated by the wind of arid thinking that saw no point in rigorous enquiry, hard thinking, and purposeful action.

This is the cure for your headache – if you are suffering from one. Accumulate lots of facts, think hard, and talk to wise people. Your vision deserves nothing less. Your future vision commands an imperative over your present activities. Acting on that is the surest way to overcome your headache and get on with business life.

GUILTY UNTIL YOU PROVE YOURSELF INNOCENT

Your audience – an investor, banker, grant-giver, partner, staff, corporate boss, or purchaser – want to be involved in success. They do not want to miss out. If you hold out to them the realistic prospect of a great opportunity, then you will win them over.

However, investors, bankers and grant-givers hear multitudes of business stories that are really fantasy tales. Your staff want to know that this is a meaningful journey before them, not a faddish flavour of the month. Your boss will (should!) want to know the truth, not what you think he or she wants to hear. A purchaser wants to know that, of all the businesses they could take the plunge with, they will not do better than yours. (By 'plunge', I mean 'to commit to purchase': it is not a forecast about their fortunes!)

This means, not cynicism, but scepticism. Scepticism is the mind of successful business people in a state of poise. You have to have a real passion for business truth to maintain a sceptical bearing. Scepticism – an open mind but not an empty one – is the disposition that winnows the grains of deep business insight from the chaff of deep wishful nonsense. You will meet sceptical backers. So do not be fazed by this; just be ready.

Your audience will start with the working assumption that you do not know what you are talking about. They do this because if they start there, and yet you can bring them round to take a positive view of you and your business, then you really must have something interesting and exciting. So recognise where your audience is starting from so that you concentrate your efforts to best effect. If you win them over from that starting point rather than a Pollyanna one, then you will also win much more enthusiastic and committed support. Consider it to be your opportunity.

At the outset, your audience will think:

- you and your team do not have the passion, energy, experience and business nous to succeed;

- your business will not get enough sales and not enough customers to generate the income that you claim;
- your costs are underestimated and will not keep a tight enough grip on margins;
- you have underestimated your competition and are blissfully ignorant of the harm they could do to your business;
- your growth forecasts are just wishful thinking clothed in silly numbers, and you have seriously exaggerated the size of the potential market both now and several years hence;
- you and your mates like your product but you have not demonstrated that you are solving real customers' problems on any kind of scale;
- you will bore us: either you will give only skimpy details or you will go on and on about irrelevant stuff;
- you won't know your stuff and will get defensive under questioning;
- you know it all and won't take advice;
- you won't give us any idea of our return and what our exit is;
- either you won't know what you want from us, or you want too much!

How do you best respond?

It is best to get your response in first. By this is meant that there is no short-cut: you must prepare, prepare, prepare! Know your stuff intimately. Commit important facts and numbers to memory. Anticipate the hardest questions you can and force yourself to mouth out loud what your answers would be. Rehearse in front of the shaving mirror (if you are a man) or the make-up mirror (if you are a woman or man). Ask family, friends and colleagues to role-play being the audience and deliver your lines in front of them. Get them to ask questions – if they do not understand anything, your intended audience will not understand it either.

This is all how you 'get your subject into yourself', as Alexander Gregg rightly commends. As for getting 'your subject into the heart of your audience', this is about delivery and also about understanding who your audience is in advance. Find out as much as you can about them. What is on their minds? How do they approach things? Who has experience of presenting to them before and what do they advise?

Let us look again at their presumptions of 'guilt' and what you can do to prove your 'innocence':

PRESUMPTION	RESPONSE
You and your team do not have the passion, energy, experience and business nous to succeed.	■ Be sure to explain the experience (especially past successes) and track record of the members of the team, pertinent to the business plan. ■ If there are gaps, acknowledge them and explain how they are being filled (e.g. access to expert advice). ■ If you can quote evidence for your people's high motivation and engagement (e.g. the results of an internal survey), then say that the whole team is very positive, engaged and motivated. ■ Make heartfelt statements of commitment: it will come out in your tone and body language. Combine passion with statesmanlike gravitas – see Chapter 8.
Your business will not get enough sales and not enough customers to generate the income that you claim.	■ Your sales forecasts should be ambitious but not ludicrous, otherwise you will not be taken seriously. ■ Pick out key pieces of supporting evidence from customer research and allude to relevant local and market conditions – see Chapter 5. ■ Be clear about the size of the market and how you will compete in it. ■ The results from any pilot or past record would be very useful here, as would any confirmed orders (not just letters expressing polite interest), and key statistics around new customer acquisition.

PRESUMPTION	RESPONSE
Your costs are underestimated and will not keep a tight enough grip on margins.	■ This is a good opportunity to show your command of the numbers. Talk about your top three areas of costs and the evidence that backs up your forecasts. ■ If you are embarking upon a cost-cutting programme, explain the key actions and why they will have the impacts expected (remember: cut 'bad' costs, not 'good' costs – see Chapter 9). ■ Talking about how you will monitor financial performance closely as part of your normal management activities will give reassurance.
You have underestimated your competition and are blissfully ignorant of the harm they could do to your business.	■ Insights from your Porter Five-Forces analysis will be relevant here. ■ Talking through the key findings from your SWOT comparison will give you the opportunity to explain how you will combat your competitors' strengths and exploit their weaknesses. ■ Talk about the counter-moves that you think your competitors will make, what impacts these will have, and how you will respond. ■ If you have any protections, such as patents, exclusive contracts (like Realcase Ltd has), rare competencies and unique features (e.g. location), then this is the time to trumpet them.

PRESUMPTION	RESPONSE
Your growth forecasts are just wishful thinking clothed in silly numbers, and you have seriously exaggerated the size of the potential market both now and several years hence.	■ You will not be fazed by this because you will have already asked yourself 'what would have to be true for things to be as I say them to be?' – see Chapter 10. So reveal your thinking with confidence, showing how the key assumptions are well-founded. This will protect you from over-inflating the potential of your business and from underestimating what it takes to take your product or service forward. ■ Talking through your 'flying-bricks' graphics (see Chapter 10) is a great way of addressing this, as they link outcomes to actions and effects to causes, and show a real understanding of the levers at work within your business. ■ A mix of relevant customer research plus some considered insights from your PEST and Five-Forces analyses will show the quality of your business thinking. ■ Talking through a strong and coherent (and contradiction-free) business narrative with a robust 'strategic logic' (see the Notes and References to Chapter 10, note 7) is your best response.
You and your mates like your product but you have not demonstrated that you are solving real customers' problems on any kind of scale.	■ You will be ready for this because you asked yourself (and answered!) lots of customer-related questions in Chapter 6, most particularly: 'Why do my customers buy from me? What is important to them?' Backers are always keen to know what your business's USP (unique selling proposition) is. ■ The findings from customer research and customer feedback are relevant here. ■ And nobody can argue with facts established by a proven track record – so be sure to know your facts and figures.

PRESUMPTION	RESPONSE
You will bore us: either you will give only skimpy details or you will go on and on about irrelevant stuff.	■ It is a balance: ideally your audience will have had the opportunity to read through your business plan document in advance of your seeing them, so send your business plan to them in good time beforehand (at least a week) and make sure it reads well (see Chapter 10), and that there are no typos.
	■ Work out ahead of time what the key messages are that you want to get across, what main facts and figures you will cite to support them, and how you will conclude. This will show your audience that you know what you and your business are about. Your business plan's Executive Summary, as a mini-version of the whole plan, will form the core of your presentation (see Chapter 10).
	■ A punchy opening gets the audience's interest from the outset, and a punchy ending leaves a positive after-image in their brains, such as: 'Realcase Ltd's new range of improved widgets will do for organisational efficiency what the needle and thread did for textiles and what the BlackBerry® has done for keeping in touch on the move'.
	■ And throughout, be brief, be focused, be done.
	■ Be enthusiastic – that is easy, because your vision really matters to you. But *show* your enthusiasm: if you do not, how can you expect your audience to?
	■ Use a few slides to guide your audience but not to slay them. This means a headline that moves the argument along, clear and brief statements, sparse text, and visual evidence. Charts and graphs are OK only if they are simple. No bullet-point blizzards.

PRESUMPTION	RESPONSE
	■ Be confident. Use the self-talk / self-image / performance cycle as part of your preparation (see Chapter 11). Choose your language carefully: 'Our business will achieve a 37 per cent uplift in sales next year as a result of ...' is much better than 'We hope that ...'; or 'Sales might go up rather a lot ...'
	■ If you are presenting as a team, then be clear beforehand who the main speaker is and who says what. The main speaker should introduce the rest of the team. He or she can pass questions around the team, but should act as the single conduit.
	■ Check the temperature: ask your audience after, say, 10 minutes or so whether the discussion is working as they wish. Are they getting what they need?
You won't know your stuff or you are hiding a skeleton in your business cupboard and you will get defensive under questioning.	■ This is entirely down to you.
	■ Do your homework – there is no short-cut.
	■ Do not let the performance also be your first rehearsal!
	■ Ask and answer a few judicious 'what if?' questions. Be open about the risks that you have identified to the successful realisation of your business plan, and talk about the avoidance and counter-measures that you have in place. This will demonstrate sure-footedness and a mature approach to business, and it will inspire confidence in your audience.
	■ Do not conceal information or be economical with the truth: this is not a game of 'catch-me-out' – it is a mature business dialogue between adults with the aim of creating trust.
	■ Remember to leave a gap between stimulus and response.
	■ Answer questions to the point and concisely. If the questioner wants more, he or she can always ask for it.

PRESUMPTION	RESPONSE
You know it all and won't take advice. **You won't give us any idea of our return and what our exit is.**	■ Be open to advice! Your business will get precious little else for free. ■ If you do not know something, please do not make it up or waffle. Take it on the chin and say what you can do to find out – and offer to get back with the answer. ■ Think like your investor: tell them what money they can make, over what period, and how they can exit (e.g. your business might buy them out, or your business might seek a public offering at a point in future). Remember: your investor does have alternatives to investing in your business!
Either you won't know what you want from us, or you want too much!	■ Know why you are there! That way you can check whether the audience has what they need to make the decision or give you the outcome that you are looking for (see Chapter 15). ■ Be ready to negotiate. The bank will negotiate on interest rate and arrangement fee, and the investor will always seek a higher stake than the one initially offered. Work out in advance your rock-bottom position and stick to it. Also, check ahead of time whether the investor is prepared to take stakes of the size you are offering. They might regard anything less than 25 per cent or even 40 per cent as not worth their while on principle. They might also have a minimum level of investment so, if your funding requirements are below the threshold, save everyone time by not bothering yourself to bother them. And do not send your business plan to the wrong people.

PRESUMPTION	RESPONSE
	■ If the audience comprises your own people, the equivalent here is making the vision connect to their own deep purposes ('the longing for the immensity of the sea') so that they feel the commitment of their talents are energies are for something worthwhile: it matters and the rewards are worth it. ■ Be realistic. Offers of a couple of per cent stakes will get short shrift! Too many businesses ask for equity funding in return for tiny stakes that imply a valuation of a business of hundreds of thousands or millions of pounds. As George Bernard Shaw said: 'Ifs and ands don't make pots and pans.' Do not overestimate today's value of tomorrow's pound. The exchange rate is always much, much higher than you think!

This advice holds good regardless of who is the audience for your business plan. An internal audience – whether your people or the corporate centre – will in all likelihood already hold a large body of common understanding and knowledge with you, so there could well be a lot of ground that you do not need to go over. Essentially, though, they are all wanting to be excited by the same key areas:

- the opportunity;
- how the business will exploit it;
- why the business is uniquely placed to exploit the opportunity better than anyone else;
- what the rewards will be.

Quality business planning culminating in a well-crafted business plan that is powerfully delivered will get your audience declaring: 'I can't miss out on this; I want in!'

SOME SPECIFIC TIPS: THE INVESTOR AUDIENCE

- You may find the investor community a tough one to engage with, but they are a crowd with a silver lining.
- Be clear what you want from them – and they will be especially keen to know their exit route; e.g.:

'We are Anothercase Ltd and as part of our ambitious expansion plans we are looking to you to invest £125,000 in our business to modernise the factory and invest in new equipment. In return, we are prepared to offer a 12½ per cent stake in our company. Our intention is to pay dividends that will give a 15 per cent return on your investment per years for the next five years. In the fifth year, your investment will be repaid in full either from the proceeds from the realisation of other long-term investments by the directors, in which case a 10 per cent bonus will be paid, or a listing on the Alternative Investments Market (AIM) will be sought and we foresee a valuation of the company of at least £7 million.'

Notice that, in this example, the investor has two possible exit routes – a plus point. However, an investor would be unlikely to be interested in the first option as the return would most probably be regarded as too low. Investors, especially if Anothercase Ltd were in a similar financial position to Realcase Ltd, would want a much higher return – perhaps five times or more (it boils down to risk/reward). So the second option is on the right lines (if it stacks up) and would be a basis on which negotiations could start.

- Realcase Ltd's business customers are interested in their widgets, but their business investors are interested in the rate of return. So, remember: to your customers you are selling your products or services, but to an investor you are selling a financial return.
- You might be concerned about losing control by offering so much equity to an investor, so choose your potential partners carefully. There is always the option of offering non-voting shares, which gives the investor appropriate claim on the business's profits and its market value, but you (or the existing shareholders) retain control over how the business is run. Certain investors will also consider providing loan capital in addition to equity finance. This latter has a different risk and reward structure (see Chapter 9 and the discussion about gearing). So consider in advance what mix of equity and loan capital you think is appropriate and what returns you will give. You might consider equity finance to fund general growth, and loan finance for the purchase of a specific capital asset. Since equity carries the highest risk, so it would expect the greatest return. Loan capital can entail reduced risk – most especially of it is secured (perhaps by the asset purchased) – and so the return would be lower.
- Also, check ahead of time whether the investor is prepared to take stakes of the size you are offering. This has been stated in the table above but this essential homework is too often overlooked.
- Some investors have a particular focus; it might be industry related (e.g. ICT) or geographical (e.g. The South West Angel and Investor Network – SWAIN). And do not send your business plan to the wrong people!
- Investors may have stipulations on how information is provided to them – find out and stick to them. They could be about the length of your business plan: a maximum two-page Executive Summary and a maximum total of 30 pages for the whole document (with details in the appendices) would not be unusual.

- Consider whether you wish to protect your business ideas by obtaining Non-Disclosure Agreements (NDAs) in advance). This is common, and is well understood by the investor community.

- Negotiate the outline of the agreement with your investor, but do not sign anything until you have proper professional advice.

- From writing your business plan and obtaining investor backing, allow at least six months and be prepared for it to take a year or more. I wish it were faster: in the modern business world, speed to market and speed of adaptation are prerequisites for business success. My advice is to hope for the best and plan for the worst.

- One more point: bear in mind that if your business is part of a larger organisation, then your presentation, albeit abbreviated because there is much common knowledge already, will resemble the task of satisfying an investor. In effect, you are pitching for investive support from the corporate centre when the centre has more funding requests than funds. Imagine your business is itself a PLC and you are presenting to a group of City analysts. You would need to convince them, as you need to convince the corporate centre, that you have compelling prospects that will deliver an attractive return, and that your business is therefore worth backing.

SOME SPECIFIC TIPS: THE GRANT-GIVER AUDIENCE

- Be ready to address the particular interests of your grant-giving audience. They might want to know what spin-off benefits there would be for other local businesses. Perhaps your hungry workers will give business to local sandwich shops; or perhaps your business will source, say, its paper-clips from a local manufacturer. Or perhaps you will link up with local schools and offer apprenticeships. Grant-givers may have all sorts of other agendas. So be prepared to talk through your environmental policy, for example.

- Grant-giving agencies can focus on a specific territory (e.g. Assisted Areas), or on specific activities (e.g. training, R&D, energy conservation) and there are likely to be specific application processes to go through. You will need to ensure that the material you submit answers the particular interests of the grant-giving agency. Bear in mind that funds are limited and, since the source of the monies is often ultimately the taxpayer, the process to go through can be arduous.

SOME SPECIFIC TIPS: THE BANKER AUDIENCE

- Banks (by which I mean the High Street banks) are not really in the business of providing equity finance ('seed capital' for start-ups; 'development capital' for expansion by existing businesses), although they might have subsidiaries that will consider such. Their mainstream activities are about providing loans, overdrafts and, usually through a separate arm, debtor-related finance (such as factoring and invoice discounting).

- Be clear what you want from them – and they will be especially keen to know how their lending will be repaid and how they will be protected until it is:

    'We are Realcase Ltd and as part of our ambitious expansion plans, we are looking to Money Bank for a loan of £125,000 to modernise the factory and invest in new equipment, together with an overdraft facility for working capital purposes of a steady £85,000 rising to a temporary peak of £120,000, in order to support a forecast uplift in trading. The loan will be for a period of five years. To secure Money Bank's position Realcase Ltd will give a debenture over the company.'

- If you know how a bank looks at a proposal from a business to borrow money, you can make your case more effectively. When considering a loan request, a bank will either explicitly or tacitly consider the following factors:

    - *Character:* the bank lender will want to make a judgement about whether the people he or she is dealing with are trustworthy and are ones with whom he or she can look to having a long-term relationship with. This is about giving the bank lender confidence that you will always do what you say you will do.

    - *Capability:* this is where you talk about the skills and experience of the team and refer to details from past track records. It is also a great opportunity to show off the coherence of your business model and the strategic logic of your business journey.

    - *Capital:* there are three main areas that a bank lender is interested in when assessing a borrowing proposal: the people leading the business ('character' and 'capability'), how the borrowing sits in relation to the balance sheet of the business ('capital'), and the extent to which the borrowing can be serviced from trading cash flows ('repayment'). As far as capital is concerned, the bank lender will look at your business's gearing (see Chapter 9) and the relationship between the bank's financial involvement in your business and that of the shareholders. Bank lenders are typically wary of a gearing higher than 50 per cent; that is, shareholders' finance should exceed outside finance by a ratio of at least 2:1. Of course there are exceptions to every rule-of-thumb; but be ready to work that bit harder on presenting mitigating factors to the bank lender if your borrowing request takes your business's gearing ratio above 50 per cent.

- *Purpose*: this is more than what it obviously means – what the borrowing is for – it is about you demonstrating that the borrowing fits into the narrative of your business and that it contributes to the successful implementation of a compelling business plan. (Naturally, the purpose of the loan must be legal and within the powers of the business – that is, not *ultra vires* – and not for any speculative purpose, no matter how certain repayment would be. Your business would not get a loan for, say, £50,000 to buy 50,000 lottery tickets even if it were secured ten times over.)
- *Amount*: you need to show that the amount of the borrowing is sufficient; that a proposed loan amount is indeed sufficient to purchase the asset and that all add-on costs are covered; that the proposed overdraft level is truly sufficient to cover future working capital needs. Your cash-flow forecast document will help with the latter, as will your 'what if' stress testing: 'What if your customers take longer to pay you'; What if your suppliers insist on faster settlement?'; 'What if sales spurt forward faster and higher than forecast?'; 'What if you purchase some sub-standard stock?' etc.
- *Repayment*: this is the third main area that the bank lender is going to focus on. An overdraft will generate interest costs, and these should show in your cash-flow forecast. A loan will require repayments and, again, these should show in your cash-flow forecast. The bank lender will want to know how bad trading would have to get before the repayments on its borrowings were in jeopardy – the breakeven point (see Chapter 10). Then the

banker will look at how the interest costs sit in the (forecast) P&L statements. Show the bank lender the calculation for the number of times that interest costs are covered by pre-tax profit. If it is tight, then be ready to adduce other factors that might put the banker's mind at ease.

- *Security*: This is the collateral to back up the proposed borrowings so that if the banker has to call in the lending there are assets which can be liquidated to repay it. Security will not be needed in all cases, but will be for larger sums. Assets owned by the business can be pledged, such as premises, either specifically or by a catch-all pledge called a debenture. This picks up all the assets of the business, not only premises but also stock, machinery and debtors. It is the job of the bank lender to judge what value there would be in these assets if they were sold. Asset finance, which is a loan to purchase a specific asset such as a machine, is usually provided by a specialist function within the bank and secured by the asset that is purchased (or it is owned by the lender until the final instalment of the loan is repaid – a hire purchase agreement). Bankers really like the directors of a company providing their personal guarantees, because they view this as a demonstration of personal commitment. Better still, from the bank lender's point of view, is that these guarantees are supported by charges over the personal assets of the guarantor (such as property). This is when the homes of the directors of a borrowing business are often put on the line. You will need to think through whether you are prepared to do this. It is a personal decision and it would be wise to seek legal advice to have the full implications explained to you by an independent adviser. If you do decide that you (and your co-directors) are prepared to give personal guarantees and pledge your personal assets, then you may find a more cost-effective route is to borrow the money in your personal capacity and then lend it on to your company. Remember that in seeking security, the bank lender is likely to want the market value of the collateral to exceed the amount of the borrowing by a margin that will reflect the banker's appetite for risk, as well as his or her judgement about the sale value of the securing asset. Property has a readily determinable value, but that is not necessarily the case with stock, especially if it is specialised. However, the mere provision of security will not itself make certain that the bank lender will advance funds. The rest of his or her analysis (character, capability, capital, purpose and amount) will have to be mostly 'green for go' in his or her mind for a positive decision to lend to be made, no matter how well covered by security the borrowing would be. This is what is supposed to separate banking from pawnbroking.

– *Terms*: this is where the details of interest rate, fees and costs are discussed and agreed. Do your homework: find out what the going rates are; talk to people in your network; seek out views from business bodies. You can try to shave off a slice from the rate of interest, but be ready to calculate the relative values of a trade-off between a reduced interest rate and a lower arrangement fee. Bear in mind that the costs of completing security, especially if property is involved, can be quite high.

■ Overdraft or loan? The overdraft is very flexible, although technically it is fully repayable on demand. Banks like to see an overdraft facility 'fully swing', by which is meant that the bank account is sometimes in credit and sometimes in overdraft. Hence an overdraft is ideal for the ups and downs of normal trading: it is a major source of working capital. Your cash-flow forecast will tell you what size of overdraft is needed and how your business's usage of it will move, month to month. A loan is better suited to a longer-term project such as the purchase of a fixed asset, and its term is usually no longer than the useful life of the relevant asset. The loan is not repayable on demand, provided that the terms of the loan are kept. Now that you understand this, you know what your business presentation should ask for.

■ When presenting your business plan to a bank, a good approach to include is what they would understand to be a multi-scenario approach. It is a rather useful way to look at your business anyway, and for the bank lender, it shows that you are a business person with commercial nous. Three scenarios are ideal in this context: you can call them 'optimistic'; 'realistic'; and 'pessimistic'. Under these scenarios, you explain what would happen to your business – and especially to your capacity to repay the bank – if, respectively, the best, likeliest and worst should happen. You will need to define the exact parameters.

- Bankers love accounting information: audited accounts going back years with balance sheets and P&L statements; forecast P&L statements and balance sheets; and cash-flow figures, both forecast and actual. So you will impress a bank lender if you demonstrate a high degree of financial literacy and show that you can read the figures, calculate a few telling ratios and interpret their meaning (see Chapter 9). Kicking around the working capital figures (debtor, creditor and stock turnover rates) and showing an understanding of the impacts of various movements in turnover, costs and profits (as part of the multi-scenarios) will be especially impressive.

- If you do get funding support from a bank, then remember that bankers hate surprises and really dislike not knowing where they are headed. So be sure that you do not ask for, say, a level of overdraft and then a short while later ask for a higher level, without a really coherent explanation. Of course bankers understand that the unexpected happens, just be sure to keep in close communication with the lender – and keep your promises. A track record of consistent positive behaviour helps to elicit consistent positive responses (see Chapter 14).

SOME SPECIFIC TIPS: YOUR PEOPLE AS AN AUDIENCE

We have used the metaphor of the potter working clay to get a sense of what the process of successful business planning is like.

It is a good metaphor but it has one important limitation: it envisages a solitary craftsman interacting with the clay, whereas successful business planning, although it is indeed a craft process, is a *social* process. Building business value is a collective effort driven along, as we saw in Chapter 14, by a network of relationships.

As far as your colleagues within your business are concerned, we have already discussed communicating to them your business journey (as envisaged by your business plan) and also the role of balanced scorecards in helping them make sense of what is expected of them and how their contribution fits in. Your role, as a leader in your business, is to make connections between the vision of the business and the deeper purposes and preoccupations of your people so that they feel that they are a real part of 'putting a man on the moon' or 'longing for the immensity of the sea'. The balanced scorecard process is about showing how this engaging vision is to be accomplished by the particular endeavours of each and every individual.

If you were an athlete, for example, your vision might be to become an Olympic champion. But then what? This is a powerful and motivating long-term ambition that will generate energy and creativity in you. But you need to know what the specifics are to achieve it, otherwise you will remain fixed solid, blinded by the brilliance of your vision. So you will have a detailed programme of sub-goals such as running a certain distance within a certain time, perfecting specifics about your technique, winning interim competitions, and so on. This is the athlete's 'balanced scorecard'.

We also talked about how story-telling can help people assimilate change more effectively by enabling them to appropriate for themselves the ways in which they can flourish in the changed business.

Story-telling can also have a wider role. One approach that would work very well when seeking to present the essence of your business plan to your people – *and to other stakeholders* – is to harness the power of narrative.

It is a very clear way of communicating how you see the game (see Chapter 14) and is more memorable. Stories are a very important way of conveying important messages and helping the process of sense-making. This is why we start stories right from early childhood. What is more, fantastic feats of memory are achieved by using stories. It might be a very simple story such as 'Richard Of York Gained Battles In Vain' which helps us to remember the seven colours of the rainbow. Or it could be a much more complex story, but a story all the same, that helps amazing individuals memorise whole decks of cards in the correct, yet random, order. These feats of memory can be achieved by assigning an image to each of the cards and then stringing the images together in the narrative of a journey. Try it! You pick up the Queen of Hearts so you think of the queen in the parlour (as in the *Sing a Song of Sixpence* nursery rhyme). A two of spades signifies two black mice that run under the Queen's table to nibble the crumbs. In fact they nibble seven crumbs because you have now turned over the seven of clubs (and 'c' stands for 'clubs' as well as 'crumbs') before being scared away by the three-legged house-cat (three of hearts) and so it goes on through the whole deck of cards. See how far you can get with your own images and story.

OK, so stories can spur people on, support individual and team sense-making, are more impactfully memorable, and are the conveyors of organisational memory that give substance to the business's ethos and personality. All this is useful and important – both for your people and for external stakeholders (including suppliers and customers, as well as investors and lenders). But stories are also much more than this; they can raise the quality of your business planning and business plan immeasurably. This is because stories can raise the quality of your business thinking and so generate truly value-adding insights. They also appropriately reflect business planning's social dimension.

The business 3M, which has a strong reputation for innovation, actively uses stories at the heart of its business planning process[2].

3M train their sales people 'to paint stories so that customers will see how using a 3M product can help them succeed. At employee award ceremonies, we tell stories about the programs and people being recognised to explain what happened and why it's significant'[3]. You can imagine the sales people that Realcase is aiming to recruit being trained to do the same with their business customers.

It goes further. A very typical way of presenting a business plan is to use slides smothered with bullet-point lists. Although bullet-points have the virtue of brevity, they also have the vice of brevity as well. They can give the headlines but not the details. It would be as if a slide presentation on becoming an Olympic champion read like this:

- Become an Olympic champion by:
  - running faster;
  - leaping the hurdles better;
  - taking in better nutrition; and
  - winning at the regional and National Championships, the Commonwealth Championships and the European Championships.

You can agree with all this but actually be none the wiser. Exactly how will these interim goals be achieved? They are not untrue but there is still no sense for what, exactly, is to be done so that, for example, the athlete will indeed run faster, or leap hurdles with greater technical proficiency, or win at various competitions. What is the athlete actually to do?

Also, a list of discrete bullet-points does nothing to illuminate key relationships between the various elements. The interaction between good nutrition, muscle development and specific forms of exercise is left unexplained. What is the value of an improved hurdling technique: a tenth of a second? A fifth? And good nutrition might mean faster recovery times from injury and also more stamina, which together mean an enhanced capability to compete in more athletics events. These causal relationships and the different impacts they have in contributing towards the athlete's goals can be left hidden by lists of bullet-points. They appear to explain things succinctly, but by leaving important interconnections unexplained, they can actually impoverish understanding.

Look again at the Notes and References to Chapter 10, Note 7. This sets out a 'strategic logic' that looks like this:

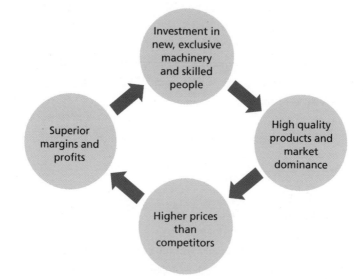

Figure 15.1

In effect, this is just a pictorial way of representing four bullet-points – plus a virtuous cycle with the elements causally linked.

But without the accompanying narrative, very different understandings of Realcase Ltd's business are possible. It all depends on your start-point.

If you start with higher prices, for example, your strategic logic could go something like this:

'We shall increase the prices of our products since higher prices will give Realcase Ltd superior margins and hence profits also. We can use these higher profits to fund investment in the business, purchasing advanced machinery and recruiting the skilled people to operate it and also the sales people to sell what the machinery produces in order to become market leader in the high-end sector. This will entitle Realcase Ltd to continue to charge higher prices for our products.'

This suggests that the implementation of Realcase Ltd's business starts with raising its prices. The assumption is that it has been getting its marketing mix wrong (pricing and promotion) and so, therefore, getting its marketing mix right is what will drive future business growth. This will likely mean that a major focus for Realcase Ltd going forward will be to maintain its ability to price its products properly.

However, what if your start-point is with higher quality products? In this case, your strategic logic could go something like this:

'Realcase Ltd will move to producing higher-specified products built from higher-quality materials and so dominate the high-end market. These high-quality products will command high prices which will give the company higher margins and so better profitability. Greater profits will help Realcase Ltd to fund investment in the business, purchasing advanced machinery and recruiting the skilled people to operate it and also the sales people to sell what the machinery produces in order to maintain our market-leading position.'

This suggests that the future growth of the business will be product-led. The assumption is that Realcase Ltd has been concentrating on the wrong sort of products and so, by moving up-market with better products, it will enter a new market that it can dominate. This will likely mean that a major focus for Realcase Ltd going forward will be to maintain its ability to design and develop new products.

In fact, as we know, Realcase Ltd starts its narrative flow with investment in new machinery and skilled people. Consequently, its strategic logic, in summary form, goes like this:

'Realcase Ltd will use the loan of £125,000 to invest in new machinery which we shall obtain from the solitary supplier in an exclusive contract. We shall exploit the full potential of this machinery to produce higher-quality, higher-specified products by investing in the skilled people to operate the machinery, and in a talented sales force that will enable us to acquire a new set of business customers, ultimately enabling us to dominate the high-end market. These high-quality products will command high prices which will give the company higher margins and so better profitability. These greater profits will enable Realcase Ltd to continue to invest in its operations and equipment to maintain our leadership of the high-end market.'

This explains what the loan is for: to kick-start a programme leading to a turnaround in Realcase Ltd's performance. It also suggests that the future growth of the business will be capability-led: it is through Realcase Ltd's enhanced operations capabilities, underpinned by its unique contractual arrangement with the machinery's supplier, that future business success will come. The assumption here is that Realcase Ltd has been too 'samey', not distinctive enough in its market. Therefore, a major focus for Realcase Ltd going forward will be to maintain its ability to sustain its operations advantage. What happens when the exclusive contract runs out? Can Realcase Ltd use the breathing space to establish new operations capabilities and quality customer relationships that will endure and so provide a competitive advantage when that time comes?

As these different strategic logics show, unless you know in your own business which perspective you hold, what assumptions you are making about where you think future business value will come from, then you will not be able to implement your business plan effectively. Nor will you be able to present it properly to your people, nor to potential investors and lenders, nor to your other stakeholders (including, but not limited to, suppliers and customers).

If you think of your presentation solely in terms of a conventional series of bulleted slides, then there is a real risk of these important inter-connections being missed. However, if you think, as 3M does, in terms of presenting to your audience in terms of a narrative flow, then the strategic logic becomes so much clearer. Any artifice or lapse of emotional logic, or convenient yet grotesque twists of plot, become immediately exposed. Also, your audience can see how they themselves fit in the story. They can see how the narrative hangs together, how the characters are playing their roles in ways that sit appropriately with the situation.

I said in Chapter 10 then the job of your business plan is to manage the view on the world of your reader. Your task when presenting your business plan is to manage the view on the world of your audience:

'Your business plan is thus a story, a narrative with a purpose and an internal logic and coherence, which are so compelling that your audience wants desperately to become a character in the tale. You have the stage, so make the promised drama hang together so that you shape and move on the audience's world-view.'

This is exactly how 3M does it: through a three-fold process which we can call:

- Our Stage
- Our Drama
- Our Way Forward[4]

Our Stage is about describing the current situation your business is in. You will talk about the key interconnections at work in your business: the key success factors and the problems – your SWOT and your marketplace.

Our Drama is where you talk about the challenges that your business faces. By now, and referring back to the D x V x I > R formula, you will have established Disturbance and Discontent; that is, you will have shown why things cannot go on as they are and why change is necessary.

Our Way Forward describes how your business can make a start on overcoming the challenges (I = Initial Implementation steps), and how you will keep the momentum going so that success is ultimately achieved (V for vision). Of course, the way forward has to be a logical response to the challenges faced on the stage on which your business is playing. By bringing to the surface your assumptions about how things are interconnected within your business and in your market, your business logic will be all the more compelling. The understanding and, crucially, the *commitment* of your audience is much enhanced.

The superiority of the narrative story over bulleted slides: an illustration with Realcase Ltd

You might find it helpful to see the contrast between describing your business through some bulleted slides and through a narrative story, by seeing an illustrative example, albeit a simplified one, based on Realcase Ltd.

I do not want to burden you with a complete reconstruction of Realcase Ltd's business plan, so if you bear with a summarised extract, then I think you will get the general idea.

So imagine that Realcase Ltd is presenting a set of slides; let us say the audience is its own people. Among the slides could be ones that look like this:

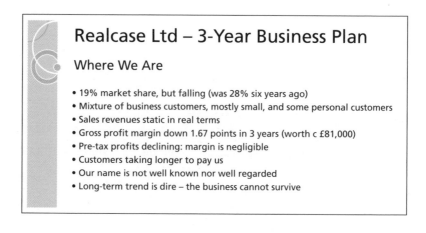

Realcase Ltd – 3-Year Business Plan

Where We Are

- 19% market share, but falling (was 28% six years ago)
- Mixture of business customers, mostly small, and some personal customers
- Sales revenues static in real terms
- Gross profit margin down 1.67 points in 3 years (worth c £81,000)
- Pre-tax profits declining: margin is negligible
- Customers taking longer to pay us
- Our name is not well known nor well regarded
- Long-term trend is dire – the business cannot survive

Realcase Ltd – 3-Year Business Plan

Where We Are Aiming For

- Higher prices
- Better products
- New, larger business customers
- Grow sales revenues to over £9m within 3 years
- Increase profit margins
- Manage working capital better

Realcase Ltd – 3-Year Business Plan

How We Shall Get There

- Buy new machine – exclusive contract
- Make high-quality, higher spec'd products starting with Widget Mark 2 and Ooji
- Develop new products
- Raise prices
- Recruit skilled machine operatives
- Recruit new sales force led by new Sales and Marketing Director
- Concentrate on larger business customers and public sector

These slides are not necessarily bad; it is just that important inter-connections are unexplained, and the understanding of the audience is diminished and their commitment is likely to be reduced.

Now, in the parlance of exams, compare and contrast the slides with a narrative approach that could go something like this:

Our Stage

Realcase Ltd provides a range of three products – Widgets, Thingamebobs, and Whatchamecallits – to over 1,500 mostly small businesses, plus some personal customers – all in the South West.

Sales of Widgets exceed sales of the other two products combined. Realcase Ltd has been selling Widgets for over 30 years. Thingamebobs and Whatchamecallits were introduced seven and eight years ago respectively.

Realcase Ltd is one of four main players here in the South West where we are based. Between us all, we account for more than 80 per cent of the total market. Our market share is 19 per cent, down from 28 per cent six years ago. Our main competitors are WidgetsOurUs Ltd, South West Stuff Ltd, and Peninsula SW Ltd.

Barriers to entry used to be quite high: providers needed a strong local reputation for local businesses to buy from them and, because average purchases were relatively low, transport costs were prohibitive. However, barriers to entry for cherry-pickers are much lower, and larger companies have been developing higher-end products which have attracted bigger customers, including the public sector. These higher-end products have been arousing interest from our traditional customer base, and some of them have been 'up-buying'. The profit margins are superior and so transport costs are less of an issue. For our other, more price-sensitive customers, our traditional local competitors have responded by undercutting us on price. They have invested in volume production, achieving economies of scale and using the Internet to market their wares and sell to customers. Price is becoming a more important consideration for our customers than having a local presence.

So we have been losing customers in two directions: our better customers are going to the new entrants, and our price-sensitive customers have been going to our traditional competitors.

We did some customer research a few months ago. The messages were rather sobering. Realcase Ltd is seen as a tired and fuddy-duddy business with serviceable but old-fashioned products. Customers buy from us out of habit, but do not feel particularly loyal. The only contact they get from us is the invoice. This was especially strongly felt by our larger business customers. Public-sector bodies in the South West said they had heard of us because we are so long-established, but they think of Realcase Ltd more like a 'fixture and fitting' of the South West business scene rather than as a potential supplier. Beyond the South West, no one has heard of us. As for large businesses who are not Realcase Ltd's customers, if they have heard of us at all, we are viewed as selling unimaginative products that do not keep up with modern needs.

In our existing market, Realcase Ltd is being pulled apart by bigger companies taking our best customers, and by our existing competitors winning over our smaller customers on price. This is shown by our much reduced – and reducing – market share. The customers we are being left with are not fast payers and this is putting pressure on our cash flow.

Potential customers have either not heard of us or, if they have, they do not believe we can produce high-quality, innovative, pace-setting products.

Realcase Ltd does not have the financial resources to build the economies of scale to compete as a high-volume, low-cost provider. This is clear from our trading performance, where a pre-tax profit of only £2,000 was made on turnover of £4.9 million. Our gross profit margin has fallen in the last three years by 1.67 percentage points. That may not sound a lot, but amounts to foregone gross profit of no less than £81,000 – a sum no less than 40 times our pre-tax profit figure. If we do nothing, we shall see the erosion of the entire customer case and the ultimate collapse of our business. We do have a potentially winning new product range, but we lack penetration in the relevant markets.

We need the skills to sell our new products and a breathing space to build-up our resources to compete in a more profitable, higher-end market. We have learned a massive amount. And this learning has led Realcase Ltd to form a more assured understanding of our capabilities and competences, and of the opportunities for us to build business value and so achieve our vision of becoming 'Most Trusted'.

Our Drama

Without change, a business on our trajectory would be looking at going to the wall. We could expect continued erosion of margins as we fought on price to keep sales. As revenues declined, so our capacity to invest in achieving a lower cost base would evaporate, and we would be in a doom loop of dwindling income unable to remedy an unsustainable cost base, and our unattractive products – that are all such a cost base can produce – discouraging customers from giving us income.

In that same recent customer research, we went on to describe the new Widget Mark 2 product and the new Ooji product that are under development. We did not reveal the identity of the manufacturer as being Realcase Ltd. The businesses and public sector bodies that we surveyed were bowled over by what these products could do – particularly in the light of impending tough legislation on energy conservation and environmental pollution – but attributed them to a totally different supplier!

It is as though Realcase Ltd is like a half-good pharmaceutical company which spends a long time developing a revolutionary drug, but then fails to get it used in every hospital, every GP's surgery.

Customers tell us they:

■ want a partner they can turn to who 'doesn't give us what we ask for, but gives us what we need';
■ want products that are exciting, flexible, of undoubted quality and regularly refreshed.

Incremental improvements within our current business will not solve our problems.

This is why our new business plan is so radical and aims to move us upmarket.

If we are to move upmarket, then we must protect our early development through an exclusive contract and, in parallel, invest in our skills and capabilities. Only raised performance will earn us the eventual right to develop committed partnership relationships founded on trust with high-end customers.

We shall be transforming our business during the next three years and this will draw on all of us within Realcase Ltd and on our stakeholders and partners beyond.

Our Way Forward

To succeed, we need our customers to believe that we so understand their business that we can solve problems and help them take advantage of opportunities before they even realise they exist.

First, that means having the capability to produce products that our high-end customers in both the private and public sectors actually want. Operationally, we do not have the means to do this at present, so we need to obtain those means. Hence, we shall use a loan from our bank, Money Bank, to invest in new machinery that will produce much higher-quality products and will extend our product range to include the Widget Mark 2 and the Ooji.

From customer research we know that there will be huge demand for these new products, as they are fantastic solutions to the challenges posed by imminent energy conservation and anti-pollution legislation.

However, that is just part of it, so we shall recruit a skilled workforce to operate the new machinery and take full advantage of its capabilities.

Producing products that our high-end customers actually want, to top-quality standards and with a high degree of bespoke specification, will enable us to charge much higher prices, more in keeping with these quality products.

This starts to build a stronger financial platform for our business. What is more, we shall finalise an exclusive contract with the supplier of the new machinery so that our competitors cannot produce similar products to the Widget Mark 2 or Ooji.

However, profits come only from sales, so we have to put some real energy into raising our ability to find, secure and nurture the upmarket customers we need. We do not have this ability at present. Accordingly, we shall recruit a highly experienced sales and marketing director. We are already at final interview stage with three outstanding candidates all of whom have excellent contacts among larger businesses and in the public sector. The appointee will open up sales opportunities and put Realcase Ltd firmly on their radar.

No more will potential customers in our chosen markets say they have never heard of us.

The sales and marketing director will need a sales team, which we do not have, as we have relied on our invoices team to be the primary point of interface for our customers. They do a great job with the important task of collecting our money, but it is unfair to expect them to have enough information to manage the customer relationship as well. Therefore, we shall recruit a skilled sales force with a proven track record in selling to our chosen customer segment. There is an early opportunity to make a flying start with this by poaching a team of able relationship managers from a smaller competitor whose overseas parent company is retrenching back to their home market.

The sales force will be groomed by the sales and marketing director with a clear brief. Their job is to achieve a partnership style of working with customers – which our potential clients are yearning for.

This is key to Realcase Ltd achieving our vision of 'Most Trusted'.

By forming such partnership relationships, we shall enhance customer loyalty and create opportunities for cross-sales. We shall never lose a valuable customer again. At the same time, we can use our close relationships to improve trading terms so that our cashflow works so much better. This will add to our stronger financial platform.

In addition, because we shall be producing some fantastic, class-leading and unique products, we believe that Realcase Ltd will be attractive for new customers to do business with. Hence our new sales force will have their skills in customer-prospecting refreshed and reinforced so that they can succeed in meeting ambitious sales targets.

Our exclusive contract with the supplier of the new machinery will give us a vital breathing space. We shall use this breathing space to build up Realcase Ltd's financial resources to fund future investment in a continually refreshed range of imaginative products that we shall co-design with our key customers, as nurtured by the new sales and marketing director.

In this way we are laying down the conditions for enduring competitive advantage and thus lasting business growth.

The right management information (MI) to the right people will also help us manage the whole value chain better. We know that a simple cost-cutting mentality is wrong. After all, if our costs were zero, then so too would be our income!

Costs are the entry card to earn the right to receive value – but what is the right relationship between the two? Better MI to those of us within Realcase Ltd who can affect that balance is essential. We cannot even begin to answer the question, for example, whether the cost of a month's product trial is or is not a legitimate entry-fee if the right people do not have the MI that explains the economics.

So, just as we believe the industry is such that the business needs to be more plainly constructed around value, so too do we believe should individual behaviours. This means a reward system that is explicit about this and an emphasis on a high-performance culture.

The competition has put some distance between them and us, so we need to raise our game to do ourselves – and our customers – justice.

Given our higher cost base than our competitors, we cannot afford to compete on price. We have to compete on the basis that we understand our customers' value-potential better, and can anticipate the products that will be needed to help them realise it.

The excitement and challenge will come first in getting us there, and then in getting better and better.

Compared with 200Z, in three years from now we shall have more than doubled sales revenues, reduced costs in real terms, and transformed profits.

It is a big map – but our journey is as big as the map that we hold!

If you perceive that there are advantages in the narrative version compared with the slides presentation version, then be clear about what you regard those advantages to be and capture them in a narrative about your own business journey.

Enabling fabling: hit and myth

You may well feel that using a story-telling approach would be effective with lots of audiences, such as investors, lenders, and other stakeholders, as well as suppliers and customers. I would agree with you[5].

Let us keep your own people in view for now. When communicating your business plan to this audience, you can see the differences in the illustrative example above between using bulleted slides and using a narrative structured around Our Stage, Our Drama, and Our Way Forward. Understanding is enhanced, sense-making is fostered, and because people can more readily make connections between the purposes of the business and their own, commitments are encouraged. People can see what it is they are a part of and how they can best fulfil their role. Balanced scorecards then agree the details.

The coherence of the business's intended journey is more open to scrutiny and in standing up to this, your business ends up with a better business plan.

So your role is to use stories and the narrative technique to communicate your business plan around your people. But you have another role: it is up to you (with your leadership team) to create the conditions conducive to story-telling around your business. This is important.

Narratives are highly context-specific in that their power in part derives from the fact they are introduced into a setting or situation in which they are highly pertinent. Contrast this with the coldness one would feel just by trawling through a database of story after story. This does not mean, however, that your business can only rely on serendipity for narratives to be shared; rather, you can actively foster the creation of situations in which story-telling is natural, effective and relevant. Stories are told in social interaction, and it is possible to create opportunities for kinds of interactions which allow certain kinds of stories to be told.

Engineered spontaneity could happen at anniversaries, presentations of monthly/quarterly/annual results, regular bulletins and newsletters, conferences, post-project implementation reviews, induction of new recruits, performance reviews, debriefs after customer interactions, team meetings, the communal coffee break, the office Christmas party, promotional videos, external advertising, issuing commemorative memorabilia, farewells to colleagues – the list could be endless. For Realcase Ltd, for example, there is likely to be a very rich source of stories in the future as the newly-formed sales force tells tales of courting customers and winning sales. No sales manual can teach trust, yet stories about behaviours that display and provoke trust can make Realcase Ltd's vision of 'Most Trusted' real and 'appropriate-able'. Indeed, with so many people joining the company, stories will be a positive force for acculturation for the enlarged Realcase team. Internal relationships founded on trust will be a necessary condition for creating external relationships founded on trust.

The point is that, rather than focusing on archival storage, it is important that your business creates social mechanisms for story-telling. Your business can then use these mechanisms and the narratives that are told as a means by which an enabling common pool of learning can be shared – and enriched. This will generate confidence in your people to make change happen successfully and to dedicate themselves to their role in your business's journey, encouraging a climate in which commitments can be made and reciprocated. They also provide your business with a co-ordination and control mechanism – provided that the 'right' stories are captured and propagated. All this takes skill.

The activity of story-telling acts as a thread that sustains learning, meaning, values and identity through time for your business – the people within it and the people connected with it[6].

Some specific tips: your buyer audience

By a buyer audience I mean a person, group or other business that is a potential buyer of your business. In this case, your business plan resembles more a sales prospectus.

Does this mean that your business planning is a wasted effort?

Not at all!

Selling a business has some important features in common with selling your house. Yes, it is undoubtedly stressful, but also just as there are activities that it makes sense to do to get the best possible price for your house were you to remain there, so there activities that it is right to complete to get the possible price for your business.

Any maintenance jobs ought to be completed; the house should be presented in its most appealing light (clean, tidy, with the smell of fresh coffee).

It is the same when selling a business: weaknesses should be identified and addressed; strengths should be capitalised on; threats should be mitigated or nullified; and opportunities should be pursued and realised.

The process of successful business planning and the effective implementation of the resulting business plan are the best ways to build a robust business and, since robust businesses are the most attractive to buyers, then these are also the best ways of achieving the best possible price for your business.

Presenting your sales prospectus to a potential buyer requires very much the same sort of approach as has already been described when presenting your plan to any audience.

Here are a few additional tips:

- Your exit can be achieved in many ways, not solely by selling the business to another entrepreneur, or other business. If large enough (and if your business satisfies other qualifying criteria), you could seek a listing on a public stock market such as the Alternative Investment Market (AIM). Perhaps your colleagues or the management team would like to buy your business in a management buy-out (MBO)?
- How much is your business worth? As with anything, the worth of something is what someone is prepared to pay for it. Without a large active market in businesses like yours, there are no ready reference points, so valuing a business is not an exact science. Also, there could be key sources of value in your business that are not obvious, such as an especially talented workforce, or some very loyal customers, or a strong brand, or a patent, or (as with Realcase Ltd) a well-crafted contractual arrangement. Here are a couple of perspectives:
  - You could look at the value of the assets of the business, less any borrowings, to get a sense of what a buyer would be getting for their money. However, this will probably get closer to the break-up value of your business, rather than the value of your business as a going concern, but it is a start.
  - As a going concern, you could look at the earnings that your business generates and then value your business as a multiple of these. What multiple to use? The key question! You might look

at similar businesses that are quoted and see what multiples (price to earnings ratio) they are operating on. In essence, it is about taking a view on the level of future earnings (usually pre-tax profit). When the economic climate is good and business confidence is high, then multiples are generally higher than when the opposite holds. Some are more sensitive than others: if times move from being bad to being good, then expect the multiples of, say, restaurants, to go up further than supermarkets.

Also consider whether to look at historic earnings or forecast earnings. If you look at Realcase Ltd's P&L statement for the year 200Z, you can see that its pre-tax profit was £2,312 (see Chapter 9). Suppose, after due consideration of comparative risks, you form the view that a multiple of seven is appropriate. This would give a valuation of Realcase Ltd of only, say, £16,000! But suppose instead you look at Realcase Ltd's potential. Their forecast figures show a pre-tax profit three years hence of, let us suppose, £973,284. Multiplied by seven, this comes to just over £6.8 million! No doubt the right valuation is somewhere in between £16,000 and £6.8 million, but what a wide pair of parameters within which to negotiate! You can see why business valuations are so tricky. And this does not even take into account any special features mentioned above, nor the fact that your business might be an especially good fit for the buying business.

- Explain why you are selling the business, in case the buyer thinks you have spotted an abyss of impending failure and you are getting out while you can. There are lots of good reasons why you might want to sell.

- Importantly, do not share a detailed and comprehensive sales prospectus unless you know the buyer is serious and genuine; otherwise, you might end up giving away key business secrets to a competitor. For enquiries, a much briefer sales memorandum would be appropriate.

- Get specialist advice. Selling a business is a specialist area and if you have decided to sell your business it deserves to achieve the best possible price. A specialist adviser can help you market your business, help you find a buyer, and support your subsequent negotiations.

MAKING A 'NO' POSITIVE

Have another look at Chapter 12.

Your path in life is not easy. When presenting your business plan, you will have visualised great success and you will have managed the self-talk / self-image / performance cycle positively.

Absolutely right.

At the same time, and paradoxically, you should also be prepared for failure. Your potential investor or your bank or your prospective purchaser might reject you and say 'no'.

You have a choice. What will be your response? You can choose to call it a day or you can press on and find a different investor/bank/purchaser.

What is the right choice? This has to be down to you.

But whatever you do, learn from the experience. Get detailed feedback. What, exactly, are their reasons for saying 'no'?

You might later reflect on these reasons and realise that, yes, they are right. You have been given a new perspective on what you had been proposing to achieve. Perhaps you realise for the first time that your business does not have a future after all. You decide to call it a day.

Lucky, lucky you!

This enlightenment at this stage, rather than after you have committed so much of your own energy and money and soul (not to mention other people's), is immeasurably precious. The ruin you have avoided, the hearts you have kept unbroken, the hope you have preserved to find a new dream are all wonderful positives.

And if you engage in the process of business planning again with a new venture or in a new setting, you will do it so much better next time. You have learned loads.

Or perhaps you are not yet ready to give up on your business. In which case remember the key steps described in Chapter 12 to find failures fascinating and deal positively with the setback:

■ Re-frame the questions about the set-back to focus on *solutions*.
■ Find and adopt the beliefs that are *useful* to hold about the set-back.
■ Find and assimilate the *learning* from the setback.
■ Resolve to *do better* next time.

Take the feedback on board; thank them for their comments (a follow-up written response is good form); learn from the comments made; work out what would have to be different about your presentation next time (style and content) to ensure that the same reasons do not crop up again. It might be a simple thing to remedy.

You will have succeeded again! You will have succeeded in learning how to raise your game yet further. Your business skills are growing all the time.

And, moreover, do all this even if your audience says 'yes'!

Remember, too, that your presentation is a two-way process; a grown-up conversation between mature business people. If you are to collaborate in a long-term relationship, the chemistry has to be right. You might conclude that, even though the audience might be saying 'yes' to your presentation, you want to say 'no' to them. It is important that you remain open to that outcome.

This will not be a failure. Again you will have succeeded in finding out something important. You will have a clearer understanding of the sort of investor or banker or whoever you want to partner with. In addition, you will have had an excellent work-out in making an effective and telling presentation. You will be in great shape for the next presentation, conceivably with a partner you will want to say 'yes' to as much as they want to say 'yes' to you.

Key takeaways from Chapter 15

1   Know your audience.
2   Relish the opportunity to present your business plan and warmly welcome questions.
3   Accumulate lots of facts, think hard, and talk to wise people.
4   Respect and embrace the scepticism of your business audience: it means they have a passion for business truth.
5   Know your stuff intimately, and prepare, prepare, prepare!
6   Make sure the structure of your presentation is simple and focused:
    a.   the opportunity;
    b.   how the business will exploit it;
    c.   why the business is uniquely placed to exploit the opportunity better than anyone else;
    d.   what the rewards will be.

7   Be clear about what you want from the audience for your business.
8   Harness the power of narrative.
9   Actively create the conditions for story-telling in your business.
10 Remember that if your presentation is rejected, you have not failed. You will have succeeded in learning what does *not* work and what to do better next time!

Notes and References

1   Bhidé, A.V. *The Origin and Evolution of New Businesses*. Chapter 2: 'Planning vs. Opportunistic Adaptation'. pp. 53ff. New York: Oxford University Press, 2000.

2   Shaw, G., Brown, R., and Bromiley, P. 'Strategic Stories: How 3M Is Rewriting Business Planning' 1998, *Harvard Business Review*, May-June, pp. 41-50.

3   *Ibid.*, p. 42.

4   In Shaw *et al*, *op. cit.*, there is a discussion of the three-fold process which comprises: 'set the stage', 'introduce the dramatic conflict' and 'reach resolution', pp. 44-47.

5   Consider, for example: 'Storytelling is the preferred sensemaking currency of human relationships among internal and external stakeholders' (Boje, D.) 'The storytelling organisation: A study of story performance in an office-supply firm'. *Administrative Science Quarterly* (1991), **36** (1), pp. 106-126, p. 106.

6   I rather like the description of stories in the workplace as 'repositories of accumulated wisdom' in Brown, J.S., and Duguid, P. 'Organisational Learning and Communities-of-Practice: Toward a Unified View of Working, Learning and Innovation', *Organisation Science*, (1991), **2 (1)**, pp. 40-57, p. 45. But they are repositories with a practical benefit since they provoke business insight or what has been called 'the situated production of understanding through narration'; see Orr, J., 'Sharing Knowledge, Celebrating Identity: War Stories and Community Memory in a Service Culture', printed in Middleton, D.S., and Edwards, D., (eds.), *Collective Remembering: Memory in Society*, p. 178, Beverley Hills: Sage, 1990.

16 - Bonus Chapter
Your Business Planning in Today's World

'It was the best of times, it was the worst of times. It was the age of wisdom, It was the age of foolishness it was the spring of hope, it was the winter of despair.' – Charles Dickens, A Tale of Two Cities

INTRODUCTION

Just like City bonuses, this bonus chapter is not performance-related.

By that I mean that I am not expecting anything from you to earn this bonus chapter. I suppose, therefore, it should be considered more like a gift from me to you. Given that there are – and will continue to be – so many lives touched for the better by you and your business, it is the least I can do as a token that represents my applause for your endeavour.

This bonus chapter is for those who find it helpful to consider the social context in which they make their business journey. If you are someone who likes to reflect on the nature of the world in which we live because, among other reasons, you believe that this will enhance the quality of your business planning, then this chapter is for you.

Like you, it helps me to focus on business in a better way when I have also thought about the world more broadly. In this bonus chapter, I would like to share my reflections with you, making links to the business journey as I do so. A proper discussion of today's world would require another book and probably also, the perspective of tomorrow's. Thus I can only offer you a few thoughts and reflections. I do not claim that my reflections are definitive (that lack of definitiveness is itself a product of the modern world), but if there is something among them that sparks off a useful thought for you and your business, then I know you have the wit to find it.

THE LAST POST

Your business plan is done, but your business planning continues.

It continues not in a vacuum, not amongst the hissing steam of the Victorian age, not amongst the austerity in the aftermath of the Second World War, not amongst the optimism of the Sixties, not amongst the decline and collapse of Communism, but amongst the opening years of the 21st century.

What is this age we live in? What is this age in which you are building your business?

Everything seems 'post-' today: UK politics are post-Thatcher; African politics are post-Colonial; geo-politics are post-Cold War; sexual politics are post-Feminist; the Christian Church is post-Reformation and religion is post-Christian; philosophy is post-structuralist; economics is post-industrial; cosmology is post-Big Bang; leadership is post-conventional.

The world is post-modern.

Or perhaps, post-postmodern!

We need a convenient label for the world of today. Perhaps you can think of one; but for now let us call the world of today the PPM world.

THE PPM WORLD: SOME MOTIFS

What is this PPM world like and what does it mean for business?

The PPM world: the motif of radical individualism

One motif in the PPM world is illustrated by that venerable soap opera *Coronation Street*.

Some years ago, I was following the story of a character called Hayley. Now Hayley is a transsexual (was a man, is now a woman). She is married – or at least has made a commitment to a male partner

– and, when I last watched it, she and her partner were looking to adopt a child.

Hayley has not let anything stand in her way of being the person she wishes to choose to be: not the biology that tried to tell her she was a man, not the religious or social mores that tried to tell her she could not marry a man, and not the rules and regulations or practices and prejudices of agencies that debar transsexuals acting as a mother to a foster child.

The modern age means that the individual believes there should be no barrier to their realising who they want to be – not even what Nature decrees. We might call this driving force of radical individualism 'the Hayley Complex'.

Anyone in the business of trying to make a living by seeking to get individuals to part with a piece of their wealth has to harness this insatiable force and function effectively within the Hayley Complex.

No more will one size fit all, no more will your business's customers accept the 'standard model', no more will customers unquestioningly fit in with company policy or procedures, no more will your staff simply do what they are told, no questions asked. It is little wonder that customers object fiercely to standardised treatment from call centres, to navigating their way through anonymous numbered options, and plead instead to speak to not just a person but a *real* person. Customer expectation to be in a segment of one is not just high, it is demanding it as a *right*.

The Hayley Complex encompasses the expectation to be treated as a segment of one, but it is much more than this. The individual soul's agenda trumps tradition, institutionalised rules, and even the once unstoppable forces of nature. True, in a sense humanity has long tried to do this from the time they first mixed herbs together to stop an illness running its course. But the Hayley Complex goes beyond this: it is about the assertion of the individual's identity. And an individual's identity is asserted as a matter of choice, not just an outworking of how Nature has dealt the chromosomal cards.

The PPM world: the motif of complexity

The Hayley Complex sits very well with other motifs in the PPM world. One of these motifs recognises the complexity of the PPM world. This is the interesting flowering that perhaps unexpectedly sprang forth from the lifeless soil that is post-modernist thinking.

For the post-modernist thinker, nothing has a privileged position: whether epistemologically, morally, philosophically, artistically, aesthetically, culturally, socio-economically, or even scientifically. This is the outlook that holds that there is no objective truth, just interpretations. Debate is not about arriving at the truth but at forming a better rather than worse interpretation. Language is not so much for expressing statements that are true, but as vehicles that are pressed into service for people to form highly contextualised relationships with each other. Hence truth is the product of social groups. It is diffuse and of-the-moment.

So what does this mean for business? Well, in the post-modernist spirit, it can mean whatever you want it to mean! The implication is that you are wasting your time trying to find enduring principles to help you run your business and find business success. It means that you should be more than usually circumspect about drawing inferences from customer data and from research about the marketplace 'out there'. This is because there is no objective truth 'out there'. There is nothing to be gained by seeking to understand the levers of your business, because it is not a functioning machine separate from you. Rather, it is a social construct that is altered as soon as you start to examine it. It would like trying to get a feel of the water without dipping your toe in. And there is no point reading books about business like this one since all authors are providing not some pieces of advice to help you and your purposes, but are merely projecting an attempt to increase their power and influence in the battlefield that is human interaction.

There is no overarching principle like progress, or scientific reason, or globalisation, or free markets, or capitalism, or Marxism to explain where the world has come from and where it is going. Such overarching principles are called meta-narratives and post-modernist thinking will have none of it. Instead of a single meta-narrative flow, post-modernism prefers to think in terms of a multiplicity of local eddies, each with its own narrative[1].

The post-modernist outlook sees the world as a multiplicity of sense-makings. Nothing is what it is; everything is open to perspective and interpretation. We see the post-modernist outlook illustrated in architecture, for example. Tall buildings, with mirrored glass that reflect their surroundings, are there, but seem also to be not quite there. They are office blocks or residential flats, but they look like sky and trees and cranes and neighbouring buildings.

We see this post-modernist outlook assumed within approaches to branding and product image. 'Bounty', for example, is not a chocolate bar, but 'a taste of paradise'. You do not just consume a particular producer's yoghurt, you 'lick the lid of life'. Consumers do not so much go to see real castles; more go to see Disneyfied versions. In the novel *The Great Gatsby*, Gatsby's library projects a carefully constructed image of learning: 'Absolutely real – have pages and everything ... It's a bona fide piece of printed matter. It fooled me ... It's a triumph. What thoroughness! What realism! Knew when to stop, too – *didn't cut the pages*. But what do you want? What do you expect?' (Chapter 3, my italics.)

We see this in popular culture: there is no such thing as good or bad television, just what has mass appeal and niche appeal. Every point of view is valid. To say otherwise, is to be mean-spirited and oppressively judgemental.

The mainstream of post-modernist thinking is ridiculous enough without holding it to account for the various grotesques that it has spawned. These range from the assumed medical efficacy of crystals through to alleged dialogues with dead people at séances and, more scarily, the propagation of literal creationism as science. These are like the anything-goes babblings so effectively lampooned in Monty Python's film *Life of Brian* when the frenzied crowd found every happenstance object to be a profound and holy 'sign'.

If everything is special, then nothing is. Not every view is valid. There are such things as facts and falsehoods. Valid views are based on facts and logical reasoning; invalid views fly in the face of facts or are confused by using poor or broken logic.

Whenever I hear anyone declare to me: 'there is no objective truth', I always invite them to step in front of a speeding truck.

This usually settles it![2] The deep irony of the post-modernist outlook is that in declaring there is no privileged position, they are privileging the human view above all else – even above the rest of reality. The outside world most certainly does impinge upon our own purposes. We can resist it, bend it, even change it, but we most definitely take it into account.

This is not to say that this is easy. 'Taking reality into account' is a complicated activity, not least because reality – especially when other people are involved – is a complicated place.

There are indeed multifarious points of view. People do indeed interpret what there is around them according to preconceived notions and their prior conditioning. 'Taking reality into account' truly does reflect a measure of construction by the individual. We only have to remind ourselves about the duck and rabbit picture (Chapter 13) to acknowledge that.

We can at the same time agree that there is an objective world against which true beliefs can be separated from false ones, correct accounts can be winnowed out of wrong ones, while at the same time agree that these beliefs and accounts can be subject to all sorts of historical and contextual determinations. This is the more constructive motif that I take to be another feature of the PPM world. It asserts the integrity of an outside reality while at the same time humbly acknowledging that our understanding of it has to be done through our individual *Weltanschauung* or world-view. We can broaden our *Weltanschauung* so that where once we saw a duck, we can also see a rabbit. But we do not see a train. Reality is not infinitely plastic; or, at least, it is not so malleable as to shape itself to just any individual's *Weltanschauung*[3].

What does this mean for business? It underlines the importance of what we discussed in Chapter 13 about keeping 'open focus'. Working out what to do for the best in business – as in any worthwhile activity – is not just about accumulating more and more truths or objects of knowledge; it is also very much about the subjects of knowledge – that is, people like you and me. This is why Chapter 8 is so keen to have you 'know thyself'. Our beliefs, as systematised in the best way we can as our own *Weltanschauung*, are crucial aspects of business life. We behave like the person we believe ourselves to be. If we think upbeat, we behave upbeat – the placebo effect can be triggered by an innocuous pill or by an effort of will. If we think we are no good at mental arithmetic, we shall get sums wrong or explain correct calculations as mere flukes or lucky guesses (see Chapter 11).

The PPM motif is that 'taking reality into account' is a complicated activity as various individuals' *Weltanschauungen* encounter one another, collide, shape and are shaped. This is what the PPM motif of the daunting complexity and ambiguity of today's world is all about.

The PPM world: the motif of multiple metaphors

The pace of life is frantic, the rate of change is ever faster, and the moments of decision ever more compressed. No wonder many writers have characterised business life as presenting business people with problems and issues that constitute a 'mess'[4], or a 'swamp'[5], are 'wicked problems'[6], and are 'multi-perspective problem situation[s]'[7]. They are best understood from the perspective of chaos theory[8].

In such a business environment there are bound to be a multiplicity of agendas, a constant ebb and flow of different concerns and views. Engaging in business planning and making the resultant business plan happen all has to be negotiated through this confusing maelstrom. This is why you will see described in this book approaches to business planning that suggest I have a wide range of views on what a business is. When I talk about understanding the levers in your business and using an engineer's charts, am I thinking of your business as a machine? Yes I am. When I talk about surviving through adapting to 'fit' with your business's environment, am I thinking of your business as a gene trying to survive a Darwinian struggle? Yes I am. When I talk about dominating a market, am I thinking of your business as an army? Yes I am. When I talk about a craft process, am I thinking of your business as in a constant state of change? Yes I am. When I talk about the life-cycle of your business, am I thinking of it as an organism? Yes I am. When I talk about the narrative of your business, am I thinking of it as on a journey? Yes I am. When I talk about the personality of your business and its purposes, am I thinking of it as a person? Yes I am. When I talk about your business as needing engaged and confident people in a culture of mutual respect, am I thinking of it as a society? Yes I am[9].

Each of these very different perspectives illuminates a different aspect of business life. And they lead to a different shaping of your business, a different behavioural disposition. Depending on circumstances, one will be more to the fore than another. Your task in business – yet another reason why being in business is so stimulating – is not so much to integrate all these different perspectives, but to hold all of them in creative tension.

There will be times when you will think and act as though you are operating your business as a machine, and there will be times when you will be nurturing it as if it were an organism. There will be yet other times when you will rally the troops and beat off a competitor's incursion into your market. Undoubtedly during the course of your business journey, you and your people will act in ways that presuppose, at varying times, one perspective or another, or a curious and perhaps uneasy mixture of perspectives about what your business is like.

To use an analogy, it is like how physicists talk about light. Looked at one way and backed up by one set of scientific instrumentation, light appears to behave like a wave and is best understood as such. However, looked at another way and backed up by a different set of instrumentation, light appears to behave as though it is made up of particles and it is best understood in that way. The voice of logic tells us that light must be one or the other; it cannot be both. Yet, at least at present, the best physicists can do is to hold both perspectives on the nature of light, since to jettison one would give an incomplete account of the information gathered.

So it is with understanding businesses. The different perspectives seem to be at odds with each other, yet to jettison any one of them would be to diminish our understanding and so impoverish our actions. This is why I talk about sense-making, since everyone in business needs to make connections between their purposes and activities and the purposes and activities of the business. It is complex and needs conscious effort rooted in open intent.

The complexity and ambiguity of today's world leads us to use of multiple metaphors to enhance our understanding of phenomena (including business) and then to inform our actions. This is surely another motif of the PPM world.

The PPM world: the motif of interconnectedness

Globalisation, the interconnectedness of trade and commerce across the world, is one manifestation of the PPM motif of interconnectedness.

The physical interconnectedness of IT communications networks is enabling the PPM motif of human interconnectedness to take root and thrive.

Another manifestation is the growing concern for environmental sustainability – the necessary condition for interconnectedness to form and flourish. Interconnectedness requires the arena of a healthy planet for it to endure, otherwise it will break down into self-reliant tribes. Also, if you and I are interconnected, we shall not put up with each of our waste being dumped on the other, nor with each of our carbon emissions ruining each other's climate, nor with our appetites allowing the other's seas to be denuded of fish stocks.

Yet another manifestation is the rising advocacy for ethical dealings – the natural outworking of a motif of interconnectedness. If you and I are interconnected, I do not want to enjoy my cup of coffee or wear my nice shirt at the expense of your exploitation, or the exploitation of your children. If you and I are interconnected, I do not want merely to look on as a calamity curses you with homelessness or famine or disease. If you and I are interconnected, we want to visit each other, communicate, and learn about each other. We might also feel interconnected not just with each other and with other people, but with other living creatures. This might lead us to conclude that the proper treatment of animals is an important ethical position. We might go further and refuse to eat meat as a matter of ethical propriety, or follow our sense of interconnectedness all the way through to a principled adoption of veganism.

What does interconnectedness mean for business? On one level it means much of what we are already familiar with: international trade, outsourcing and offshoring, the systemic inter-dependence of national economies, and the idea that relationships are fundamental to business activity (see Chapter 14). It also means the fair trade agenda, responsible sourcing, and the likelihood that whoever makes hydrogen fuel cells work and can set up the infrastructure to support them, will be a multi-billionaire. It is also why we see new businesses based on social networking like Facebook. Indeed, there are businesses that are doing very well whose offering *is* their network. But this motif of interconnectedness means a lot more than all this for business.

Being interconnected is an essential part of who each of us is.

This PPM motif of interconnectedness is wrapped up with the dawning realisation that the true actualisation of the full potential of our individual identity is bound up with other people. We cannot show respect and be respected unless there are other people in our lives. We cannot converse without others. Games of solitaire are soon boring; laughing at your own jokes is a thin joy. We cannot care and nurture and love unless there are others. We cannot form a true sense of self except in interaction with other selves.

The wonderful and awesome irony of radical individualism, as it is actualised in the PPM world, is that it is a profoundly socialising, other-regarding phenomenon.

Who you are cannot be separated from your history, your family, your friends, your colleagues. Your world-view is the product of your beliefs, habits, attitudes, expectations, values, behaviours and actions, both individual and social. A matrix of patterns of cognition, perception and action produces, in interplay with your social context, your world-view – and thus who you are. You shape your context and you are shaped by it. The self is essentially a 'web of relationships' and 'the constitution of the self happens only in community'[10].

One of the distinctive features about the PPM world's motif of interconnectedness is that although it is energised by radical individualism – the notion that the identity of the self is primary and a matter of individual choice – it is also understood to have this inescapable social dimension. That is, the full potential of the true self cannot be realised except through committed social relationships in a community.

This alone is very interesting. But in the PPM world, this motif has a moral underpinning. Unlike the post-modernist outlook which sees the Enlightenment agenda as bereft, the PPM world is recognising that reason, properly understood, continues to guide us forward. If, like Kant, I see myself as not merely a means to an end but as an end in myself, then, rationally, I cannot help but see you – and everyone else – in the same way. It would be irrational to see just myself as more than just means, as an end in myself, but to view you as somehow lesser, as a potentially convenient route to achieve what fulfils me. Hence, if I am to proclaim something as right for me, then reason obliges me first, to put myself in the shoes of affected parties to check that I can still truly call it 'right'; secondly, if it passes this test, then I must also agree that it is right for others as well[11].

So, if I count the full realisation of my potential as the driving force in my life, then I must, rationally, recognise the same importance of realising your potential for you.

It is reason, then, that is the objectivity 'out there' that holds the PPM world together – just as reason was held dear by the Enlighten-ment and *contra* the post-modernist outlook. Reason does not favour the rich or the powerful. It has no favourites. It is not swayed by supe-rior eloquence or material bribes or anyone's status. It truly does see all people as equally worthy and significant – but not as *identical*.

There is in people a longing for significance, an urge to find Meaning in our lives. You do not have to be religious to recognise that this impulse is there. As Aristotle said: 'The only way to achieve true success is to express yourself completely in service to society.'

The PPM motif of interconnectedness combines this spiritual impulse with clean, unprejudiced reason to give us radical individual-ism as a socialised agenda that values the uplift of all.

YOUR BUSINESS: SELF-IDENTITY AND ACTION

The assertion of personal identity as a matter of choice universally prescribed as a collective, social endeavour, is just as much an issue for organisations, including individual businesses.

We talked about the personality of your business in Chapter 8. It is also possible to talk about your business as having its own self-identity with its own *Weltanschauung*[12]. This is an emergent property of the business. An emergent property is exhibited by a system as a whole that is not exhibited by any one of its constituent parts. Emergence is a self-organising behaviour that comes out of multi-agent-to-agent interaction and multi-agent-to-environment interaction. Emergent properties cannot be described fully by consideration of each agent in isolation – the whole is more than the sum of the parts. For example, we speak about the properties of a flock of birds or a shoal of fish without any one bird or fish itself having those properties. This is one reason why we can be taken unawares by unintended consequences: the bringing together of various components into a complex system can generate novel emergent properties not exhibited by any of the components separately.

The business's sense of self-identity will filter in and filter out that which accords with its world-view and that which discords with it respectively. This is the phenomenon known to us as 'group think'[13]. This activity is another emergent property which we can call the 'collective will'. It is a force that can be cohesive across the individuals in a business, but it can also lead to collective myopia. The Royal Bank of Scotland, for example, had a clear sense of its self-identity to 'make it happen'. In 2000, its collective will ruled in the action of acquiring NatWest in a £21 billion deal – the largest takeover in British banking history. The integration of RBS and NatWest, a huge challenge, was achieved ahead of time and very effectively. RBS's collective will proved to be a cohesive force. Some years later, and again consistent with its emergent sense of self-identity to 'make it happen', its collective will also assembled a consortium that successfully acquired ABN-Amro in 2007 for £48 billion. In the following year, and amidst a huge furore, RBS was taken under government control in order to avoid collapse. Its collective will made more happen than it intended because of enormous blind spots in its world-view. As the bank itself admits: 'Some of our major strategic decisions were subsequently shown to be bad mistakes, making us more vulnerable than we would have been otherwise'[14].

The claim here is that the collective will is an emergent property reflecting the effective outworking of a business's commitment to act, which in turn represents the engagement with reality of what are called here the emergent properties of a business's (or any organisation's) sense of self-identity, its *Weltanschauung*. In short: a business's self-identity is projected through its collective will.

It is not oblivious to the activities of people within and outside the business, nor to PEST forces nor to Porter's Five Forces. The organisation's self-identity shapes the identities of others, and is shaped by those identities. It is a structuring construct, and a structured construct. The collective will can realise itself through the business's power structures and gain traction through, for example, instruments of co-ordination such as balanced scorecards. This is why open focus is so important: to keep the positives of business action without its potential myopia.

OPEN FOCUS AS A DISPOSITION TO LEARN: THE IMPLICATIONS FOR YOUR BUSINESS

Open focus (Chapter 13) is a proper response to many of the PPM motifs: that the world is complex and that no one metaphor or perspective captures complete understanding. It entails a disposition to learn. Learning is an individual and social process to accumulate 'justified true beliefs'. These include not just statements of fact, but also activities, values, and virtues.

It is the people in a business interacting with each other that provides the generational dynamic for beliefs. It is then in the business's construction of meaning that the beliefs cohere. It is in the business's sense of self-identity ('Who have we been?'; 'Who are we?'; 'Who ought we to be?') that the framework of validity – 'truth' – of the business's beliefs is found. It is in the outworking of the business's sense of self-identity, its values, its *Weltanschauung* in the collective will in action that 'justification' is provided.

In the RBS example, its myopia was that its collective will indeed 'made it happen', but failed properly to project its more fundamental value of business survival. Its action, therefore, was not 'justified'.

Many writers firmly secure the commercial prospects of businesses in generating enduring competitive advantage to its learning capabilities[15]. In short, if you want to be a successful business, then you must be a learning business. This makes sense given the motifs of the PPM world. Even a thinker like Michael Porter who, as we know from Chapter 5, locates the determinants of business performance in the external market environment, stresses learning as an integral feature of the successful organisation[16].

Learning poses many practical issues for your business. We talked earlier about the value of embedding learning in your business as routines. However, there is also value in jettisoning old routines that become out of place and replacing them with new routines. This is the tension between exploiting existing practices to the full, and exploring for new ones[17].

A business that engages exclusively in exploration is liable never to make any returns on its learning. On the other hand, a business that engages exclusively in exploitation is liable to see its learning suffer from obsolescence. Thus your business has to maintain a balance but this is not an easy challenge to overcome. Both activities (exploitation and exploration) compete for scarce resources, so choices have to be made both explicitly (e.g. the contents of your investment portfolio) and implicitly (e.g. in the informal activities of your business). But, in a sense, it is not an equal fight. The returns from exploration are much less certain and usually far more remote in time. It is harder to construct the necessary business case by comparison with activities of exploitation where the feedback loops are clear and tighter. Short-term pain (and short-term gain, similarly) is more keenly felt than the 'if-and-maybe' of long-term gain, particularly when overlaid with the time horizon of the tenure of the relevant decision-making managers.

You may find that your business is inundated with exhortations to spend significant sums on all sorts of knowledge-related technologies such as data-mining, intranets, video conferencing, webcasting and the like. This is all very well, but if your business's investment effort is targeted exclusively at the technologies that hold information, your precious funds will be wasted. This is because your business cannot afford to overlook the vital investment necessary in the people in whom knowledge is embedded, and between whose interactions new knowledge is created, and by whom actions are taken. Interpretive flexibility – the PPM motif of multiple metaphors – is what is required.

Learning and knowledge management are about addressing the critical issues of business flexibility, survival and competence in the face of increasingly discontinuous environmental change. It is about synergising the technical processes of information acquisition, processing, combination, storage, retrieval and sharing, with social human processes of collaboration, creative sense-making, innovation and purposive team-work. Social networks are no less important than IT networks[18].

Consider also your own attitude towards learning. One writer has observed that 'many professionals have extremely 'brittle' personalities' which can entail 'a formidable predisposition against learning'[19]. He tells companies that 'success in the marketplace increasingly depends on learning, yet most people don't know how to learn'[20]. This might be because, understandably, you tend to favour stability over change, since stability and predictability are core elements of co-ordinated behaviour. You might view that it is important for your business to emit predictable responses to outside stimuli as the basis for forming long-term relationships. But there is a difference between consistency of behaviour and being closed to new learning. Ask yourself how well you think you are managing this difference in your business.

Sometimes it takes a crisis to shake things up and create the conditions for new learning. The pertinence of established routines diminishes in a changing marketplace until crisis-point is reached; or a crisis is engineered to catalyse the jettisoning of familiar routines. This is the 'D' – Disturbance – that is necessary to overcome inertia or Resistance: D x V x I > R. In your business, you must be prepared to manufacture a sense of crisis in advance of environmental change so as to force out fresh thinking and new learning. This is 'shaking things up around here'. It can entail setting very challenging goals, calling it a day with inflexible workers and bringing in new blood.

The risk, however, with such induced crises is that the wrong problems might be set. One of the tricks to pull off if your business is to learn effectively is to ensure that the right problems are being framed for solution. Hence, effective business learning does not begin once a problem has been set from outside; rather such learning includes the framing of the problem in the first place. This is why in Chapter 13 on open focus, we stressed the importance of re-framing the issue properly.

COMPLETING YOUR BUSINESS'S JOURNEY IN THE PPM WORLD THROUGH WISDOM

We can now begin to pull our reflections on the nature of today's world together.

A business – your business – interacts with its environment, affecting it and affected by it – both externally (PEST forces, Porter's Five Forces, etc.), and internal (units, teams, individuals, etc.). And, moreover, each person in the business is affected by the business and affecting of the business. There are some predictable affects – orientations and constraints – but not necessarily mechanical determinism: there is necessity mixed with chance, creativity mixed with conditioning.

Learning, both individual and organisational, introduces uncertainty into social behaviours since it gives rise to invention – the possibility of new responses to similar stimuli, new behaviours in similar social situations. This entails knowledgeable, creative, *learning* actors. Individuals create the business of which they are members and are also the created results of that business. There is dialectic.

We now pull together our reflections on the nature of today's world and so describe the context in which you are undertaking your business journey. It comprises the notion of identity as an emergent property of businesses that is projected by the collective will (itself an emergent property of the business) through change management processes into the socially-structured, community-based activity of learning practice.

At all levels, whether for the individual or for a group or for a business or for a society, issues of identity are overarching (the PPM motif of the Hayley Complex).

The projection of identity ('action') can be understood in agency terms in respect of an individual, and in terms of collective will for a business. Action is about resolving disconnects between who we are and who we ought to be.

Your role in your business is to create the conditions for effective learning by achieving a shared world-view and a shared vision. You will need skills in judgement to devise actions that flow backwards from common goals. Future goals give present meaning. Throughout, you will be measuring your business against an objective yardstick: the extent to which it is getting closer to the vision. You will also need skills in control in order to maintain conformity to common purposes while being buffeted by a turbulent environment. This means holding your nerve, and the nerve of your people, and a continual public reaffirmation of the vision and the shared identity. It is a tough place for recidivists or mavericks! And potentially unattractive to outsiders!

What the PPM motif of radical individualism poses to business is the challenge of reconciling identity maintenance with identity change.

For an identity to amount to being an identity that provides either an individual or a business with essential cohesion, without which cohesion no sense of the world can be made, there must be some measure of continuity and resilience.

The tension is that resilience of identity is a prerequisite of sense-making, yet malleability of identity is a prerequisite of learning.

But there is a deeper paradox. If there is no resilience of identity, there can be no learning at all either, since new experiences must be made sense of in the context of the world-view of the individual (or business), which world-view is integral to self-identity. Otherwise there is deep-seated, systemic angst since the 'self' is as the air that touches the surface of the sea – constantly giving way to every incursion of every wave.

So how is the individual – or business – to have both the resilience and the malleability that are each necessary for learning to take place?

The answer is wisdom[21]. It is the role of wisdom to overcome this paradox between the resilience of identity that is a prerequisite of learning and the malleability of identity that is also a prerequisite of learning.

Wisdom, which includes the realisation that the question of self-identity is always open plus notions of respect and trust, becomes the hardwired, in-the-DNA guarantor of a continuous capacity for deep learning. This is why businesses with strong cultures can struggle: rigidities can reduce learning capacities and result in dysfunctionality.

The activities you must do to make a successful business journey in our PPM world start to become clear: first, a climate of trust needs to be created; then there needs to be a process of creating productive social relationships, and then an alignment of purposes and intentions.

Once these conditions are right, then you can encourage what has been called 'critical self-reflexivity'[22]. This is where existing world-views that support the business's current sense of self-identity are challenged, and ideas about the potential new identity that the business is working towards are developed. This is a business confronting the motifs of the PPM world with a disposition of deep learning. Conceived as such – a sense of self-identity that entails openness to the question of self-identity – this leads to 'the attainment of wisdom'[23]. Wise individuals and wise businesses have the maturity to self-question as part of shaping and re-shaping their identities.

In this way, therefore, wisdom resolves the paradox. It assumes environmental complexity and the openness of self-identity. At the same time, it engenders a shared identity that can undertake complex sense-making and pattern-forming. Wisdom both provides the necessary resilience and the necessary malleability of self-identity.

Thus wisdom can embrace the PPM motif of interconnectedness. At the same time, in Yeats' phrase, we do not know 'the dancer from the dance'[24].

Learning for a business is an holistic combination of capability with wisdom[25]. This embraces not just cognitive processes, but also feelings, emotions, values, morals and spirituality. Hence, teams that learn together must not just think together but also feel together – and play together.

Your role in a wise business is to reflect critically upon the various self-concepts that form the basis of your business's identity. Conflicting views should be surfaced, re-integrated, and the wounds of such self-reflexivity healed. A wise business understands, and is secure in, its limits. Its learning helps it to negotiate identity change as part of its continuing strategic development[26].

This was RBS's problem that led to its comeuppance: it was not a *wise* business. It did not have sufficient wisdom.

THE NEW NARRATIVE FOR THE PPM WORLD

It does not matter that wisdom might be an idealised state that can never be fully attained. The point of it all, the power of it all, is that the deep learning business's quest for wisdom acts as a regulatory vision which is approached asymptotically.

The gap between the business which people can ever create and the truly wise business may become infinitely small after an infinite time. Yet, as a regulatory vision, it provides the sparkle of meaning and purpose in the here and now.

Because humanity's bittersweet lot in life is forever to be at a distance, even an ever-decreasing distance, from this vision, people need to proceed in life with wisdom.

The business's journey, understood as a quest for wisdom, is normative and acknowledges that it is idealised and visionary. It aims to lift one's gaze to something aspirational and meaningful – a *summum bonum* which is approached asymptotically as a regulatory principle of human nature that provides point, purpose and meaning to human existence.

We can accept that people live in a world of multiple narratives, but my conclusion from my reflections on the motifs of the PPM world is that the post-modernist interpretation is a passing fad. The PPM world's complexity is a stimulus for enriched learning and for a renewed coming together with a newly-created synthesis of ideas and behaviours. Radical individualism socialised by the power of reason into a highly positive interconnectedness means that individuals and businesses can participate in new and ever-evolving social linkages.

This is the potential 'meta-narrative' for the human condition that post-modernists deny is even possible.

Thus, the human lot moves from being fractured splinters of individual discovery to being fractal glints of the collective construction of meaning and self-identity. This is the new 'myth' for the 21st century from which sub-meanings and sub-sensemakings across the multitude of forms of life will draw.

Notes and References re Chapter 16

1   If you have the stamina to read some of the endless literature on post-modernist thinking yourself, then not only do I commend your staying power, I also feel a vicarious sense of loss for all your opportunity costs. Reading a work of post-modernist thinking is like being put in a black room, without a photon of light, while wearing a black hood with a blindfold on. There is just no escape from the darkness. Let me help you by giving some references to you so that you know that I am not making this up and see if that saves you the effort which you can redirect more profitably elsewhere. On post-modernist thinking as seeing the end of meta-narratives, consider Jean-François Lyotard:

'Simplifying to the extreme, I define *post-modern* as incredulity toward metanarratives. This incredulity is undoubtedly a product of progress in the sciences: but that progress in turn presupposes it. To the obsolescence of the metanarrative apparatus of legitimation corresponds, most notably, the crisis of metaphysical philosophy and of the university institution which in the past relied on it. The narrative function is losing its functors, its great hero, its great dangers, its great voyages, its great goal. It is being dispersed in clouds of narrative language elements – narrative, but also denotative, prescriptive, descriptive, and so on. Conveyed within each cloud are pragmatic valencies specific to its kind. Each of us lives at the intersection of many of these. However, we do not necessarily establish stable language combinations, and the properties of the ones we do establish are not necessarily communicable ...There are many different language games – a heterogeneity of elements ... Where, after the metanarratives, can legitimacy reside?'

Lyotard, J.-F., *The Post-Modern Condition: A Report on Knowledge.* p. xxivf. Translated by Bennington G., and Massumi, B., Manchester: Manchester University Press, 1984.

In Lyotard's view, decision makers (who would include business leaders), for example:

'... attempt to manage these clouds of sociality according to input/output matrices, following a logic which implies that their elements are commensurable and the whole is determinable. They allocate our lives for the growth of power. In matters of social justice and of scientific truth alike, the legitimation of that power is based on its optimising the system's performance – efficiency. The application of this criterion to all of our games necessarily entails a certain level of terror, whether soft or hard: be operational (that is, commensurable) disappear.' (*Ibid.*)

It is easy to manufacture cardboard foes in order to seem the hero when you vanquish them. For someone who eschews meta-narratives, Lyotard's meta-narrative of business, the growth of power as legitimised by ever-greater efficiency of performance, is curiously two-dimensional. We say more about the 'profit motive' in Chapter 17, but meanwhile you might like to consider whether Lyotard's account adequately describes your own motivations for being in business.

For a better account of post-modernist thinking, see Harvey, D., *The Condition of Postmodernity*, Oxford: Blackwell, 1990.

2   You might think I am being somewhat flippant. After all, even post-modernist thinkers would not step in front of a truck and expect to survive unscathed from that particular collision with objective reality! The debate is about the objectivity of the theories that explain objective reality. For example, we take in certain experiential inputs and might, for example, pronounce grass to be green. We see similarly coloured objects and call them green as well, or *vert* if we are French, or *grün* if we are German, and so on. But suppose an English speaker said that grass and all similarly coloured objects are 'grue', by which she means 'green before the 1st January 2050' and blue after that date. Everything that we call 'green' is exactly co-extensive with what she calls 'grue'; it is just that her concept is more complicated than ours. Sure, what

happens on the 2nd January 2050 will prove either us or her right but what if the threshold date were, say, a billion years in the future? We would still dismiss her concept of 'grue' as being an unnecessary complication and, in accordance with commended scientific practice, we would prefer the simpler concept, 'green'. And this is the point: one of the axioms of science is to prefer the simpler explanation, even though the more complicated one could be true (just as grue objects are as exactly consistent with all the available the data as green ones). We just think it is good science to go for the simpler explanatory framework. Why? Where does the principle that the simpler explanation is right come from? It is around this area of the philosophy of science that a genuine debate can be had; but it would take us well beyond the scope of this book. (The 'grue' example is an amended version of an argument devised by Nelson Goodman in Goodman, N., *Fact, Fiction and Forecast*. Cambridge: Harvard University Press, 1951.)

3   Centuries ago, a geocentric view of the solar system (earth at the centre) fitted with the Catholic Church's *Weltanschauung* rather than a heliocentric view (sun at the centre). And they felt they had the moral and spiritual authority to ensure that everyone believed the same. They had the power to project their view and ensure that it prevailed – but only for a time. Despite the combined forces of a powerful institution and a sense of righteous zeal, the fact that the earth (and the other planets) go round the sun, and so this is a solar system, not a 'terra- system' – remained unassailed, whether believed or not. Then the Church's *Weltanschauung* changed and it, too, now accepts the fact of our solar system. We can explain why the Church held the belief that it did, why it was so important to them, why they were so reluctant to change, and how different people responded to the Church's view and its behaviours, but this is always a different academic activity from the one that determines how the solar system itself operates.

4   'Managers are not confronted with problems that are independent of each other, but with dynamic situations that consist of complex systems of changing problems that interact with each other. I call such situations messes. Problems are abstractions extracted from messes by analysis; they are to messes as atoms are to tables and

chairs'; Ackoff, R.L. 'The future of operational research is past', *Journal of the Operational Research Society*, 1979, **30**, pp. 93-104.

5   'In the swampy lowland, messy, confusing problems defy technical solution. The irony of this situation is that the problems of the high ground tend to be relatively unimportant to individuals or society at large, however great their technical interest may be, while in the swamp lie the problems of greatest human concern. The practitioner must choose. Shall he remain on the high ground where he can solve relatively unimportant problems according to prevailing standards of rigour, or shall he descend to the swamp of important problems and non-rigorous enquiry?'; Schön, D.A. *Educating the Reflective Practitioner: Toward a New Design for Teaching and Learning in the Professions*. p. 1. San Francisco: Jossey Bass, 1987.

6   Rittel, H.W.J., and Webber, M.M. 'Dilemmas in a general theory of planning', *Policy Science*, 1973, **4**, pp. 155-169.

7   'Any situation in which human beings try to act together will be complex simply because individuals are autonomous. Shared perceptions – essential for corporate action – will have to be established, negotiated, argued, tested, in a complex social process. Any human situation, in fact, will be characterised by more than facts and logic...But the facts and logic will never supply a complete description of a human situation. Equally important will be the myths and meanings by means of which human beings make sense of their worlds'; Checkland, P. (2001) 'Soft Systems Methodology', printed in Rosenhead, J., Mingers, J. *Rational Analysis for a Problematic World Revisited*. Chichester: Wiley, 2001.

8   For example, see Levy, J. 'Chaos Theory and Strategy: Theory, Application, and Managerial Implications', *Strategic Management Journal*, 1994, **(15)**, pp. 167-178.

9   For an excellent and stimulating discussion of how different metaphors can illuminate the nature of organisations and organisational life, see Morgan, G. *Images of Organization*, 2nd ed., London: Sage, 1996.

10 Kofman, F., and Senge, P.M. 'Communities of Commitment: The Heart of Learning Organisations', *Organisational Dynamics*, 1993, **22 (2)**, pp. 5-23, p. 14.

11 It is listening to the lectures of Professor Richard Hare on moral philosophy in around 1980 that set me thinking along these lines. Prof. Hare writes beautifully clearly, and his views are accessibly described in a series of books: Hare, R. M., *The Language of Morals*, Oxford: Oxford University Press, 1952; Hare, R. M. *Freedom and Reason*, Oxford: Oxford University Press, 1963, Hare, R. M. *Moral Thinking: Its Levels, Method, and Point*, Oxford: Oxford University Press, 1981.

12 For example, see Kim, D.H., 'The link between individual and organisational learning', printed in Starkey, K., Tempest, S., McKinlay, A., *How Organisations Learn: Managing the Search for Knowledge*, 2nd ed., pp. 29–50 London: Thomson, 2004 (originally published in *Sloan Management Review*, 1993, **35**, pp. 37-50); also Weick, K., Roberts, K., 'Collective minds in organisations: heedful interrelation on flight decks', *Administrative Science Quarterly*, 1993, **38 (3)**, pp. 357-381. One writer has claimed, perhaps provocatively: '... companies collectively constitute a sentient, intelligent, non-human species at a relatively early stage in its evolution'; Lloyd, T., *The 'Nice' Company*, p. xiii, London: Bloomsbury, 1990.

13 Janis, I.L., *Victims of Groupthink*. Boston: Houghton Mifflin, 1972.

14 See www.rbs.com/about-rbs/heritage/our-story/history-highlights/from-1727-to-today/2000-to-present.ashx

15 Among many examples are:
a. Drucker, P. *The Age of Discontinuity: Guidelines to Our Changing Society*. New York: Harper & Row, 1968.
b. Hutchins, R.M. *The Learning Society*. p. 130. London: Penguin, 1973.
c. Schön, D.A. *Beyond the Stable State*. p. 28. London: Penguin, 1973.
d. Bell, D. *The Coming of Post-Industrial Society: A Venture in Social Forecasting*. p.20. New York: Basic Books, 1973.
e. De Geus, A.P. 'Planning as Learning', *Harvard Business Review*, March-April, 1988, pp. 70-74, p. 74.
f. Levitt, B., and March, J.G. 'Organisational Learning', *Annual Review of Sociology*, 1988, **14**, pp. 319-340.
g. Senge, P.M. *The Fifth Discipline: The Art and Practice of the Learning Organisation*. p. 4. New York: Doubleday, 1990.

h. Senge, P.M., 'The Leader's New Work: Building Learning Organisations'. *Sloan Management Review*, 1990, **1**, pp. 7-23.

i. Toffler, A., *Powershift: Knowledge, Wealth and Violence at the Edge of the 21st Century*. New York: Bantam Books, 1990.

j. Useem, M., Kochan, T.A. 'Creating the learning organisation', 1992. Printed in Kochan, T., and Useem, M. (eds.), *Transforming Organisations*, Oxford: Oxford University Press, 1992.

k. Kofman, F., Senge, P.M. 'Communities of Commitment: The Heart of Learning Organisations', *Organisational Dynamics*, 1993, **22 (2)**, pp. 5-23, p. 22.

l. Bennet, K.J., and O'Brien, M.J. 'The building blocks of the learning organisation', *Training*, June, 1994, pp. 41-49.

m. Wishart, N.A., Elam, J.J., and Robey, D. 'Redrawing the portrait of a learning organisation: inside Knight-Ridder Inc', *Academy of Management Executive*, 1996, **10 (1)**, pp. 7-20.

n. Wenger, E.C., Snyder, W.M. 'Communities of Practice: The Organisational Frontier', *Harvard Business Review*, Jan-Feb, 2000, pp. 139-145, p. 139.

o. Castells, M., 'Information technology and global capitalism', printed in Hutton, W., and Giddens, A. (eds), *On the Edge: Living with global capitalism*. p. 52. London: Vantage, 2001.

16 Porter, M. 'Creating tomorrow's advantages', printed in Gibson, R. (ed), *Rethinking the Future*, pp. 48–60, p. 59, London: Nicholas Brealey, 1997.

17 See March, J.G. 'Exploration and Exploitation in Organisational Learning', *Organization Science*, 1991, **2 (1)**, pp. 71-87. Also see Nyström, P.C., and Starbuck, W.H., 'To Avoid Organisational Crises, Unlearn', *Organizational Dynamics*, 1984, **12 (4)**, Spring, pp. 53-65: 'Organisations learn. Then they encase their learning in programs and standard operating procedures that members execute routinely. These programs and procedures generate inertia, and the inertia increases when organisations socialise new members and reward conformity to prescribed roles. As their successes accumulate, organisations emphasise efficiency, grow complacent, and learn too little. To survive, organisations must also unlearn' (p. 53). And also see: Hedberg, B., 'How organisations learn and unlearn', printed in Nyström, N.C., Starbuck, W.H.

(eds.), pp. 3–27, *Handbook of Organisational Design*, Oxford: Oxford University Press, 1981: 'In fact, it seems as if slow unlearning is a crucial weakness of many organisations', p. 3.

18 See Swan, J., Newell, S., Scarborough, H., and Hislop, D., 'Knowledge management and innovation: networks and networking', *Journal of Knowledge Management*, 1999, **3 (4)**, pp. 262-275.

19 Argyris, C. 'Teaching Smart People How to Learn', *Harvard Business Review*, May-June, 1991, pp. 99-109, p. 104.

20 *Op. cit.*, p. 99.

21 Wisdom is 'a stable attitude of the personality toward life and the world, an attitude that is formed through the integration of cognitive function with humour, acceptance of transience, and a firmly cathected system of values ... [Wisdom represents] the ego's ultimate mastery over the narcissistic self, the final control of the rider over the horse' in Kohut, H., 'Forms and transformations of narcissism', printed in Ornstein, P.H. (ed.), *The Search for Self: Selected Writings of Heinz Kohut: 1950-1978*, vol. 1, New York: International Universities Press, 1978, pp. 427-460, pp. 458-459.

22 Brown A.D., and Starkey, K. 'Organisational identity and learning', printed in Starkey, K., Tempest, and S., McKinlay, A., *How Organisations Learn: Managing the Search for Knowledge*, 2nd ed., London: Thomson, 2004, pp. 571-597, p. 583.

23 *Op. cit.*, p.587.

24 W. B. Yeats, *Among School Children*, VIII, last verse.

25 See Cunningham, I., *The Wisdom of Strategic Learning*, Maidenhead: McGraw-Hill, 1994.

26 See Brown A.D., and Starkey, K., 2004, *op. cit.*, pp. 588-589.

Chapter 17
Parting Is Such Sweet Sorrow

'You are today where your thoughts have brought you; you will be tomorrow where your thoughts take you.' – James Allen

Profits and prophets

The expression 'profit motive' is bandied about a lot. It is often used to mean making a financial return; that is, making a financial gain in excess of financial outlay. I shall come back to this.

However, I prefer to think of the profit motive as that reward, not necessarily financial, which induces and incentivises a person or group to accomplish and gain something. It is about what it takes to commit something of oneself – physical and emotional resources, effort, skills, thinking, etc. – to achieve value-add (where the value-add is by no means necessarily financial).

Understood in this way, it is the absolute opposite of a something-for-nothing outlook. It is the basis for human endeavour. The gain could be for oneself, for a loved one, for a collective (such as local community or nation etc.), for a cause, and it could be financial, material, educative, spiritual – even fun! This profit motive is a creative force.

Not having a profit motive is impoverishing in every way.

I would not presume to tell you what your personal profit motive – or value motive – is. It probably has a lot to do with your vision and this is individual and precious to you. How do you keep on course?

This is where profit – as financial gain – comes in! Think of 'profit' in this financial sense as a proxy for whatever your value motive is. The value motive is different from, yet is illuminated by, the accountant's profit motive.

It is like the map of the London Underground. What is important is how the underground trains actually progress under the streets of London. This is what gets passengers from station to station. They would get nowhere if the trains tried to follow routes exactly as depicted by the London Underground map.

However, if the map were a faithful depiction of the actual routes of the tracks between stations, it would be much less usable – if, indeed, it were usable at all. Sometimes a loss of what is the full picture actually enhances our understanding – provided that we know what we are looking at.

We use the London Underground map very successfully to navigate our way, but we do not confuse it with what is actually the path of the train. We know, of course, that the tracks are not differently coloured, that the trains do not run in straight lines with occasional bends, and that the distances between stations are not to scale.

We use the London Underground map and it is important for that, but we do not confuse it with being a literal map with all the relationships between stations accurately portrayed to scale at every point.

It is the same with profit. It is extremely useful as a very sincere form of feedback on your business's performance. If your business is making repeated losses, then you are doing something silly. You might be doing the wrong thing or you might be doing it in the wrong way – or both. If your customers like what you are doing, then they will signal this through the number of times they buy from you, and through what they pay you when they do buy.

It s hard to get a handle on a complete set of measures to judge your progress towards acting on your value motive, but the financial performance of your business is a good indicative proxy. Just do not confuse the two and recognise the limitations of pursuing profit only.

THREESOMES: A SUMMARY

You will have covered a lot of ground in engaging in the process of successful business planning.

A summary organised as questions clustered in groups of related threes that feed into 'profit' will help you.

First, let us remind ourselves what profit is. It is the excess of income over expenditure (a deficit is called a 'loss'). Just as you orientate your travels around London by using a London Underground map, so the profit performance of your business can orientate your business journey. Just as you keep the map on your person and review it regularly to assess progress and to help at key decision moments, so too should you examine frequently the profit performance of your business.

More precisely, profit is what we call the result of the following calculation:

(Price minus average cost) multiplied by the quantity sold

$$(P - AC) \times QS$$

Consider each of these components in turn:

- *Price*: This focuses attention on customers, how you reach them, the problems you are solving for them, and the value they put on your business's products and services.
- *Average cost*: This focuses attention on the efficiency and effectiveness of your processes, the skills and motivation of your people, the quality of your communication and leadership, the nature of your relationships with your suppliers and other stakeholders. It also highlights how well you are marshalling all the resources – such as cash, assets, stakeholders, partners, and good and bad costs – to make your business plan happen and the business that you are *really* in successful.
- *Quantity sold*: This focuses attention on the size of the market and how much of it your business can have versus your competitors (including potential new entrants). It also raises issues about how your customers access your products and services (distribution) and how you keep your offering up to date (prolonging the life-cycle and creating new life-cycles)[1].

Figure 17.1 opposite offers a useful visual summary.

Each of the three main components that make your business's profit – price, average cost, and quantity sold – is itself the outworking of constituent components. These constituent components are, in turn, the outworking of yet more fundamental forces. For example, take average cost. One component here is your people. How confident are they in fulfilling what is expected? Yet this confidence is itself the outworking of how well they understand what is expected of them,

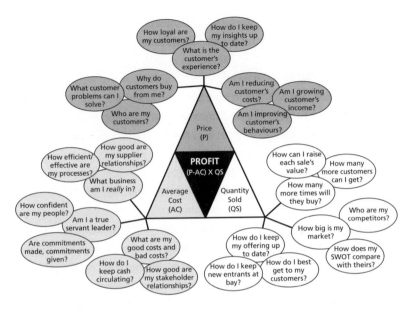

Figure 17.1

how well-informed they are about how they are performing, how skilled and well trained they are, how motivated they feel, how well connected they are to the vision of the business, how well they manage their individual self-talk / self-image / performance cycle, and so on. To address all these issues you will be obliged to ensure that balanced scorecards are in place and properly used, that there is regular and effective communication, that there are good learning and development processes in operation, that rewards mechanisms are effective and felt-fair, that leadership is strong, clear and supportive.

What is more, you will be obliged to make these component forces work together or make trade-off decisions. For example, you might decide to increase profits by raising your price. But what will this do to customer demand? What will it do to enticing new entrants to come in to your market? Or perhaps you decide that you will aim to increase profits by raising the quantity sold by lowering your price. Will the increase in quantity sold truly make up for the reduced income from each individual sale? Will your operations still be efficient as they try to make the extra output to keep up with demand?

This summarising pictorial representation of the performance factors of your business, centred on profit, leads you to understand the workings of your business and its interactions with its marketplace, so as to make your business planning all the more effective.

GROWING PAINS

I wish you every personal and business success.

And that is not meant to hurt you! As you successfully make your business plan happen and your business grows, so you will face some real challenges. Perhaps some of these have come your way already. When the business is just its owner, the owner is involved in every decision. Control is total and communication full and immediate. As the business grows and more people join the journey, so challenges around ceding control and communication also grow. There is just too much to do for the original owner to be involved in every move and to control every decision. Delegating, ceding power and letting go can be desperately difficult. Speaking as a parent, it is as difficult and as wrenching as saying goodbye to your child on their first day of school.

Be ready for this challenge, this trauma. It will happen more than once as your business grows and grows. You will have to be ready for different ways of organising. How? Cultivate business realism embraced by a disposition of trust – and pick the best people. Have great people around you – better than you – and let them loose. As with parenting, the best tribute to your business is when it can grow on its own, without you.

Ideas that will change your world will come out. Implement them brilliantly. The challenge will always be in the implementation. Overcome the challenge of implementation with proper business planning. Grow business planning skills widely around your business. These business planning skills and good conversations between great people will see you through the growth pains[2].

TAKING THE PULSE

Different people will find different forms of summary useful. If you incline towards words, then my recommendation to you is to review and *act on* the key tips at the end of each chapter.

If you incline towards pictures and mind-maps, then think through and *act on* the tree of threesomes in Figure 17.1. You can even develop your own mind-map since, as explained, the components identified (such as having confident people) themselves comprise more fundamental components.

I would like to leave you the latitude to make up your own list of business do's and don'ts – if you are the sort of person who finds such shopping lists helpful.

What I shall do is give you my recommendations on the key aspects of the health of your business journey that you should check regularly. If your plate is already full, then I recommend you get a bigger plate. To pick up the analogy used in Chapter 13, these check-ups and the consequential actions they provoke should be counted among the rocks with which to fill your bucket first.

Regularly making these check-ups, and taking the actions identified as a result, will keep your business healthy and on its journey's course.

I describe the check-ups first in words and then pictures.

Your Business

    a.   Do a SWOT analysis on your business regularly and compare it with a SWOT on your competitors. As your business evolves and grows, and in an ever-changing world, what count as strengths, weaknesses, opportunities and threats will also change. Drifting out of touch with business realities is a sure way to business ruin.

    b.   Keep the cash flowing around your business by regularly reviewing your cash-flow forecast and comparing it with actual results. As with your own health, good circulation is essential for continued wellbeing. You will die if your circulation stops.

    c.   Review your products and services regularly to ensure that they truly solve important problems for your customers better than any alternative. (These problems will change over time.) Look continually to augment your offering to stay ahead. The alternative is to lapse into being yesterday's news.

Your Relationships

    a.   Be sure to undertake bubble-bursting every week (see Chapter 14, Figure 14.4). When times are tough and when times are good, it will be the quality of your relationships that will see your business through.

b. Let your customers design your offering. Business health starts with your customers, for it is they who give you the best kind of money.

c. Surround yourself with the best people – better than you. Check that you are creating the conditions for great people to be great.

You

a. Review your own performance regularly. In the spirit of continuous improvement, every day is the worst that you will be. Work out how you can raise your game. Keep your self-talk / self-image / performance cycle positive. If you do not, you will not last the journey.

b. Review your own approach regularly. Keep open in your focus (see Chapter 13), because both a closed mind and a distracted one will dissipate any business success.

c. Review the balance of your life regularly. For your business to be the best it can be, you must be the best that you can be. What kind of profit will your business have earned if it has cost you your soul?

If you prefer words as your tools of understanding that prompt action, then after reading this book, a combination of the key tips at the end of every Chapter plus the above action-points in the check-ups will give you a fully loaded, ready-to-hand tool-kit.

On the other hand, you might be someone who prefers to deal with pictures. For you, here is a pictorial representation – a MindMap™ opposite – summarising all the key tips at the end of every chapter, plus the action-points comprising the check-ups (these are closest to the heart of the picture). I should also add that there is no significance in the different sizes of the texted ovals – apart from that this helped me fit the picture on a single page!

If you cannot quite call to mind what a texted oval is referring to or what an individual image means, then the full explanation will be in the appropriate chapter.

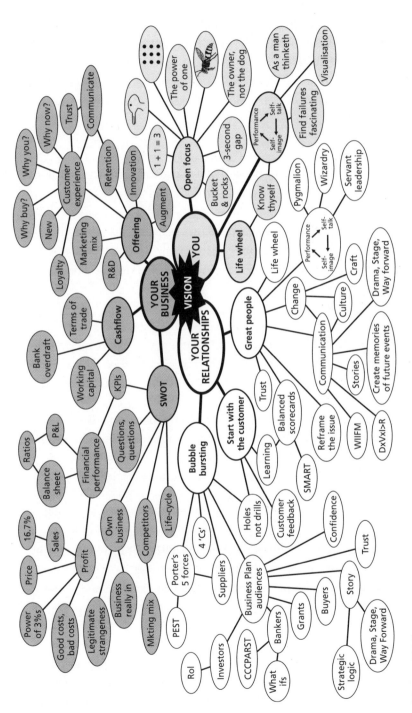

Figure 17.2

'GO FORTH TO MEET THE SHADOWY FUTURE WITHOUT FEAR AND WITH A BIG, BRAVE, BOLD AND BEATING HEART'[3]

Whether you are a start-up business or an established one, the next phase of your journey starts now. The ship is slipping anchor and leaving harbour.

It is exciting!

You will surf on the waves of an adrenalin rush, you will have joys that glint like diamonds of happiness, you will punch the air in life-affirming 'YES!!' moments. And, also, there will undoubtedly be challenges and setbacks along the way. There will be unexpected twists and turns. You will have times of queasiness, panic and doubt.

If your business plan is a chart, then remember that business planning is the all-important process of navigation. Anyone can read a chart, but it is the navigator who gets you home.

Whether seas are calm or choppy, whether the wind is stormy or favourable, a proper engagement with the process of business planning, as described in this book, will keep you on course. Darkness precedes dawn. This means that, when you are wrestling with anxious doubt, just ask yourself two questions: 'Am I doing the right thing?' and 'Am I doing it in the right way?'

If you can put your hand on your 'big, brave, bold and beating heart' and answer 'yes' to both of those questions, then hold your nerve and keep going.

This is the ship that will keep on course: it is called 'leadership'.

You will have succeeded, through the process of business planning, in turning your vision into your cause. It is your 'cause' in both senses of the word. It is your cause in that it is an arresting goal of profound personal meaning that draws you towards itself and feels bigger than you are. You are a committed servant of your cause.

It is also your cause in that it stimulates you to action and to make an impact, just as a cause stimulates an effect. You are given energy by your cause.

Your business plan is now done; but your business planning continues. Aligning your business's character or 'legitimate strangeness' with the vision and purposes that you set, and then pursuing this mission with a coherent and pertinent set of actions, is what the process of business planning is all about. You reach both outwards to your customers' real root-needs, and also inwards into your business's authentic personality. The coherent, systematic and deliberate outworking of this momentous conjunction into your business's vision and your business's behaviours, captures the essence of successful business planning. No wonder it is continuous!

In the final analysis, however, the ship is your business and the journey is yours to make. Yes, please use all in this book that you find helpful, but your success will be yours. It will be down to you. Develop your own style and approach – there is no one way. A star shines its own light.

I wish you every success. I can see you at journey's end, embracing your vision, pausing only briefly before creating your next vision. Your journey goes on. I am convinced that you will either find the right course or make it.

As you steer your business ship along, if you should hear a clapping sound in the distance, that will be the roar of my applause for your endeavour.

I really want you to make a successful journey – I know it matters to you and to those who care about you. The purpose of this book is to help you.

I wish you fair winds and following seas.

Notes and References

1   We are familiar with the notion of the life-cycle from Chapter 11. Taking this idea further, there have been developed models that seek to describe the characteristics of the various phases of growth that a business (or any organisation) goes through. One such model has been developed by Larry Greiner who first talked about five and, later, six main stages of evolutionary growth, punctuated at each transitional point by crisis and revolution. His model looks like this:

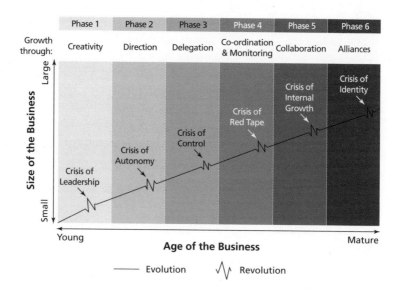

Figure 17.3

2 Based on Greiner, L., 'Evolution and Revolution as Organisations Grow' *Harvard Business Review*, **50** (4), July–August, 1972,
pp. 37-46; and modified by Larry Greiner in the *Harvard Business
Review*, **76** (3), May–June, 1998, pp. 55-64.

As with all models (and just like the map of the London Underground), Greiner's growth model is not literally true in every
respect but through a model's distortions is reality illuminated in
an interesting way. Our understanding is deepened.

Greiner's growth model might not depict a neat linear progres-
sion that all businesses will experience in the stated sequential
order, nor does it explain fully what the underlying dynamics
are: the forces that power the stages and the punctuating crises.
However, that there is a relationship between business size and
difficulties of communication, of coping with ever-rising work-
loads (scale and scope), and of control (the setting of direction)
seems intuitively right. You will probably be able to locate your
own business on the Greiner growth path as your business grows.
Part of the secret of coming through the crises successfully is to
acknowledge that they are likely as your business grows. Once
you begin to expect them as 'normal', you can anticipate them and

ready yourself and your business to face the crises. If you continually engage with the process of business planning as described in this book, especially with issues of organising in mind, then you will win through.

3   With apologies to Longfellow: 'Look not mournfully into the past, it comes not back again. Wisely improve the present, it is thine. Go forth to meet the shadowy future without fear and with a manly heart.'

Index